Legal Protection of Scheduled Castes and Tribes

Constitutional Safeguards and Social Justice

Legal Protection of Scheduled Castes and Tribes

Constitutional Safeguards and Social Justice

DR. DEEPAK KUMAR SRIVASTAVA
Assistant Professor (Law)
Hidayatullah National Law University
New Raipur, Chhattisgarh

Foreword by

PROF. (DR.) ANIRUDH PRASAD
Visiting Professor of Law
Hidayatullah National Law University
New Raipur, Chhattisgarh

DEEP & DEEP PUBLICATIONS PVT. LTD.
F-159, Rajouri Garden, New Delhi - 110 027

LEGAL PROTECTION OF
SCHEDULED CASTES AND TRIBES
Constitutional Safeguards and Social Justice

ISBN 978-81-8450-409-5

Typeset by RAHUL COMPOSERS
358, Pocket-B, Phase-2, Sector-16B, Dwarka, New Delhi - 110 075

Printed in India at MAYUR ENTERPRISES
WZ Plot No. 3, Gujjar Market, Tihar Village, New Delhi - 110 018

Published by DEEP & DEEP PUBLICATIONS PVT. LTD.,
F-159, Rajouri Garden, New Delhi - 110 027 • Phone : 25435369, 25440916
E-mail : ddpubs@gmail.com • ddpubs@yahoo.com
Showroom :
2/13, Ansari Road, Daryaganj, New Delhi - 110 002 • Telefax : 23245122

Contents

Foreword

Scheduled Castes and Scheduled Tribes are the classes of the Indian citizens who had been persecuted, discriminated and deprived of human face of Justice for long. Their suffering had endless destination because they had been victims of graded inequality resulting into perpetual degradation and gigantic cold-blooded repression. They had been lamenting since long:

"Hush my child; don't cry, my treasure:
Weeping in the vain,
For the enemy will never
Understand our pain.
For the ocean has its limits
Prisons have their walls around,
But our suffering and our torment
Have no limit and no bound".

The Scheduled Castes and Scheduled Tribes categorization is the secularised as well as constitutionalised version of degraded lot searched in 1930s. Prior to that, they were known by different names inviting analogous discriminatory treatment to slaves, Negroes, aboriginals, etc. in different parts of the world based on deep-rooted prejudices and heartlessness. Speaking of American situation *Ronald Dworkin* very aptly remarks that, "racial discrimination that disadvantages blacks is unjust, not because people cannot choose their race, but because that discrimination expresses prejudice".[1]

Since all Homo sapiens are creation of the same God, equality among them is not only an ideology but also the natural fate of the entire human race. In practice for selfish motive people, who matter, have broken the image of God and forgot his words. The Supreme-Being created man in his own image but the human race forgot the Divine message to live with love and affection with a sense of brotherhood based on the sensibility of togetherness. It created its own image of dominance, superiority and inferiority which gave birth to acute discrimination.

The history of discrimination, more or less, has similar trend of psychological domination by some group of persons over the other constructing racial images encouraging hierarchical social order. The outcome being that some became privileged on the basis of the accident of birth and relegated others to the disadvantaged position. The disadvantaged position of such unfortunate people caused perpetuation of formal as well as material subordination. They are deprived of social and political equality with the fortunate privileged people on the one hand and economic subordination on the other. In most of the countries the victims of societal hierarchical structure may be few (i.e. in minority) like USA or UK but in a country like India they may be many (in majority). It is thought that racism in U.S.A. and Castism in India are not aberrant but rather natural to the socio-economic life and they have become ingrained feature of the life. It is also viewed that how whites in America or caste superiority loaded (rather overloaded) higher castes people in India tolerate and encourage advancement of disadvantaged people in their respective country is not above board as they do so only to the extent they also promote their own self-interest.

Human experience, scientific temper and rational thinking have disapproved earlier ill conceived and motivated notions that whites (in India high castes) possess all virtues—they are industrious, intelligent, moral, knowledge, enabling culture, law abiding, responsible and pious (virtuous) and blacks (in India

1. Law's Empire, p. 388.

SCs, STs) possess all vices—they are lazy, unintelligent, immoral, ignorant, disability culture, criminal, shiftness and lascivious.

JURIDICAL JUSTIFICATION FOR SPECIAL SAFEGUARD FOR THE UNFORTUNATE LOT

The Justification for the very existence of the ordered society is to ensure justice to all including the unfortunate disadvantaged people. Justice to them has many considerations beyond traditional thinking about it. Equalitarian Justice may not serve the purpose. Of course, among the equals law should be equal and should be equally administered. But injustice may breed either way—if equals are treated unequally or unequals are treated equally. All citizens or inhabitants of a country are not equal. In many countries negroes—African Americans, aboriginals could not have even voting rights for a long time. They were deprived of common freedoms and citizenry privileges and to quote Chief Justice Roger Taney "at the time when the Constitution of the United States was adopted, Negroes were regarded as persons of inferior status, not as citizens; that the constitution did not include them in the term citizens".[2] The learned C.J. realised that to be contrary to the prevailing standards of civilized society and sympathised Negroes as unfortunate race, but could not help. So had been case in Australia in relation to aboriginals. Entrenched caste-ridden Indian society with predominant non-contractual status and hierarchical structure had its own discriminatory method of ousting some people from education and other avenues of development. To quote *Justice P.B. Sawant*, "hither to, for centuries, there have been cent percent reservations in practice in all fields, in favour of high castes and classes, to the total exclusion of others. It was a purely caste and class based reservation".[3] Thus, in view of the graded and degraded social structure making people inherently unequal equalizational Justice is to be preferred. What American Sociologist, *Lester*

2. Dred Scott *v.* Sanford, 60 U.S. (19 How.) 393 (1857).
3. Indra Sawhney *v.* Union of India, 1992 SCC (L and S) Supp. 1 para 4 to 7 at p. 217.

Ward says, "Justice consists in the enforcement by society of an artificial equality in social conditions which are naturally unequal". There may be some debate whether unfortunate people are naturally unequal or forced to become unequal by active societal degradation. Efforts to provide equalizational opportunity may involve a tinge of inter-generational Justice. There are forceful arguments for providing Justice to disadvantaged classes through compensatory discrimination method. *Paul W. Taylor* very succinctly and forcefully justifies such measures: "When an injustice has been committed to a group, compensation and reparation must be made to that group. Group rights to compensation are not rights against wrong doers but against society as a whole. The obligation to offer such benefits to the group as a whole is an obligation that falls on society in general, not on any particular person. For it is society that through its established social practice brought upon itself the obligation". Even President *William, J. Clinton* in his visit to Africa in 1998 while dealing with the horrors of slavery said, "European Americans received the fruits of the slave trade and we were wrong in that". And *Vincene Verdun* argues of "continuing liability for racism: Because society perpetuated and benefitted from the institution of slavery, all of society must pay".[4] With a view to make the Justice-oriented plans more effective the proponents of Critical Race Theory overthrew the study of liberal scholars propagating colour-blindness. For them colour consciousness makes the search of identifiable disadvantaged groups possible separating them from Anglos in America. They subscribe the view that "colour-blindness and equal process makes no sense in a society in which identifiable groups had actually been treated differently historically and which effects of this difference in treatment continued into the present".[5] In actuality the Critical Race Theory group adopts an extreme view. A proper rapprochement can be found in observation of the American Supreme Court in *U.S.* v. *Jefferson County Board*. "Our Constitution is both colour-blind and

4. If the shoe fits, wear it : An Analysis of Reparation to African Americans, 67 *Tul. L. Rev.* 597 1993 at p. 621.
5. Kimberie Crenshaw' Race, Reform and Retrenchment : Transformation and Legitimation in Anti-Discrimination Law (1988) 101 *Harv. Law Rev.* 1331).

colour-conscious. To avoid conflict with the equal protection clause, a classification that denies a benefit, causes harm or imposes a burden must not be based on race. In that sense the Constitution is colour-blind. But the Constitution is colour-conscious, to prevent discrimination being perpetuated and to undo the effects of past discrimination. The criteria are the relevancy of colour to a legitimate governmental purpose".[6] So is the case in India. Articles 15(1); 15(2); 16(2); 29(2) ensure non-discriminatory provisions prohibiting discrimination on the grounds of race, caste and religion, but it retains a tinge of caste-consciousness in ensuring preferential treatment or protective discriminatory measures in favour of disadvantaged and socially persecuted groups, as caste has become had reality in India deciding status of individuals from womb to tomb or even after.

The other juridical basis for special provisions for deprived, depraved and disadvantaged group is psychological. Unwanted degradation breeds reaction. There is natural human urge for respect, for equal treatment and human desire to be free from domination by others. The sense of injustice revolts against whatever is unequal by caprice. *Bodenheimer* rightly says, "The struggle for emancipation of classes, races and female sex, which occupies a prominent place in legal history, is evidence of this psychological fact".[7] History is evidence that slaves did not find justice even from the hands of the Supreme Court in *Dred Scott* which accelerated reaction against slavery and American Civil War (1861-68) was revolt against the institution of slavery. Similarly, psychological reaction could be found in French Revolution of 1789, American Revolution and European Chartist Movement. The added merit of compensatory discrimination or protective measures for disadvantaged people is that it not only compensates the degraded classes by creating an atmosphere to assert their status, personality and independence on equal footing with others, it also widens the freedom of such classes to have their own choices like others. *Ramaswamy J.* very aptly observed that "Equality prohibits the State from making discrimination amongst citizens on any

6. 372 Fel. 836 (1967).
7. Jurisprudence.

ground. However, inequality in fact, without differential treatment between the advantaged and disadvantaged subsists. In order to bridge the gap between inequality in results and equality in fact, protective discrimination provides equality of opportunity. Those who are unequal they cannot be treated by identical standards. . . . The State must, therefore, resort to protective discrimination for the purpose of making people who are factually unequal, equal in specific areas".[8]

Akin to the above justification is wider societal problem/ purpose solved through protective discrimination policy. *Ronald Dworkin* remarks, "affirmative action is justified, not because those who are given preference are entitled to an advantage, whether in compensation for past discrimination or for any other reason, but simply because helping them is now an effective way of attacking a national problem".[9]

In *M.R. Balaji* v. *State of Mysore Gajendragadkar J.* had expressed similar views; "The interests of the society at large would be served by promoting the advancement of the weaker elements in the society that Article 15(4) authorises special provision to be made".[10] Thus it has social as well as a national purpose as the interests of the society at large would be better served by promoting the advancement of the weaker elements in the society or as helping them is now an effective way of attacking a national problem and therefore, *in elevating the depressed classes we are but elevating ourselves (emphasis added)*. In *State of Kerala* v. *N.M. Thomas, Krishna Iyer J.* expressed the view that "to protect harijans is not to prejudice any caste to but promote citizen solidarity".[11]

In the above backdrop of the multi-dimensional ramifications of providing special protection to the disadvantaged people throughout the world the specific study of "Legal protection of Scheduled Castes and Tribes" (constitutional safeguards and social justice) conducted by Dr. Deepak Kumar Srivastava, Assistant Professor,

8. Ashok Kumar Gupta *v.* State of U.P. (1997) 5 SCC 201.
9. "Why Bakke Has No Case", *New York Review of Books*, 24, (Nov. 1977) p. 12.
10. (1963) supp. 1. SCR 439 at p. 467.
11. AIR 1976 S.C. 490 at p. 534.

Hidayatullah National Law University, Raipur is most timely and alive presentation of the entrenched problems posed by caste ridden hierarchical Indian society relegating the degraded people to the periphery and constitutional commitment to ameliorate their status so as to ensure their effective and meaningful participation in the mainstream of the national life. The author has caught the nerve and root of the problem by locating continuous persecution of Scheduled Castes and Scheduled Tribes people by pointing out that they are the children of the 'Endless night', i.e. perpetual misery. With this opening line, the author has very succinctly introduced the book with note how the social stratification developed in historical perspective from casteless and classless Vedic society to brahminical priesthood germinating caste system. Not only this, some people were relegated even below to the Charturvarna—the fifth class-untouchables and even 'Unseeables'.[12] The author rightly narrates commitment of our founding fathers with responsibility to ameliorate the conditions of the weaker sections of society, who had suffered in the past[13] and the different constitutional safeguards provided under our Constitution.

Chapter II deals with different dimensions of social justice starting from Aristotalian distributive and corrective Justice to Rawlsian justice as fairness. After presenting indepth study of the facets of Social Justice and its interpretation by the Supreme Court of India, the author narrates permissible departure in favour of Scheduled Castes and Scheduled Tribes which may be formalised as equalisational Justice or protective discrimination.

Chapter III deals with 'Historical perspective and origin of the Scheduled Castes and the Scheduled Tribes'. It also narrates how the expression 'Scheduled Castes' came to be adopted under the Government of India Act, 1935 after covering the journey through 'depressed classes', 'exterior castes' and 'excluded class'. 'Depressed class' was wide enough to cover both Scheduled Castes and Scheduled Tribes as Indian Legislative Council clarified in 1916 the term 'depressed classes' should include criminal and wandering tribes, aboriginal tribes

12. p. 3.
13. p. 4.

and untouchables. Depressed class possessed traits of 'unclean profession', 'unclean caste' and untouchable. Now scheduled castes is defined under Article 366(24) read with Article 341 which means such castes, races or tribes which have been notified by President of India to be Scheduled Castes. So is the case with Scheduled Tribes Article 366(25) read with Article 342 which means such tribes or tribal communities or part of a group within such tribes or tribal communities declared so by the President in his order. The author rightly discusses the Supreme Court's decisions on the interpretation of 'Scheduled Castes' and 'Scheduled Tribes' and analyses how the Supreme Court has given literal and restrictive interpretation to the castes and tribes enumerated in Presidential orders. The Supreme Court has not allowed the benefit of conversion, marriage or adoption for the purpose of reservational/protective discrimination benefit.[14] The Court also denies the benefit of Scheduled tribe status to a person who moves to another state where that tribe is not recognised as Scheduled Tribe.[15] Attaching too much importance and giving due deference to Presidential order, the apex court declared its considered opinion in *State of Maharashtra* v. *Milind*[16] that "the Scheduled Tribe order must be read as it is. It is not even permissible to say that a tribe, sub-tribe, part of or group of any tribe or tribal community is synonymous to the one mentioned in the scheduled Tribes order if they are not specifically mentioned in it". In view of the need of the amelioration of the condition of the Scheduled Castes and the Scheduled Tribes by taking liberal and beneficial approach judicial legalism may require realism and serious research of the impact of reservational benefit to such classes be conducted and author's submission that the Supreme Court's pronouncement in *Bhaiya Ram Munda* v. *Anirudh Patar*[17] though departed and undone in *Milind case* requires restaging with progressive and meaningful approach adopted in that case : "Because some sub-tribes of Mundas are enumerated in order and others are not, no inference will arise

14. Valsamma Pal *v.* Cochin University (1996) 3 SCC 545; Sobha Hemavathi Devi *v.* Setti Gangadhar Swamy (2005) 2 SCC 254.
15. Marri Chandra *v.* Dean, Seth G.S. Medical College (1990) 3 SCC 130
16. (2001) 1 SCC 4 at p. 31.
17. AIR 1970 SC 2533.

that those not enumerated are not Mundas". The problem of under inclusion in Presidential order may be real due to the source of information not based on realistic survey of all the castes. As regards the denial of reservation benefits to converts or married or adopted Scheduled Castes and Scheduled Tribes it needs serious rethinking whether allowing of reservational benefit in such cases will strike at root of caste consciousness prevailing in the Indian society and make the path of assimilation of different shades of people? The spirit of judicial review of reservational benefit placing much emphasis on gigantic reality or avoidance of misuse of reservational benefit is one constitutional value, but the constitutional value of amelioration of Scheduled Castes and Scheduled Tribes and removal of caste consciousness is not less important. Between the two, Scheduled Tribes need more sympathetic treatment because Scheduled Castes have been excommunicated from mainstream culture, the tribal people have been excommunicated from civilization.

Chapter IV of the book presents the study of the causes for degradation of Scheduled Castes and Scheduled Tribes. The root cause lies in deep-rooted prejudices and complexes. The author rightly refers the story of not only denial of admission of Eklavya, a tribal boy as his pupil by Dronacharya but also claiming undeserved *gurudakshina* by treacherously cutting his thumb (angutha) of right hand, so he was incapacitated to use his Dhanurvidya and put challenge to his pupils. The incidence may be narrated as a prosecution for merit dissuading other tribals and depressed lot to make effort to excel in any walk of life. The author rightly narrates the irrational discriminatory arrangements of house in separate streets for Brahmins, Sudras and Panchamma and in last Pallans, Paraiyans and Chakkilians in Trichinopoly district, in Marathas dominated area the practice of not allowing entries of Mahars and Mongs through gate of Poona between 3 P.M. to 9 P.M. because during that period their body cast too long a shadow which falling upon higher castes especially Brahmins defiled them.[18] The author presents the study of different factors contributing towards degradation of depressed people. Factors being impurity and pollution, low

18. p. 78.

origin, caste associated occupation (menial jobs), undesirable habits of eating, economic dependence and above all psychic feeling of superiority among higher caste men and inhered inferiority among depressed people and intolerance on the part of higher caste to see any kind of association or interaction with such degraded lot.[19] The author rightly draws conclusion from that all the factors contributed miseries and suffering of depressed people and discrimination resulted into segregation of haves and have nots.

It was not so that everybody was of the same coin. Since discrimination was ingrained in social evils many large hearted, virtuous and righteous persons made efforts to provide respectability to the virtuous men of these communities. Lord Krishna did not allow completion of Rajsuya Yagya of Yudhishthira so long as Bhakt Supan (a Chandal) was not honoured by offering foods with due respect. Lord Buddha wiped away the wall of superiority and inferiority by admitting low caste people with equal status in his Sangha.

In Chapter V author has elaborately discussed the role of religio-social reformer groups like Buddhism, Jainism and Sikhism and great individual souls like Vivekananda, Kabir, Dayanand Saraswati and many others. On the point of state sponsored invaluable effort, the author cites Chhattrapati Sahuji Maharaj of Kolhapur State, who excelled all earlier efforts by arranging community *bhoj* with depressed and untouchables, making arrangements for their education, enforcing 50% reservation in his state in 1902 (which has been Judicalised by our Supreme Court in *M.R. Balaji* v. *State of Mysore*[20]) and passing Mahar Vatan Abolition Act, 1918. The author must be congratulated for giving due place to the every laudable reformatory and human touching efforts of Sahuji who had performed unparalleled contribution towards equality and equalizational justice, but remained neglected by class biased historians. To quote the author, "The Mahars thereby became outright owners to their land and were freed from doing a hundred odd jobs for the village in return for a small piece of land they were allowed to cultivate. He recruited Untouchables

19. p. 99.
20. AIR 1963 SC 649.

as clerks in the state services and admitted a few educated Untouchables at Bar. In 1919 he legally prohibited the segregation of Untouchable children in schools.[21] And at the last contribution itself, i.e. desegregation of touchables and untouchables may be regarded as most transformative, revolutionary and assimilating force in the every caste-ridden society. It was precursor of the world-wide moving phenomena—the direction in which the law moves is often guide for the decision of particular cases[22] or what *Warren C.J.* declared in *Brown* v. *Board of Education*.[23] "Education is the very foundation of good citizenship" and any sense of segregation is bound to breed inferiority and that may affect their hearts and minds in a way unlikely ever to be undone. The author has critically evaluated the great contribution of the two great-men in pre-constitution era struggling for amelioration of the lot of the unfortunate untouchables, though sometimes appearing on surface to differ on certain principles but core of their heart aiming to arrive at the same goal of wiping out of any sort of disability and ensuring equality to depressed people. B.R. Ambedkar and Mahatma Gandhi both made their most sincere efforts to end the evil of untouchability and its offshoots. The former had experience and lived the life of degradation and persecution, the latter had a great soul devoid of any sense of complex and wishing good for all and his preference for the expression Harijan (people dear to God) coined by the great saint Narasimha Mehta was due to his large heartedness and desire to wrong semblance of nomenclature 'Adi dravidas', 'Antayajas', 'Ati Sudras', 'Avarnas', 'Bhangis', 'Pariahs', 'Panchamas', 'Chamars', etc. It was his large heartedness and he learnt from experience and mend himself when he uttered that "if caste is an essential to Hinduism he would not be a Hindu" or "if untouchability lives Hinduism dies". Gandhi lived for depressed both by words and deeds. By living in Harijan Basti and cleaning night soils he practised. The author has also presented study of attempts made by the depressed classes themselves. On failure from all side and bearing intolerable

21. p. 105,
22. Frank Further J. in Universal Camera Co. *v.* NLRB 474 U.S. 340 at 497 cited by Bodenheimer, Jurisprudence at p. 371.
23. 349 U.S. 294 (1955).

discrimination and persecution and inhering the resentment against high caste Hindus and search of respectability and equal treatment untouchable groups adopted the path of conversion to Buddhism, Islam, Sikhism and Christianity.[24] The author also discusses different legislative measures from princely states and Legislative Assemblies in direction of eradication and upliftment of untouchables in pre-constitution era[25] culminating in secularised term 'Scheduled Caste' under the Government of India Act, 1935.

Chapter VI covers the main target of the study—safeguards provided for the Scheduled Castes and Scheduled Tribes under the Constitution of India. It covers the survey of all the relevant provisions relating to social, educational and economic, service, political and administrative safeguards. After a critical appraisal of non-discriminatory provisions, abolition of untouchability and efforts to assimilate these Scheduled Castes and Scheduled Tribes in the mainstream of life; provisions against exploitation, provisions relating to temple entry on equal footing, the author appreciates the comprehension of the founding fathers that without ending disparity, discrimination, injustice and segregation no fruitful end might be achieved and therefore, they provided for that.[26] Without economic and educational upliftment social equality cannot be achieved or retained and therefore the author has discussed the constitutional safeguards provided for the advancement of Scheduled Castes and Scheduled Tribes, reservation of seats for Scheduled Castes and Scheduled Tribes in private educational institutions, promotion of the educational and economic interest of Scheduled Castes and Scheduled Tribes. The author rightly concludes that "our Constitution-makers not only wanted to eradicate the social evils but they were willing for all-round upliftment of Scheduled Castes and Scheduled Tribes".[27] While dealing with service safeguards, the author deals with all relevant cases relating to the socially and educationally backward classes including *Indra Sawhney* v. *Union of India*,[28] but the author has

24. p. 114.
25. pp. 114-20.
26. p. 156.
27. p. 173.
28. AIR 1993 SC 477.

been conscious of the fact of basic difference between the two types of backward classes i.e., socially and educationally backward classes (suspect class) and Scheduled Caste and Scheduled Tribes (definitely and undisputably backward classes). That is reason why the Supreme Court limited creamy layerisation formula to SCBCs and specifically said that it would not cover Scheduled Castes and Scheduled Tribes. In *Indra Sawhney,*[29] Court overruled *Rangachari*[30] and declared reservation in promotion as violative of equality clause. With a view to provide special safeguard to Scheduled Castes and Scheduled Tribes the Parliament removed this lacunae by inserting clause 4-A to Article 16 by the Constitution (Seventy-seventh) Amendment Act, 1995 and secured reservation for Scheduled Castes and Scheduled Tribes even in promotions. Krishna Iyer J. very aptly distinguished the position of Scheduled Castes and Scheduled Tribes from that of OBCs when he observed in *State of Kerala* v. *N.M. Thomas*.[31] "The Scheduled Castes and Scheduled Tribes are no castes in the Hindu fold but an amalgam of castes, races, groups, tribes, communities or parts thereof found on investigation to be the lowliest and need of massive state aid and notified as such by President. To confuse, this backward most social composition with the castes is to commit a constitutional error, mislead by compendious appellation. So that, to protect Harijans is not to prejudice any caste but to promote citizen solidarity".[32] The author has rightly discussed relevant cases in post-1995 period and proviso to Article 335 permitting lowering the standard of evaluation and relaxation in qualifying marks in relation to Scheduled Castes and Scheduled Tribes. After having have the in-depth provisions for political and administrative safeguards, the author emphasizes the need of the effective implementation of the relevant Commission's report.[33]

Chapter VII of the study draws certain conclusions and proposes certain suggestions. The author rightly focuses on the

---

29. *Ibid.*
30. AIR 1962 SC 36.
31. AIR 1976 SC 490.
32. *Ibid.*, p. 534.
33. p. 234.

reality of the Indian societal impact that 'there is some progress in breaking the mould of social inequality and caste oppression and in the economic and educational spheres but there is a long way to go before social equality, educational equality freedom from caste oppression, freedom from economic dependence are achieved. The author rightly laments that in spite of many facilities the intended goal is not achieved due to lack of planning and imaginative leadership and lack of co-ordination among the different branches of the government. And, therefore, the suggestions of the author needs serious concern that there must be better co-operation and understanding between the Government departments so that the constitutional objective to uplift the Scheduled Castes and Scheduled Tribes could be achieved'.[34]

The problem of Scheduled Tribes who had been secluded from civilization itself needs handling with special care so as to integrate them with rest of the society. The author very appropriately quotes Nehru: "What we ought to do is to develop a sense of oneness, with these people a sense of unity and understanding. That involves psychological approach". The author also quotes the reports of the Scheduled Castes and Scheduled Tribes Commission: "The problem of problems is not to disturb the harmony of tribal life and simultaneously work for its advance; not to impose anything upon the tribals and simultaneously work for their integration as member and part of Indian family".[35]

The evaluation of the functional impact of constitutional safeguards presented by the author that much has been done much more is needed as, "Even after more than six decades of the commencement of Constitution, the position of Scheduled Castes and Scheduled Tribes has not been substantially improved".[36] It speaks loud of the realism about the implementation of constitutional safeguards in favour of Scheduled Castes and Scheduled Tribes. It is more important for our continuous endeavour in view of multi-dimensional problems of development, ecology and tribal rights. There is

34. p. 251.
35. *Ibid.*
36. p. 252.

flood of litigation raised by public and justice-oriented people but solution does not appear very satisfactory in near future. Keeping in view the seriousness of ouster of Scheduled Tribes forest dwellers due to developmental programmes, Parliament has enacted, The Scheduled Tribes and other Traditional Forest Dwellers (Recognition of Forest Rights) Act, 2006 with specific view to recognize and vest the forest rights and occupation in forest land in forest dwelling Scheduled Tribes and other traditional forest dwellers who have been residing in such forest for generation but whose rights could not be recorded. The objective of the said Act is also to address the long standing insecurity of tenurial and access rights of forest dwelling Scheduled Tribes and other traditional forest dwellers including those who were forced to relocate their dwelling due to state development interventions. The Act has come into force from 31.12.2007. Maharashtra has been the first state to recognise rights of the forest dwellers and allocate 2349 hectares to two tribal villages[37] but much is needed to be done. Scheduled Tribes ousters are not receiving proper rehabilitation by way of land allotment or adequate compensation. The new law will be effective only if forest management becomes sensitive to social, economic, ecological and cultural realities of forest dwellers. It is also hoped that as the Court has not found it helpless to grant relief in a case of violation of the right to life and personal liberty, it should also be prepared to forge new tools and devise new remedies for enforcing the rights of Scheduled Castes and Scheduled Tribes.

It is true that the Constitution provides sufficient safeguards for the betterment of the Scheduled Castes and Tribes but fruitful result can be perceived only through societal outlook of assimilation, not dissimilation. The recognition of the Scheduled Castes and Scheduled Tribes talent and giving them position of prestige should be honestly and sincerely perceived and not politically perceived e.g., the caste leader is pronounced as great Indian leader, but a Scheduled Castes or Scheduled Tribes leader is termed as Scheduled Castes and Scheduled Tribes leader. We know that when Meera Kumar became speaker of Lower House she was publicized as first woman

37. Down to Earth, Sept. 1-15, 2009, Vol. 18, No. 8, CSE, New Delhi.

Scheduled Caste speaker. They should be treated, acclaimed and accepted as Indian leader.

In the backdrop of continuing societal conflicting interests, values and aspirations the book written by Dr. Deepak Kumar Srivastava under caption "Legal Protection of Scheduled Castes and Tribes (Constitutional Safeguards and Social Justice)" is most timely, informative, challenging and full of well considered solutions. I am of firm view that the book will inspire all those who have sincere concern for implementation of socio-economic, cultural, educational and political measures ensuring social justice to the Scheduled Castes and Scheduled Tribes people. It will be of great interest of the law students, scholars, teachers, political thinkers, framers of policy and all those who have to think of humanitarian touch and equality for the long persecuted lot Scheduled Castes and Tribes. I strongly recommend the publication of the book and hope and trust that it will serve the intended purpose of social justice efforts for Scheduled Castes and Tribes.

ANIRUDH PRASAD
Visiting Professor of Law
Hidayatullah National Law University
New Raipur, Chhattisgarh

Preface

The founding fathers of our Constitution felt that the inequitable forces in the socio-economic system and political organizations had created imbalance in the society and placed certain people particularly the Scheduled Castes and the Scheduled Tribes in the disadvantageous position. The Constitution of India provides to all the citizens, social, economic and political justice and equality of status and opportunity. For achieving this objective safeguards and protective measures were provided in the Constitution for the deprived, weaker and vulnerable sections to ensure their all round development so as to bring them into the mainstream of the nation and at par with the other section of the society. This book is directly associated with these provisions which are there in Constitution to make a society devoid of inequality through by the way of discrimination. I must admit candidly that because of the topic being associated with Constitution certain provisions, which I too have dealt with, have been a matter of hot debate before our Supreme Court and in legal, social and political sphere. But still there seems to be a lack of organised study of all those provisions which are there for the Scheduled Castes and Scheduled Tribes in Constitution in such a way as could give a lucid understanding of the problems and the solutions provide for them from time-to-time by the legislature. To compile these provisions and study them under relevant head was the driving point for me to choose the caption of the book. It gives me immense pleasure to write for the cause of those who have been marginalised since ages. This is what can be called as humanitarian face of my work. Above all the idea of our Constitution to spread justice to each and everyone has always fascinated me. So by the way of this I have tried to justify the core of our Constitution.

This book is based on the provisions of our Constitution which are there for the protection, benefit and upliftment of Scheduled Castes and Scheduled Tribes. But the extent of the book is not confined to the provisions of our Constitution only. It includes in its ambit the concept, historical aspect, chronology of origin of Scheduled Castes and Scheduled Tribes the miseries suffered by them. Other than this, certain pre-constitutional scenario whether social or political and different enactments of the then states have also been included at relevant places to make the book more vivid and clear. The scope of the book also extends to different judicial pronouncements of our Courts whether they are in favour or against in the interest of Scheduled Castes and Scheduled Tribes. In this book, I have dealt with these against cases also and the correction of judicial decisions whether by the way of constitutional amendments or by the judiciary itself. I have included those provisions also which impliedly are there for the upliftment of Scheduled Castes and Scheduled Tribes as Articles 23, 24, 243D, 243T. All relevant recent amendments and the object for the amendment also find place in it. Above all, I, with my best efforts, have tried to put forward some valuable suggestions which are of practical importance to integrate the Scheduled Castes and Scheduled Tribes in the mainstream.

The book is an attempt to examine the different Legal protections regarding the Scheduled Castes and the Scheduled Tribes. The book is divided into seven chapters including Introduction and Conclusion. Chapter One introduces the subject and points out the relevance of the Constitutional provisions which are incorporated by the framers of our Constitution to uplift the condition of the Scheduled Castes and the Scheduled Tribes.

Chapter Two includes the discussion on the very concept of justice and further elaborates the concept, growth, scope and different aspects of Social Justice which are there in our Constitution and reiterated by our Supreme Court.

Chapter Three deals with in-depth study of the Historical perspective and origin of the Scheduled Castes and the Scheduled Tribes. It is a fact that if the Historical perspective and origin of any subject matter is clearly established then it becomes easier to understand the subject matter. Keeping this view in mind an attempt has been made to study the systematic historical perspective and origin of the Scheduled Castes and the Scheduled Tribes.

Chapter Four explains different causes for degradation of Scheduled Castes and Scheduled Tribes. This chapter throws light on the miseries suffered by the Scheduled Castes and the Scheduled Tribes, their inhumane condition, their depression and their poverty and segregation from the rest of the society. This work is an attempt to enumerate those factors which could be held responsible for the degradation of the Scheduled Castes and the Scheduled Tribes.

Chapter Five is "Pre-Constitutional Measures for upliftment of the Scheduled Castes and the Scheduled Tribes." In this chapter, I have discussed different measures which were adopted for upliftment of Scheduled Castes and Scheduled Tribes. This chapter has been divided in two parts; in part first I have discussed the attempts made by social reformers and by the member of depressed class itself. In second part the description of that the Legislative attempts have been made which were made by before application of Government of India Act, and under Government of India Act, 1935. Finally, in Chapter Five a brief reference of Constituent Assembly Debates has been discussed. These debates are the foundation on which the Constitutional safeguards have been given to Scheduled Castes and Scheduled Tribes.

Chapter Six is the crux of our study. The heading to Chapter Six is Safeguards under Constitution of India. This Chapter further contains five sub-heads, namely:

- (i) Social Safeguards,
- (ii) Educational and Economic Safeguards,
- (iii) Service Safeguards,
- (iv) Political Safeguards, and
- (v) Administrative Safeguards.

Each sub-head contains relevant Constitutional provisions regarding these safeguards which have been discussed in that sub-head.

At last in Chapter Seven the conclusion of the study has been done and it has been endeavored to make some valuable suggestions, so that these measures could not only become a mere piece of paper but a mighty weapon to uplift the status of Scheduled Castes and Scheduled Tribes.

First and foremost, I express my heartfelt gratitude to my teacher Prof. (Dr.) Anirudh Prasad, visiting professor, Hidayatullah National Law University, Raipur for kindly consenting and sparing his valuable time to write the Foreword of the book. I am thankful for his humble words which will inspire upcoming authors like me to undertake similar work in future.

I wish to express regard to my parents for their blessings, my wife and colleague Mrs. Balwinder Kaur Sandhu for her constant support and encouragement and my friend Mr. Kanderpesh Dwivedi, Assistant Prosecution Officer who also prompted me to complete the book, without whom this work would have not been completed. Through this book I also acknowledge the love and affection rendered to me by my students. Their appreciation and admiration is an important source of encouragement and motivation.

Lastly, I express my gratitude, thanks and appreciation to Mr. G.S. Bhatia, Deep and Deep Publications Pvt. Ltd., New Delhi for not only publishing this book but for giving me opportunity, rendering all the help and assistance, anytime I required it. Without his cooperation, this book would not have become a reality.

DEEPAK KUMAR SRIVASTAVA

1

Introduction

> "Every night and every morn,
> some to misery are born
> Every morn and every night,
> some are born to sweet delight
> some are born to sweet delight,
> some are born to endless nights."[1]

The Scheduled Castes and the Scheduled Tribes were the children of the "Endless night." Their birthright was the badge of shame; their inheritance the overflowing cup of humiliation; their constant and closest companion degradation; the bride of their marriage lifelong poverty; and their only fault to be born to their parents. They were denied jobs except the lowest menial tasks and they were denied contact with other persons. And all those wrongs were done to them by those who candid

1. William Black, 'Auguries of innocence'. As quoted by Supreme Court in State of Kerala *v.* N.M. Thomas, AIR 1976 SC 490.
2. For a detailed historical background of the social structure in India see Churye, Caste and Classes in India (Bombay 1959) : B.R. Ambedkar, The untouchables 1948, K. Subba Rai, Social Justice and Law (1974); A.N. Bharadwaj, Problems of Scheduled Castes and Scheduled Tribes in India (1979).

themselves their superior. The rationale behind their condition can be found if we examine the Indian social structures in its historical prospective.[2] The prehistoric record of the Hindu culture reveals that social stratification did not exist in ancient times. The civilization of Vedic times gives information about the social structure of the then society and confirms equality in the Hindu society. During those days all human beings were equal and enjoyed equal status and there was no trace of social disintegration into castes and classes. The entire society was bound by a feeling of brotherhood and enjoyed unrestricted social intercourse. But, in the course of time, the society was divided into caste and classes.

The origin of social stratification is lost in antiquity. One view is that divinity ordained the social order in which each caste has the particular function to perform in furtherance of *dharma*. According to this view, caste is a part of religion and every person born in a caste has to obey the divine injunction and discharge the duties of that caste. The other view is described as the organic theory of society. According to that theory, each section of the community has its allotted place and function and each is as important as the rest for the achievement of the common welfare. Each caste is a natural focus of loyality, but together they constitute an interdependent community.

The sociological origin of caste system has a rational basis. The fourfold division of the society was based not on birth but type of work performed. The division of society was not merely functional, it was also a division by standards of culture and excellence. Persons belonging to lower groups could claim and enter the higher strata of society by personal achievement. Likewise persons belonging to higher groups could come down to a lower strata by personal degradation. But as time passed by, the social stratification had become crystallized into watertight compartments and became rigid. Earlier spirit of fraternity got eclipsed and the division in the society became visible leading to castes and sub-castes based on birth. Caste had become a symbol of status; one was born and die in the same caste.

Orthodox historians trace the origin of caste system prevalent in Indian society to the time of Aryan advent and consequent subjugation of local residents. Originally, the Aryans were grouped into three Varnas : Brahmins, Kshatriyas and the Vaishyas. A man could aspire to rise in the heirachy either by his wisdom or prowess. As the progress of integration of the Aryans with the local residents continued, the local residents were admitted as one more class and they were called Shudras. It is from this categorization that caste which was in a way a religious revolution-tried to destroy the caste system. But with the decline of Buddhism, caste system got revived. And with the passage of time, a complicated network of castes became the stronghold of Hindu social structure and orthodoxy.

The last position among the Varnas and association with unclean occupations led the Shudras on to untouchability—which became a lasting social stigma. The vocations, admittedly essential for the wellbeing of the society but involving physical handling of dirty and putrefying matter, were assigned to this class of society. They were employed or asked to do the dirtiest possible jobs such as flaying of dead animals, tanning hides, manufacture of leather goods, sweeping streets and scavenging. In addition to this, Smritis and Shastras ordained them as social segregates. In order to perpetuate their hold and position in social heirachy, the Brahmins propounded a sense of defilement and pollution with these unfortunate people. They were asked to live outside the village. In some parts of India, not only were there 'untouchables but there were also 'unseeables'.

Earlier period of Indian history reveals indirect support to caste heirachy.[3] It was only in the later part of the British period that some steps were taken to ameliorate the conditions of people at the lowest rung of the social heirachy. In addition to anti-disability measures such as temple-entry, etc., certain ameliorative measures were taken to help the lowly. But these steps were more of political nature. In the absence of any special leverage, the lower castes could not avail of opportunites provided under law for their advancement. On the other hand, the usurpation of available opportunites by more advanced classes created wide economic disparities in Indian society. The socially advanced classes got the advantage of the traditionally inherited skills, education and employment opportunities. They were also fortunate in getting into the government service in good numbers. Resultant socio-economic deprivation gave rise to a new class called 'depressed classes'. Subsequently the tribal

3. See Marc Galanter, "Untouchability and the Law", *Economic and Political Weekly*, (1969) p. 131.

people, people of denotified tribes and the depressed classes were lumped together.

It is with this historical background that the leaders of free India visualized a social reconstruction while framing the Constutution. The Constitution Assembly, appointed a sub-committee with *Thakkar Bappa,* a dedicated leader of the downtrodden, as its Chairman to suggest the necessary sanctions to undo the evil of age-old social stratification in the form of castes and classes. The historic recommendation of the said committee, later on accepted as a national policy by the Constituent Assembly, was that "the new democratic state has a responsibility for the welfare of the weaker sections of the society, who have suffered in the past." In pursuance of the policy, the Constitution prohibited discrimination against citizens on various grounds and removed all forms of disabilities. Further, special provisions were made to ameliorate the conditions of these neglected sections.

The framers of the Constitution were great social engineers and the Constitution of India is an excellent piece of social engineering.[4] The Constitution of India aims to wipe out all possible socio-economic and political imbalances and achievement of justice—social, economic and political[5] is its real goal. Having the experience of important democratic countries,[6] the Constitution ruled out discrimination on grounds of religion, race, caste, sex or place of birth or any of them.

4. Social Engineering is a principle coined by Dean Roscoe Pound, the great American Sociological Jurisprudent, by which he meant a process of balancing conflicting interests and securing the satisfaction of the maximum of wants with the minimum of friction. Interpretation of Legal History, 156.
5. Preamble to the Constitution of India and Article 38. The latter provides interalia that the State shall strive to promote the welfare of the people by securing and protecting as effectively as it may a social order in which justice, social, economic and political shall inform all the institutions of national life.
6. In important democratic like America, there has been racial discrimination and segregation for a long time which was done away with in 1954 in Brown v. Board of Education. The framers of the problem of discriminatory governmental treatment under political pressures and therefore they ruled out discrimination of the grounds enumerated in Articles 15(1) and 16(2).

Guaranteeing such equality in law, the Constitution also seems to be aware of guaranteeing equality in fact. With this view it protects the interests of Scheduled Castes, Scheduled Tribes and other weaker sections of society by providing for Protective Discrimination.[7]

The Constitution aims at peaceful social change by balancing the conflicting interests in the Indian Society and protective discrimination is one of the measures of balancing the societal interest at large with that of interests of weaker sections of Indian society. The expression weaker section of the society is comprehensive and includes backward classes, Scheduled Castes and Scheduled Tribes. The Constitution explicitly safeguards their interests.

Underlying our Constitution is an egalitarian philosophy which makes no discrimination between individuals on grounds of caste, creed, race, religion, birth, sex, position, power, wealth or influence. This is clearly echoed in the preamble which states that 'We the People of India have solemnly resolved to secure to all its citizens :

JUSTICE social, economic and political;
LIBERTY of thought, expression, belief, faith and worship.
EQUALITY of status and of opportunity.[8]

The resolution aims at social reconstruction guaranteeing socio-economic justice through the mechanism of political

---

7. Articles 16(4) and 15(4). "Equals must be treated equally, unequals must be treated unequally", says Mr. R.K. Gupta, "not to perpetuate the existing inequalities but to achieve and maintain a real state of effective equality, if the notion of equality were so defined as to include unequal but inseperate treatment to the deprived, it would ensure Justice to the people across their ideological bounds". 'Justice; unequal but inseperate', *Journal of Indian Law Institute*.
8. The above phrase has been carved out of the Objective Resolution of the Constituent Assembly adopted on January 22, 1947, which states *inter alia* as under : The Constitutent Assembly declares its firm and solemn resolve to proclaim India as an Independent Sovereign Republic and to draw up for her future governance a constitution... (5) Wherein shall be guaranteed and secured to all the people of India justice, social, economic and political; equality of status and opportunity before the law.

democracy and individual liberty. This preambulary concept of socio-economic justice has been translated by the framers into specific provisions in Part III (Fundamental Rights) and Part IV (Directive Principles of State Policy) of the Constitution. As observed by Granville Austin.[9]

"The Indian Constitution is first and formemost a social document. The majority of its provisions are either directly aimed at furthering the goals of the social revolution or attempt to foster this revolution by establishing the conditions necessary for its achievement. Yet despite the permeation of the entire Constitution by the aim of national renascence, the core of the commitment to the social revolution lies in Parts III and IV, in the Fundamental Rights and in the Directive Principles of State Policy. These are the conscience of the Constitution."

It was felt that the socio-economic justice ushering a social reconstruction of Indian society is a *sine qua non* for effective exercise of all other basic rights guaranteed in free India. As Laski says :[10]

> "The more equals are the social rights of citizens, the more likely they are to be able to utilize their freedoms in realms worthy of exploration. The more equality there is in a state, the more use in general, we can make of our freedoms."

In a caste-ridden and economically imbalanced society like ours, wherein due to historical reasons certain castes and classes were for centuries socially oppressed, economically condemned to live the life of penury and were coerced to learn the family trade or occupation the strict application of social equality would have meant perpetuation of agelong distinction based on caste and class. It was thus contended that the doctrine of social equality ensuring socio-economic justice would be meaningful

9. Granville Austin, The Indian Constitution : Cornerstone of a Nation (1966), p. 50. The purpose of the fundamental rights is to create and egalitarian society to free all citizens from coercion or restriction by society and to make liberty available for all. The purpose of the directive principles is to fix certain social and economic goals for immediate attainment by bringing about a non-violent social revolution.
10. Herold Laski, The Modern State (1948), p. 52.

in the context of Indian society only if 'Protective Discrimination'[11] or initial advantage or privilege is given as an equalizer to those who are too weak, socially, economically and educationally, enabling them to avail of the guaranteed freedoms and rights on the footing of equality. In pursuance to this social policy, certain provisions are made in the Constitution giving 'favoured treatment' to various castes and classes.

The Constitution of India is a Charter of a peaceful democractic social revolution.[12] Such a social revolution is meant to get India out of the medievalism based on birth, religion, custom and community and reconstruct her social structure on modern foundations of law individual merit and secular outlook. It is to give a socio-economic content to our freedom obsessed with this desire, the framers of the Constitution laid down a scheme.[13] The scheme operates in two-fold manner :

(i) By treating every person as equal in the eyes of law and removing all forms of discrimination or disabilities; and

(ii) By undertaking special measures for the advancement of weaker sections of society by giving them adventitious aids and preferential treatment over others.

---

11. The term 'proctective discrimination' was coined by Professor C. H. Alexandrowicz to indicate the measures of protection including reservation of seats in colleges and posts in government services sanctioned by the Indian Constitution, by way of exception to the general principle of equality and non-discrimination embodied in Articles 14, 15(1), 16(1) and 16(2) of the Constitution, and in favour of the Scheduled Castes and Scheduled Tribes. See Alexandrowicz, Constitutional Developments in India, 56(1958); The synonyms used for protective discrimination in legal literature are mostly 'reservations', 'quotas', 'compensatory treatment' or 'preferential treatment'; and 'adventitious aids', etc.
12. As observed by Mrs. Indira Gandhi, the Prime Minister of India, on Feb. 1975 at a function held to celebrate the 25th anniversary of the Constitution.
13. As early as 1931, the Indian National Congress at its Karachi Session had adopted the famous resolution on Fundamental Rights and Economic and Social Change. The resolution, *inter alia*, stressed the need for a constitutional framework to bring about a social revolution in India.

Article 14 to 18 of the Constitution guarantee the right to equality to every citizen. Article 14 embodies the general principle of equality before law. In specific contexts the State is further forbidden to discriminate on ground of race,[14] religion,[15] caste,[16] sex,[17] place of birth,[18] residence,[19] descent,[20] class[21] and language.[22] Additional provisions outlaw untouchability[23] and protect the citizen from certain kinds of discrimination by private persons and institutions.[24]

In a society of uneven basic social structure, the doctrine of equality, howsoever comprehensive, would fail to afford an equality of opportunity in the real sense. So to make the right of equality meaningful, the Constitution-makes a number of provisions to ameliorate the socio-economic conditions of socially, culturally and economically backward communities, or of those which are in a depressed state and to bring them up to a level comparable with the advanced sections of society. This policy is epitomized in the Directive Principle contained in Art. 46, which states :

> "The State shall promote with special care the educational and economic interest of the weaker sections of the people, and in particular, of the Scheduled Castes and the Scheduled Tribes, and shall protect them from social injustice and all forms of exploitation."

The Constitutional imperative and the madate for securing and protecting a social order in which justice, social, economic

---

14. Articles 15(1), 16(2) and 23(2).
15. *Ibid.*
16. *Ibid.*
17. Articles 15 and 16.
18. Articles 15 and 16.
19. Article 16(2).
20. Article 16(2).
21. Article 23(2).
22. Articles 29(2), 30(2).
23. Article 17.
24. Articles 15(2) prohibits discrimination by private individuals in regard to use of facilities and accommodations open to the public.

and political shall inform all the instructions of the national life necessitated some form of 'preferential treatment' in favour of the weaker sections of society.

In the broad compass of 'preferential treatment' policy, we find special provisions for certain backward areas[25] provisions guaranteeing minority rights,[26] provisions for the welfare of children and women[27] and provisions aimed at helping the weaker sections of the society.[28] But in the narrow sense of the term, the policy of 'prefential treatment' in the form of 'protective discrimination' has been made to ameliorate the conditions of the Scheduled Castes, the Scheduled Tribes and other backward classes. Not only are they favoured in benefit like housing, scholarships etc., but exceptions have been carved to some of the non discriminatory provisions of the Constitution to uplift these people. The scheme of preference or 'protective discrimination' is introduced not with the purpose of affording equal opportunity to these weaker sections of the society (which they already have, atleast theoretically) but for the purpose of giving them greater opportunity to achieve success. The scheme is justified on the ground that these sections are deficit in background socially and educationally which make them unable to compete on terms of equality. The whole scheme of preferences introduces a factor of historical balance or compensation; the backward are to be given a more than equal chance in order to overcome the deprivations and inequalities of the past.[29]

---

25. Part X of the Constitution (Art. 244-244A).
26. Articles 25, 26, 27, 28, 29 and 30.
27. Articles 15(3), 24, 39 (f), 42 and 45.
28. Articles 15(4), 16(4), 46, Part XVI of the Constitution (Arts. 330-342).
29. Gajendragadkar, J., in General Manager V. Rangachari, (1961) II S.C.J. 424-431.

2

Dimensions of Social Justice

Justice is the constant and perpetual will to render to everyone that to which he is entitled.

—ULPIAN

Social Justice is not a blind concept or an irrational dogma. It seeks to do justice to all the citizens of the state.

—P.B. Gajendragadkar

The very existence of society depends upon the communities forming it and the harmony amongst communities. The society existing in our country is diverse and plural. If we look at the developmental process of society we find that it is the family which comes first at the level of social organization after that the community and gradually the society. When we talk about society at macro level we have the society as told above, looking calm and organized and well placed.

But when, deal with the nature of society at micro level, we find different segment having their own inerest and a vast disparities between those segments. These segments can be named as different castes based on religion or different religion themself. Historically and mythologically it has been prevailing in our society since ages.

The differences and conflicts between priviledged and oppressed class is very common phenomenon when the instrument named "State" was used to follow the concept of 'Laissez faire'. Them conflicts were more evident and priviledged used to enjoy the major chunk.

Now there has been a radical change in concept of State, i.e. welfare State. Now the state not only provides security from external aggression but it also endeavour to minimize or remove the disparities or differences between different groups.

The State as it exist today realizes the fact that the problem of disparity and oppression of have nots which concern an overwhelmingly large number. If its citizens can not be successfully met unless it wisely uses its mighty weapon of law and attempts to restore balance by the way of justice.

(I) IMPORTANCE OF JUSTICE IN CIVILIZED SOCIETY

Justice is the concept which existed along with the existence of the universe itself. One can find the prevalence of justice in the very creation of the creator. For every living group of organisms nature set norms for the smooth survival with the sense of coexistence. The Almighty is the embodiment of justice and the same he expects from every creature, every society and every set-up. Along with the revolutionary development of human race and society the concept and sense of justice became its part and pareel and even now in the extremely advance society of twenty-first century the quest and concept of justice is the fundamental base of a superior system. Even in the primitive society the virtues and ideals were ordained with justice and the supreme people preferred to die but not to leave the path of justice. One can quote the famous Sanskrit verse:

अद्यैव वा मरणमऽस्तु युगान्तरे वा।
न्यायात् पथ प्रविचलन्ति पदम् न धीराः।।

It means that the people who are ordained with heavenly boon they always prefer to follow the path of justice even at the cost of their life. The modern system of justice is critically studied and looked from various angles and from various doctrines, while the ancient idea of justice evolved out of the natural and religious consciousness of the noble thinkers. In every act and conduct of the people justice prevailed as a basic norm of humanity. In every act and conduct of the people and the king the sense of justice was inherent.

Speaking of justice in the broadest and most general terms, we might say that justice is concerned with the fitness of a group order or social system for the task of accomplishing its essential objectives. The aim of justice is to coordinate the diversified efforts and activities of the members of the community and to allocate rights, powers and duties among them in a manner which will satisfy the reasonable needs and aspirations of individuals and at the same time promote maximum productive effort and social cohesion.

Kelsen remarks with special reference to the ethical concept of justice "To determine whether this or that order has an absolute value, that is, is 'just', is not possible by the methods of ethical knowledge. Justice is an irrational ideal. However, indispensable it may be for the willing and acting of human beings, it is not viable by reason. Only positive law is known, or more correctly is revealed to reason."[1]

In the opinion of Swedish legal realist *A.V. Lundstedt,* the often heard assertion that law-makers and courts should be guided by ideals of justice is "completely senseless".[2] Such skeptical viewpoints have their origin in an unconscious or conscious belief that expressions of ethical judgements are more "ejaculations"[3] that is, irrational articulations of emotions, feelings and subjective preferences. *Plato* in his 'Republic,' fashioned a doctrine of the just commonwealth strongly embedded with collectivistic ideals. In his view, justice consists in a harmonious relation between the various parts of the social organism. Every citizen must do his duty in his appointed place and do the thing for which his nature is best adapted. Since

1. Kelson, General Theory of Law and State, transt. by Wedberg, A. (Cambridge, Mass., 1945), p. 13.
2. "Law and Justice", in Interpretations of Modern Philosophies, ed. Sayer, P. (New York, 1947), p. 450.
3. Bordenheimer, Jurisprudence, p. 178.

Plato's state was a class state, divided into rulers, auxiliaries and the producing class, Platonic justice signified that the members of each class must attend to their own business and not to meddle with the business of the members of another class. Some people are born to rule, some to assist the rulers in the discharge of their functions, and others are destined to be farmers or artisans or traders. A man who attempted to govern his fellow men and he was only fit to be a farmer or craftsmen must be deemed not only foolish but also unjust. The rulers of the state, assisted by their aides, must see to it that each person is assigned his proper station in life, and that he adequately performs the duties of this station.[4]

A different approach to the concept of justice was taken by *Aristotle*. Justice in his opinion, consists in "some sort of equality." It demands that the things of this world shall be equitably allotted to the members of the community or state, it also requires that this just distribution of things shall be maintained by the law as against any violations. According to this two-fold function of justice, Aristotle distinguishes between two forms of justice. The first he calls Distributive Justice. This form of justice is meted out primarily by the legislator and consists in the distribution of offices, rights, honours, and goods to the members of the community according to the principle of proportionate equality. Equal things should be given to equal persons, unequal things to unequal persons. According to *Aristotle*, it is the person of highest civil excellence, making the greatest contribution to the good life in society, who should be entitled to the greatest recognition in matters of monetary reward, honour, political office, and the like.[5]

The second kind of justice in the Aristotelian scheme is called Corrective Justice. Assuming that an allocation of rights, duties, and office has been accomplished by legislative or other means, it is the function of justice to guarantee, protect and maintain this distribution against illegal attacks and to restore the distributive equilibrium after it has been disturbed. This corrective function of justice is chiefly administered by the

4. Plato, The Republic transt. Lindsay, A.D. (Everyman's Library, ed.,, 1950), BK. IV, 433-34.
5. See The Politics, BK. III 1281a.

judges. According to *Aristotle* distributive justice demands a relative, proportionate, "geometrical" equality which takes account of the natural differences in the physical and mental endowments of men. The equality postulated by corrective justice, on the other hand is an "arithmetical" one, being concerned with the computation of losses suffered and the restoration of gains illegally made.

According to *Ulpian*, "Justice is the constant and perpetual will to render to everyone that to which he is entitled."[6] This description of the aim of justice can be traced back to Cicero, for purposes of brief identification it might be called the *'Suum cuique'* ("to each his due") formula of justice. There is implicit in the *Suum cuique* notion an assumption that two persons to whom the same things are "due" are entitled to equality of treatment.

A fundamentally divergent attitude towards justice was taken by the English philosopher and sociologist *Herbert Spencer*. The supreme value he linked to the idea of justice was not equality, but freedom. This concept of justice was cast by Spencer into the mold of a celebrated formula: "Every man is free to do that which he wills, provided he infringes not the equal freedom of any other man."[7]

Law is a manifestation of the spirit of the people and a legal system is the sum total of laws. Furthermore, we can define a "law" as the command of the sovereign for regulating various aspects and conducts of citizens in that particular country or society. The law is most effective and standard norm for regulating a civilized society through a legal system to achieve justice therein.

Justice is the administration of law in a fair and reasonable way through a legal system prevailing in society. The essence of justice lies in equity, evenhandedness, fairmindedness, fairplay, impartiality, legality, neutrality and objectivity. Justice is integral to the concept of a legal system, the etymology of the word 'law' itself derives from what is fitting and right. The achievement of a minimum of justice is a condition *sine qua non* of the continuity of a legal system and orderly smooth running of society.

---

6. Dig. 1. 1.10 : Iustitia est constans et perpetua voluntas ius suum cuique tribuendi.
7. Justice (New York, 1891), 9. 46.

The notion of accountability is spread throughout public life and the duties of judiciary were not owed to electorate, they were owed to law which was there for peace, order and good government of the whole community. The impartiality of a judge means that he has no personal stake in the outcome. Absence of bias is essential to judicial process. With impartiality comes objectivity, it means making judicial decisions on the basis of considerations that are essential to the judge and that may even conflict with his or her personal views. The preconditions for realising the judicial role are independence of judiciary, judicial objectivity and public confidence in judiciary. An essential condition for analysing the judicial role is public confidence on judges. This means confidence in judicial independence, fairness and impartiality. Public confidence was ensured by the recognition that judges are doing justice within framework of law and its provisions.

Judiciary is the true index of the responses of the enlightened conscience of the community to the surest road of national protection. Our judiciary have accumulated vast powers. There are no checks on the exercise of power by the apex court except self-restraint. Judiciary is the backbone of democracy.

The accountability of judiciary is not only to the conscience of judges but also to the people in whom the ultimate sovereignty vests. Since the legislature, the executive and the judiciary are none other than the servants of law and function for the society, they are definitely accountable to it. Delivery of justice is one of the main attributes of Almighty. The judges and lawyers working in the legal system for justice delivery are called noble. The nobility means rendering selfless service to others, relieving the oppressed and reaching justice to all. Every member of this justice delivery system is performing most sacrosanct and holy act. If truly performed it sanctifies the very person rendering service, which brings peace and happiness to society. The primary duty of judges and lawyers is to be within the law. Any transgression from it cannot render true justice.

The law existed from the very inception of the universe. The main purpose of law in every legal system is to protect the individual against oppression, and bring coherence in functioning of society.

The law truly devolved on man from nature. There is an inherent relationship between man and nature. Man is a part of nature. According to *Wayne Morrision,* there is interconnection between eternal law and divine law. In God's intellect there exist a plan expressing the order of all things to their ends, this plan we may refer to as eternal law. All creatures bear the imprint of this eternal law and for man this imprint has special bearing due to his rationality. Divine law is available to man through revelation is found in the scriptures.

The basic percepts of natural law are the preservation of life, propagation, education of off-springs, the pursuit of truth and the construction of a peaceful society. The natural law consist of broad general principles reflecting God's intention for man in creation. The specific statutes of Government or human laws ought to be derived from general percepts of natural law.

What gives law a character of law is its moral dimension, in conformity with the percepts of natural law. Thus, human law would only be law if it is based on moral law and within its moral dimensions.

Through various evolution by *John Austin* and later on by Thomas Hobbes the proposition of legal positivism, all traditional forms of natural law was rejected. *Thomas Hobbes* assert law to be the command of the sovereign which is enforced through power. He states positive human laws replaces natural law.

Now the purpose of law is to bring peace and happiness to individuals with orderly society. So, we have to achieve the objective through the law and justice, viz., a peaceful and coherent society. On the contrary, we find that anarchism and terrorism is on increase. In spite of scientific and technological developments which are taking us to sky height, there is chaos and disorder in the society.

The judges alone cannot achieve the desired objective in the administration of justice. Lawyers too play an important and significant part in the administration of justice. They are the vehicles through which justice is reached to the people at large. Their purity, dedication, sincerity, diligence—all play an important role in the administration of justice. One is reminded here that *Justice V.R. Krishna Iyer* has said: "Law without lawyer loses its locomotion; Lawyer without law misses his function, that is why, a lawyer is an officer of justice not only of courts. Lawyers are the foremost in protecting violations of one's dignity, equality, freedom and life. These are basic human rights of human being. By this lawyers are serving the people, serving the cause of truth by their sincere efforts and assistance in the administration of justice.

Lawyers are the instrument through which justice is rendered of the instruments are tarnished one gets polluted justice.

Every civilized society has own laws and traditional customs having the force of law to regulate the society to a standard norm, so as to lead a peaceful orderly life with all sorts of security and protection. Justice is everybody's business. Crimes constitute a major challenge to public order, the proper maintenance of which is essential to a well ordered society. To meet this challenge effectively and to eradicate this evil from society, governments all over the world have resorted to enforcement of criminal law through police and criminal courts. But the steady increase in the number of crimes inspite of these measures raise the question whether the existing methods of enforcement of law and administration of justice are not adequate to the task. Laws are made to meet the challenges but mal-administration of criminal justice and enforcement of criminal laws by corrupt officials are also a reason for enormous increase of crimes in the society.

After independence, the emphasis shifted from the protection of individual interest to the protection of public and social interest. The reason for these trends appear to be in tackling numerous problems arising from crowded conditions of life. Thus the increased social evils gave birth to new penal statute and new forms of regulations. But inspite of all we are witnessing today a steadily growing stream of offences.

In every social set-up penal sanctions are attached to those behaviours which are legally disapproved, when they are applied by competent authorities, they reflect the sentiment of the community. It is necessary that sanction also must change with changing conditions. If the punishment is to be made effective it must be severe so that it may not only prevent the criminal form repeating his act but others may also take a warning from his punishment. The sentence should serve as a deterrent to others who may be thinking of adopting a criminal career.

Thus, it is quite evident that in absence of a legal system and institutionalised law enforcement, mechanism, individual would seek to redress his grievances on his own. The modern state has provided a more civilized substitute for such primitive practice, i.e., the system of administration of justice.

"Private vengeance is transmuted into administration of criminal justice; while civil justice takes place of violent self help". The evils of state of nature were too great and obvious to escape recognition even in the most primitive societies. Every individual was a judge in his own cause, and might was recognised the sole measure of right. Later on, gradually with the growth of power of state, the state ventured to suppress with strong hand the ancient and barbaric practice, and laid down the principle that all disputes shall be brought before the courts of law for the settlement. As royal justice grew in strength, the law was enforced with the establishment of modern theory of the exclusive administration of justice by the tribunals of the state, by the courts of law.

Distinction between crimes and civil wrongs is roughly that crimes are public wrongs and civil wrongs are private wrongs. According to Blackstone, "Wrongs are divisible into two sorts, or species, private wrongs and public wrongs." Private wrongs are an infringement or privation of the private or civil rights belonging to individuals, considered as individuals, and are frequently termed as civil injuries; the public wrongs are a breach and violation of public rights and duties which affect the whole community, considered as community. A crime then is an act deemed by law to be harmful to society in general, even though its immediate victim is an individual.

The purpose of criminal justice is establisment of peace by award of punishment. Furthermore the punishment can be looked from two different aspects. Punishment is a method of protecting society by reducing the occurrence of criminal activities, or in other way it is an end in itself. Punishment has an objective of protecting society by deterring offenders, by preventing the actual offender from committing further offences and by reforming and turning him into a law abiding citizen.

Other object of criminal justice is disabling or preventive. The aim of punishment here is to prevent a repetition of the offence by rendering the offender incapable of its commission. Imprisonment has not only a deterrent value, possible a reformative; but it serves also as a temporary preventive measure. Disablement is just like an order to disqualification for instance a disqualified from driving get disabled from committing motoring offences.

Next object is reformation aimed at actual offenders. The attempt to use prison as a training centre rather than a place for pure punishment, and the greater employment of probation, parole and suspended sentences are evidence of this general trend. The reformative theory admits only such form of punishment as are subservient to the education and discipline of the criminal. Death is in this view no fitting penalty; we must cure our criminals, not kill them.

According to retributive theory of administration of justice evil should be returned for evil and that as a man deals with others so should he himself be dealt with. An eye for an eye and a tooth for a tooth is the underlying principle of this theory. Retribution basically means that the wrong doer, must pay for his wrong doing. This notion is clearly connected with that of revenge.

Akin to the idea of retribution is that of expiation, according to it, crime is done away with, cancelled blotted out or expiated by the suffering of its appointed penalty. To suffer a punishment is to pay a debt due to the law that has been violated. Guilt plus punishment is equal to innocence. The wrong whereby he has transgressed the law, has incurred a debt. Justice requires that the debt be paid, that the wrong be expiated. The first object of punishment is to make satisfaction to the outraged law. The object behind redress is to restore the position demanded by the rule of justice, to substitute justice for injustice.

The right enforced in civil proceeding is either a primary or a sanctioning right. A sanctioning right is one which arises out of the violation of another right. All others are primary right; primary rights are those which have some other source than wrongs. Thus my right not to be libeled or assaulted is primary; but my rights to obtain pecuniary compensation from one who has libeled or assaulted me is sanctioning. My right of the fulfillment of a contract made with me is primary, but my rights to damages for the breach of contract is sanctioning.

A sanctioning right almost invariably consists of a claim to receive money from the wrong doer.

The enforcement of a primary right may be conveniently termed as specific enforcement. For the enforcement of a sanctioning right there is no suitable generic term, but we venture to call is sanctioning enforcement.

Example of specific enforcement are proceedings whereby a defendant is compelled to pay a debt, to perform a contract to restore land or chattels wrongfully taken or obtained to refrain from committing or continuing a trespass or nuisance or to repay money taken or obtained by mistake or fraud. In all these cases the rights enforced is primary rights itself, not a substituted sanctioning right.

(II) SOCIAL JUSTICE

(A) Growth of the Concept of Social Justice

Nature blessed man with the gift of reason and under standing which enabled him to make steady strides in the transformation of himself and the surroundings through explorations, inventions and innovations. Though emergence of society brought in its wake various other problems as well.

> "The first man who having enclosed a piece of land he thought himself at saying this is mine and found people simple enough to believe him was the real founder of civil society."[8]

Man began to attach self esteem and pride in his view of others and himself and this was reciprocated by others.

Rousseau Pointed

> "Whoever sang or danced himself best, whoever was the handsomest, the most dexterous or the most eloquent came

8. Rousseau, as quited by Chaturvedi, R.C., Natural Justice and Social Justice p. 401, Law Book Company, 1970 edition.

> to be of most consideration and this was the first step towards inequality and at the same time towards vice. From these first distinctions arose on the one side vanity and contempt and on the shame and envy."[9]

The idea of self-preservation resulted in a notion of self eminence and self respect paving foundations for exploitation the arising conflict had to be bridled by self-imposed restraints without which society would have vanished. It was a strange paradox that man had to invent all types of checks. balances and restraints in his endeavour to enjoy freedom, which resulted in the anguished cry of *Voltaire*.

"Man is born free and he is every where in chains".

Thus primarily laws were the self imposed restraints, which arrived as a necessity to prevent society from perishing and withering away. Law is to be viewed not in isolation but in the context of the society. Law has necessarily with it the notions of liberty, equality and justice. The harmonious blending of the three provides the basis for freedom and rights of man, which are natural and necessary for the development of man as well as the society.

The role of law must be considered in its relation with social justice as a flexible instrument of social change and adjustment. It is precisely the functional aspect of law, which makes it much more significant than merely a command of a monarch.

As a social institution, democratically evolved in order to achieve the object of making social adjustments to meet the challenge which necessarily and incessantly flows from unsatisfied legitimate human desire and ambitions.[10]

Cohen considered law as a means of social adjustment which is regarded as social aspect of law for providing justice.

Lord Macmillan had observed that :

> "Law is the guardian and vindicator of the two most precious things in world "justice and liberty". Its ideal remains constant and unchanging. But justice and liberty

9. *Ibid*.
10. Gajendragadkar, P.B., Law, Liberty and Social Justice, 1964, pp. 77-99.

> are not to be sought in isolation but in a mutual synthesis as there can be no liberty without justice and no justice without liberty.[11] The earlier outlook on justice was essentially involved to otherwise. But the concept as grown in recent times is positive approach of identifying tasks which can enable the society to secure equitable distribution of social wealth and opportunity to all members of the society.

The terms like "happiness" were found to be relative and changing and inturn affecting other concept. So justice was more related to balance and adjustment in society. Arbitrary discrimination base on caste, creed, religion, race, sex, etc. were to be countered to make way for the journey of justice. So journey of justice from political rights to social and economic rights had begun to leave its impact on history. The march of justice has crossed the geographical barriers the states and the nations and the concept of justice in the relationships between states is now an accepted fact.[12]

In the administration of justice law plays the most vital role. Law is the means whereas justice is regarded as the end. The concept of law itself has undergone many changes. Different jurists have looked at law from different angles. Each has emphasized a particular aspect of it.

In the words of *Holmes*.

Law is not brooding omnipotence in the sky but a flexible instrument of social order,[13] but as *Kelsen* remarked:

> There is no eternal law. The law that is suitable for one period many not be for another. We can only strive to provide every culture with a corresponding system of law. What is good for one may be ruin to another.[14]

Law must adapt itself to the constantly changing conditions of civilization and it is the duty of the society, from

11. Lord Mac Millan, Law and other things, Cambridge 1937, pp. 111-12.
12. Ginsberg, M. on Justice in Society.
13. Helmas, J. as quoted by Ganjendragadkar, P.B., Law, Liberty and Social Justice.
14. Kelsen, Philosopy of Law.

time to time to sharp the law in conformity with new conditions.

Law has to keep track of the past and keep in view the future to strike a balance as *Cordozo* remarked:

> "Today we study the day before yesterday, in order that yesterday may not paralyse today and today may not paralyse tomorrow".[15]

So, law has to be dynamic in its conception. if it has to succeed. In the words of *Friedman*:

> "It would be tragic if the law were so petrified as to be unable to respond to the unending challenge of evolutionary and revolutionary change in society. To the lawyer, this challenge means that he cannot be content to be a craftman. His technical knowledge will supply the tools but it is his sense of responsibility for the society in which he lives that must inspire him to be a jurist a well as lawyer."[16]

Analysing Rawls's theory of justice Dworkin reaches the conclusion that "justice as fairness rests on the assumption of a natural right of all men and women to equality of concern and respect, a right they possess not by virtue of birth or characteristic or merit or excellence but simply as human beings with the capacity to make plans and give justice."[17] He goes on to say, "Rawls's most basic assumption is not that men have a right to certain liberties that Locke or Mill thought important, but that they have a right to equal respect and concern in the design of political institutions."[18] Thus, according to Dworkin, "right to equal concern and respect" is the most fundamental of

15. Hall, M.E., ed. Selected writings of Benzamin Nathan Cordoze, p. 128.
16. Friedmann, "Law in changing Society", p. 503.
17. R. Dworkin, Taking Rights Seriously, 182 (1977).
18. *Ibid*.

all the rights.[19] This right, according to Rawls "is 'owed to human beings as moral persons', and follows from the moral personality that distinguishes humans from animals"[20] Thus, human being already possessed this right when they agreed on the two principles of justice enunciated by Rawls.[21] This right "is more abstract than the standard conceptions of equality that distinguish different political theories. It permits arguments that this more basic right requires one or another of these conceptions as a derivative right or goal."[22]

Any arrangement for the allocation of social positions and goods should thus proceed on the basic assumption that everyone has a right to equal concern and respect. Any arrangement that pays unequal respect or shows unequal concern towards any one violates this basic right of all.

From the earliest times to which the idea of justice can be traced, equality has been at its centre. Injustice, according to Aristotle, arises when equals are treated unequally, and also when unequals are treated equally. Professor Hart calls this precept as "a central element in the idea of justice."[23] But, this precept to "treat like cases alike and different cases differently" is yet incomplete as it lays down no satandard for determining the likeness or differences and, therefore any characteristics of

19. *Id.* at xii. See also at 1811 where he says :
    This is one right, therefore, that does not emerge from the contract, but is assumed, as the fundamental right must be, in its design.
20. J. Rawls, A Theory of Justice, 511 (1972) quoted in R. Dworkin.
21. Rawls's two principles of justice are :
    First: each person is to have an equal right to the most extensive basic liberty compatible with a similar liberty for others.
    Second: social and economic equalities are to be arranged so that they are both (a) reasonably expected to be to everyone's advantage, and (b) attached to positions and offices open to all.
22. R. Dworkin, *supra* n. 17 at 23.
23. H.L.A. Hart, The Concept of Law, 155(1961). He says: "Justice is traditionally thought of as maintaining or resorting a balance or proportion, and its leading precept is often formulated as 'Treat like cases alike': though we need to add to the latter, and treat different cases differently". And further, "Treat like cases alike and different cases differently", is a central element in the idea of justice".

individuals may be picked up to differtiate between them. In view of the experience in the past, as to how men have been differentiated arbitrarily for different characteristics, it has been recognized that the characteristic or criterion for differentiating must be relevant to the object or the good to be distributed and that no characteristics beyond one's control, such as race, caste, sex, colour, etc. can be relevant criteria for differentiating between individuals.

Justice is generally divided into legal and social justice. "Legal justice concerns the punishment of wrongdoing and the compensation of injury through the creation and enforcement of a public set of rules."[24] Social justice requires equitable or just distribution of the social goods and evils or of burdens and benefits.[25] The task of just distribution in the present day society has to be performed primarily by the state and, therefore, though social justice may cover even private, or in Aristotles's language "corrective", justice, yet it is mainly concerned with distribution through the agency of the state.[26] To operationalise the general notion of social justice from time to time thinkers have laid down several principles of distribution. Some of these principles are :

1. To each according to his need;
2. To each according to his worth;
3. To each according to his merit;
4. To each according to his work;
5. To each according to the agreements he has made; and
6. To each according to his claims.

---

24. D. Miller, Social Justice, 22 (1976). Distinguishing social justice from legal justice he says : Social justice..... concerns the distribution of benefits and burdens throughout a society, as it results from the major social institutions, property systems, public organizations, etc. For other division of justiçe see the works cited in nos. 4 and 5 in D. Miller, *id.* at 21. Also see N. Rescher, Distributive Justice, 5(1966).
25. Miller, *Ibid.*
26. See the distinction drawn between the distributive and corrective justice by Aristotle in Nicomachean Ethics, V. 1-7.

To these western principles may be added an Indian Shastric principle of doubtful application—

7. To each according to his Karma.[27]

The principles are neither completely mutually exclusive nor exhaustive.

The social awarness and consciousnees of the prevailing social problems have answered history at different items in different societies. However, it is a fact that the realization and awareness as understood in the present day is of a recent origin.

The four major ideas which catalysed the process of awareness of social problems were:

1. Equality,
2. A new image of human nature,
3. The belief that conditions which are deplorable can be rectified, and
4. Humanitarianism, the heart of the matter, the expression of concern for others.[28]

Lets have a brief disucussion on the above mentioned heads—

(1) Equality

The concept of equality no doubt an ancient thought, had not been effectively expressed till recently while the other major factors affectintg social problems can be said to be of historically recent origin. Most of the modern social problems are concerned with the improvement of the lot of lower status person. The first step in social problem awareness as traced in history, was to combat this peculiar problem.

Concern about equality have long though thin roots in human history. Ancient Greeks and Roman thinkers did reflect the noble ideas that basically all men were equal. But they appeared to be into clear understanding or agreement about the

27. See P.V. Kane, 5, History of Dharamasastra, Pt. II, 1573 (1962).
28. Green, Arnold W., Social Problems, Arena of Conflicts.

'equality' than what the present day society appears to be. However, the modern notions to concede that—

(a) Everyone deserves respect as human being no matter what this status may be, and
(b) Some degree of equal opportunity must be open to every adult.[29]

The struggles at political, social and economical levels did deny the men equal opportunity of competition. It is adversely affected by the other face of equality rewards to all alike or literal equality.

(2) A New Image of Human Nature

One of he ideological allies of equality was the concept of human nature, its innate potentials to a positive nature, one of optimism, a conviction of the intrinsic goodness of man and of mans ability to win happiness, in contrast to the old belief that human nature is basically evil. The arguments of the original sin were strongly replaced by a belief in the innate good nature of man is born good and is made evil only by social institutions.

Although faith in man's goodness have waned in recent decades enough of it has been retained to provide a continuity of hope that social problems can be solved.[30]

(3) The Belief that Conditions which are Deplorable can be Rectified

Reasoning capacity for rectification was considered the panacea for all social problems and the new spirit of humanitarianism owes its birth to this mistaken assumption. Age-old notions of pity and charity got displaced enabling injustice and suffering to lay claims to the attention of the social order itself.

(4) Humanitarianism

The institutionalization of compassion is what we mean by humanitarianism. Something inseparable from the modern

29. Tiger, L., Men in Groups.
30. Green, Arnold W., Social Problems, Arena of Conflicts.

sentiment of equality. The extention of humanitarianism "to include literally all human beings in society", was quite slow, however and was only achieved in the last few decades.

(B) Concept of Social Justice

The concept of social justice grasp although many have a vague notion of what it is and even this varies in content and meaning with each person confusion prevails its real import.

The transition observed in the concept of social justice in the history of mankind has been traced to identify the emergence of positive conceptions and newer dimensions of social justice from a traditional and outdated *laissez faire* approach of the society. The slow subtle and yet perceptible changes seen in the content and extent of the concepts like liberty, equality and justice have substantially affected the concepts of social justice. These noble ideas have been continuously experiencing a dynamic. The meaning and value of these basic idea held a few centuries ago are potential different from the present day notion.

Admittedly during the last few hundred years "religion" played an important role to shape the just and unjust social, political and economical values of the day. It was Karl Marx who gave a new twist to the economic relations between labour and capital and has rightly been termed as the eman-character of human society from economic exploitation. He was responsible for the synthesis of the concept of economic justice as a vital part of Social Justice.

When during the Second World War Britain was engaged in the battle of survival, its intellectuals and thinkers were making desperate efforts to seek solution to the ideological conflict which had been sparked of the war. *Lord Beveridge* was asked to head a committee to seek answer for the various socio-economic problems. In an effort to find the much needed answers the "Beveridge Report" evolved the concept of a welfare state which has a tremendous historical significance.[31]

In its crusade to seek the ideas of welfare democracies biggest ally is law and thus the role of law is integrated with the

31. Lord Beveridge, "Beveridge Report".

object of democracies in its obligation *vis-à-vis* the citizens of the state.[32] The concept and spirit of social justice have infused newer dimensions in the man's quest for a richer and more meaningful existence on this planet. The concept of social justice is revolutionary and dynamic one which gives sustenance to the rule of law. It also endeavours to bring in through the help of law, a social structure by removing causes of social and economic tension. At the same time it ensures the freedom for the individual personality to grow and develop.

The concept of social justice is primarily based on the idea that all men are equal in society. Acceptance of the idea of welfare puts the claims of social justice on a higher plane and thus has to be achieved by regulation of individual liberty and rights. Social justice as the name itself indicates, must and should seek justice in all its social aspect.

The concept of social justice is thus a revolutionary concept which gives meaning and significance to the democratic way of life and makes the rule of law dynamic. It is a concept of social justice which creates in the minds of the masses of this country a sense of participation in the glory of India's political freedom. Social justice to all the citizens of the state Indian political thinkers has coined the doctrine of "Samanvaya" (harmonious synthesis) to balance between the rival claims of social justice and of individual liberty and freedom. Social justice must be achieved by adopting necessary and reasonable measures with courage, wisdom, foresight, sense of balance, and fair play to all the interests concerned. In short, it is what is the concept of social justice.

(C) Meaning and Definition of Social Justice

As discussed carlicr terms like equality, liberty, justice, etc. have different connotation in their respective society. Nevertheless, these terms are not vague and have definite meaning but still a concrete definition is yet to be found rather it would be impractical to define these relative and dynamic terms. So is the case with the definition and meaning of social justice.

32. Gajendragadkar, P.B., Law, Liberty and Social Justice, 1964, pp. 77-99.

As has been said—

> We hear much today of social justice. I am not sure that those who use the term most glibly know very clearly what they mean by it. Some interpreted it as equality of opportunity itself a misleading term. Since opportunity can never opportunity can be equal among human beings who have unequal capacities to grasp it, many I suspect, mean simply that it is unjust that anybody should be fortune than themselves and the more intelligent mean that it is just. I would rather as benevolent that every effort should be made at least to mitigate the disparities of natural human in equality and that no obstacle should be offered, but rather help afforded, to practicable opportunities of self- improvement.[33]

According to *P.B. Gajendragadkar, J.*

What is social justice? I have already referred to the welfare plan evolved by the Beveridge report and I have pointed out that according to the plan of social security put forward by the said report, democracy took upon itself the task of attacking five giant evils: want, disease, ignorance, squalor, idleness. Basically all these five giant evils thrive on the fundamental evils of poverty. Therefore, under the concept of welfare state, the primary function of state to attack the problem of poverty assumes considerable significance. Democracy realizes that this problem which concerns an overwhelmingly large number of its citizens cannot be successfully met unless it wisely uses its mighty weapon of law and attempts to restore balance to the economic structure and to remove the causes of economic tension from the body politic of the community.[34]

All the attempts made by democratic legislatures to meet the challenge of poverty constitute attempts to give to the citizens of the state economic justice. Equality of opportunity to all the citizens to develop their individual personalities and to participate in the pleasure and happiness of life is the goal of economic justice. Social justice as distinguished from economic

33. Allen, C.K., Aspects of Justice, p. 3; Stevens and Sons, London, 1955 (edition).
34. Gajendragadkar, P.B., Law, Liberty and Social Justice, pp. 77-99.

justice has a special significance in the context of Indian society. As were all aware, the Hindu social structure is based on caste and communities which create walls and barriers of exclusiveness and proceed on the basis of considerations of superiority and inferiority.

This vice of social inequality assumes a particular reprehensible form in relation to the backward classes and communities which are treated as untouchables, and so the problem of social justice is as urgent and important in India as is the problem of economic justice. . . . Here the term social justice is being used in a comprehensive sense so as to include both social and economic justice. The concept of social justice thus takes within its sweep the objective of removing all inequalities and affording equal opportunities to all citizens in social affairs as well as in economic activities.

Social justice is people justice where the tyranny of power is transformed into the democracy of social good.[35] Hon'ble Supreme Court in a case[36] realised to lay down any rigid definition when it said that "social justice" is a very vague and indeterminate expression and no clear-cut definition can be laid down which will cover all situations, but it added that concept of social justice does not emanate from the fanciful notion of any adjudicature.[37] The Supreme Court, however, regarded the concept of social justice as living concept of revolutionary import, it gives sustenance to the rule of law and meaning and significance to the ideal of a welfare state.[38]

(D) Nature, Object and Scope of Social Justice

Change in the concept of state has introduced the objective of social justice forcefully. The nature of social justice is to be explained in context of present scenario.

As we all know inequality is rampant nowadays. Inequality whether it is social, economic or political is causing great damage to our society. Because of this inequality Marx had said that capitalism will destroy itself by a cycle of wars, and

35. Iyer, J., Social Justice, Sunset or Dawn, (1987), pp. 17-18.
36. Per Bhagwati, J. 1955 S.C.A. 321 at pp. 330-31.
37. *Ibid.*
38. Per Ganjendragadker.

that proletariat can rise to power only by successful and violet class struggle.

But the Indian thinkers in past had adopted a doctrine of Samanvaya to minimize the inequality. This doctrine can be termed as the nature and objective of social justice.

Roscoe Pound has classified social interests under six heads, which the law should take into account in order to achieve the objective of social justice—

(i) Social interests in general security, e.g. peace public health, security of acquisition, etc.
(ii) Social interests in security of social institutions, e.g. marriage, religious institiutions, etc.
(iii) Social interests in general morals, e.g. gambling drinking, immoral traffic, etc.
(iv) Social interests in conservation of social resourccs, e.g. food minerals, etc.
(v) Social interests in general progress, e.g. freedom of trade encouragement of research.
(vi) Social interests in individual rights, e.g. wages conditions of work.

The above mentioned social interests reflects the nature of social justice. The objective of social justice can be strengthened by applying social obligation and social consciousness in individual action. To promote the welfare of the people by securing and promoting a just social order with a view to provide social justice to common man comes within the nature and objective of social justice.[39]

The ancient nature of social justice was to render to a person what is due to him without making an effort to define what is just. Utilitarians propounded the theory of greatest happiness to greatest number as the objective of social justice.

The main objective of social justice is to fight against social inequality and economic exploitation of individuals amongst the fellow members. It also aims to provide equal opportunities to all citizens in all social and economic activities. The significance and vital feature is in arriving at the social justice

39. R.G. Chaturvedi, *Supra* note 8 at 20.

spread to all in the community, to achieve justice and equality political, social and well as economic in a peaceful way by keeping rule of law as the beakon light.[40]

Thus, the nature of social justice has from a theoretical beginning as a doctrine of social philosophy over the years developed itself into a practical means of human welfare. The objective is to achieve a social structure that is steady but not static, stable but not stationary.[41]

(E) Social Justice and Constitution of India

Social justice is the ideological signature of our Constitution we are directly concerned with social justice spelt out by our Constitution. So whatever may be its wider or narrower connotations we have to understand the concept as envisaged in our Constitution.

According to *Granville Austin,* The Indian Constitution is the first and foremost a social document. The majority of its provisions are either directly aimed at furthering the goals of social justice or attempt to foster this revolution by establishing the conditions necessary for its achievement. The core of the commitment to the social justice and social revolution lies in Parts III and IV, in the Fundamental Rights and in the Directive Principles of State Policy. These are the conscience of the Constitution.[42]

The foundation of the Constitutional arch and the philosophy enshrined in the Constitution have been well summarized in the preamble to the Constitution. The preamble declares:

> WE, THE PEOPLE OF INDIA, having solemnly resolved to constitute India into a SOVEREIGN SOCIALIST SECULAR DEMOCRATIC REPUBLIC and to secure to all its citizens:
> JUSTICE Social, Economic and Political;
> LIBERTY of thought, expression, belief, faith and worship;
> EQUALITY of status and of opportunity;
> and to promote among them all

40. Friedmann, Capitalism and Freedom, pp. 3-4.
41. Allen, C.K. Aspects of Justice.
42. Austin, G., The Indian Constitution—Cornerstone of a Nation, 41, 1966.

FRATERNITY assuring the dignity of the individual and the unity and integrity of the Nation;
IN OUR CONSTITUENT ASSEMBLY this twenty-sixth day of November, 1949, do HEREBY ADOPT, ENACT AND GIVE TO OURSELVES this CONSTITUTION.

The preamble to the Constitution is not merely a decorative preface but is a meaningful indicator reflecting the ideas of the people who have cherished a dream to be realized and interpreted in their daily lives through the Constitution.

The language of the Preamble, the spirit and aspirations of the people, is a clear indicator of the approach of the various other goals enshrined in the Constitution.

In the words of Gajendragadkar J.[43]

"It would, I think be fairly accurate to say that the basic philosophy of the Constitution is to be found in the preamble itself. India is one country and there is only one citizenship. India is committed to the idea of welfare State and it has to establish socio-economic justice. India is committed to democracy and respect individual liberty; and India wants to give all its citizens equality of status and opportunity, thereby attempting to create a mighty brotherhood of Indian citizens, which would assist the Sovereign, Democratice, Republic reaching its proclaimed objectives. That, in substance is the message of preamble".

The word justice social, political and economic used in the preamble broadly reflects the aspirations of the people of India and at the same time it can be viewed as the controlling parameters of the Constitution as well. The primary objective of ensuring justice, social, economic and political as envisaged in the preamble has to be appreciated in a wider perspective. The word 'justice' used in the preamble to the Constitution has to be understood in a deeper and wider connotation. The word justice employed by the framers of the Constitution in the preamble refers to the whole philosophy by which our Constitution is guided.

43. Gajendragadkar, P.B., The Constitution of India—Philosophy and basic postulates.

There are certain other provisions of our Constitution which further the principle of social Justice. The Constitution gurantees to all its citizens right to equality and freedom from discrimination on grounds of religion, race, caste, sex, place of birth, residence, etc. The Constitution sets forth a programme for the reconstruction and transformation of Indian society on secular model. But in a caste ridden society like ours, any strict application of the doctrine of equality would have in fact meant perpetration of age long distinctions based on caste and class. There is therefore, a Constitutional commitment to accord favoured treatment to the weaker sections of our society. The Constitution classifies the Scheduled Castes and Scheduled Tribes as a separate class for their special treatment and provides for reservation of seats in legislatures, in government jobs and in educational institutions. This commitment is in full realization to raise the sunken status of these pathetically neglected classes. Article 15(4) authorizes the 'state' to make preferences in favour of any socially and educationally backward classes of citizens or for the Scheduled Castes and Scheduled Tribes in all its dealings and Article 16(4) enables the state to make preferences in favour of these classes in the field of public services. Article 17 in itself is a unique piece of principle for the cause of Social Justice as it abolishes the ages old malpractice of untouchability. It was long cherished dream of *Mahatma Gandhi* which reflects in Article 17. Article 335 requires the State to take into consideration the claims of the members of the Scheduled Castes and Scheduled Tribes for appointment in various services under the Union and the States consistently with the maintenance of the efficiency of administration. Articles 330, 332 and 334 provides for the reservation of seats in the legislatures for the Scheduled Castes and Scheduled Tribes. Articles 338 and 338A provides for the appointment of National Commission for Scheduled Castes and Scheduled Tribes to investigate all matters relating to the safeguards provided to them by the Constitution. Articles 341 and 342 authorizes the President to designate the Scheduled Castes and Scheduled Tribes for the purpose of the Constitution.

It is envisaged that the state shall take positive steps to remove or eliminate existing social inequalities by special measures. Article 46 directs the State to "promote with special care the educational and economic interests of the weaker sections of the people and, in particular, of the Scheduled Castes and Scheduled Tribes and to protect them from social injustice and all forms of exploitation." The Constitution itself provides the method and an agency for the identification of the Scheduled Castes and Scheduled Tribes.

(F) Social Justice and Supreme Court of India

The Supreme Court of India is conscious that the Constitution makers "adopted the democratic ideal which assures to the citizens the dignity of the individual and other cherished human values as means to the full evolution and expression of his personality"[44] and the Constitution "is intended to be a social document in which the relationship of society to the individual and of the Government to both and the rights of the Scheduled Castes and Scheduled Tribes are clearly laid down. This social document is headed by a preamble which epitomizes the principles on which the Government is intended to function."[45]

The Supreme Court in *Muir Mills Ltd.* v. *Sutt Mill Mazdoor Union*[46] realized the difficulty of defining the phrase 'Social justice' and refused to lay down any rigid-definition when is said that "Social Justice is a very vague and indeterminate expression and no clear-cut definition can be laid down which will cover all situations", but it added that "concept of social justice does not emanate from the fanciful notions of any adjudicator[47] nor the phrase means that, "reason and fairness must always yield to the convenience of a party-convenience of the employee at the cost of the employer... in an adjudication proceedings."[48] The Supreme Court, however, regarded the concept of social justice "as living concept of revolutionary

44. Per Patanjali Shastri, J. in A.K. Gopalan *v.* State of Madras, AIR 1950 S.C. 27.
45. Per Hidayatullah, J. in Golak Nath *v.* State of Punjab, AIR 1967 S.C. 1643.
46. Per Bhagwati, J. 1955, S.C.A. 321.
47. *Ibid.*
48. Per Das, S.K., J. in Panjab National Bank *v.* Sri Ram Kanwar, 1951 S.C.A. 598.

import, it gives sustenance to the rule of law and meaning and significance to the ideal of a welfare state."[49]

Thus, "the judiciary was to be an arm of the social revolution upholding the equality, that Indians had longed for during colonial days, but not had gained—not simply because the regime was colonial and perforce repressive, but largely because the British had feared that social change would endanger their rule,"[50] but with the dawn of independence the judiciary has to discharge the function assigned to it in the Constitution. In particular, the Supreme Court has to guard and guide in administration of justice and come upto the expectations of the people.

The delicate task of administering social justice by balancing of individual's rights and the needs of society in imposing social control, falls on the shoulders of judiciary in general, and the Supreme Court in particular.

Referring to the aspect of social justice Subba Rao, C.J.[51] as he then was had observed:

> "The rule of law under the Constitution has a glorious content. It embodies the modern concept of law evolved over the centuries. . . . It enjoins to bring about a social order in which justice, social, economic and political shall inform all the institutions of national life. It directs it to work for an egalitarian society where there is plenty, where there is equal opportunity for all, to education, to work, to livelihood, and where there is social justice. . . . It, therefore, preserves the natural rights against the State encroachment, and constitutions the higher judiciary of the State as the sentinel of said rights and the balancing wheel of the right subject to social control. In short, the Fundamental Rights, subject to social control, have been incorporated in the rule of law. . . . By this process of scrutiny, the court maintains the validity of only such laws as keep a just balance between freedom and social control. . . . The standard is an elastice one; it varies with time,

49. Per Gajendragadkar, J. in State of Mysore, AIR 1958 S.C. 926.
50. Austin, Granville, *Supra* at Note 42.
51. Golak Nath *v.* State of Punjab, AIR 1967 S.C. 1643.

space and condition....(it)... serves the needs of the people without unduly infringing their rights. It recognizes the social reality".[52]

Supreme Court of India has delivered many judgements to strengthen the concept of Social Justice. Some of these cases are *M.H. Hoscot* v. *State of Maharastra,* AIR 1978 SC 1548, *P.U.D.R. v. Union of India,* 1982 SC 1473, *Bandhua Mukti Morcha* v. *Union of India,* AIR 1982 SC 849, *State of Kerala* v. *N.M. Thomas,* AIR 1976 SC 490, *Indira Sawhney* v. *Union of India,* AIR 1993 SC 497, *Neerja Chaudhary* v. *State of M.P.,* 1983(3) SCC 243.

(III) PERMISSIBLE DEPARTURE IN FAVOUR OF SCHEDULED CASTES AND SCHEDULED TRIBES

The policy of special treatment of weaker sections of the society is called protective discrimination, it is also known as "reverse discrimination" because it involves discrimination in favour of those who until recently had themselves been the victim of discrimination. It is given the name 'protective discrimination' because the avowed purpose of special or preferential treatment is not to award any special privileges but to give protection to those who, because of cent . . . to get exploited despite the removal of legal sanctions behind exploitation which had been practiced so far.

As stated above, the old norms which sanctioned or tolerated exploitation and domination of many by a few and of one section of population (i.e. Scheduled Castes and Scheduled Tribes) by another (upper castes) are no more valid.

The Supreme norm which governs the Indian polity is the Constitution of India which ushered a new era from Jan. 26, 1950. In place of exploitation it aspires to bring about justice, social, economic and political and also guarantees equality of status and opportunity. These aspirations are to be achieved by popularly elected and accountable Governments at the Centre and in the States in a manner so as not to infringe constitutional norms and limitations. The problem becomes complex when we realize that the socio-economic structure which the independent

52. *Ibid.*, pp. 1655 and 1656.

India inherited was that of extreme inequality and bridging the wide hiatus which separated one section of population from the other was by itself a formidable task; achieving of this objective without violating the guarantee of equality of opportunity in the process made the task doubly more difficult.

In order to reconcile conflicting pulls and pressures of aspiration actively the framers of the Constitution drew a sharp distinction between long term goals and short-term means without at the same time making the goals and means inherently incompatible with each other. Thus, as stated above the Preamble of the Constitution promises to secure to all its citizens justice, social, economic and political and equality of status and opportunity. This wider objective is further repeated in a slightly different language in Article 38 which is one of the Directive Principles of State Policy. Another Directive Principle contained in Article 46 enjoins the State to "promote with special care the educational and economic interests of the weaker sections of the people and enjoins it to "protect them from social injustices and all forms of exploitation." However, the objective has to be achieved without violating the right to equality guaranteed in Articles 14, 15, 16 and 29. The guarantee is specific that no discrimination whatsoever can be practiced on the basis of religion, race, caste, creed, colour or sex. In other words, differential treatment normally permissible by the State can't be based on the above consideration. But this is a long-term objective. As short-term measure our Constitution permits reservation of jobs in services to weaker section of citizens generally. Articles 15(4), 15(5) and 16(4); 16(4A) and 16(4B) are exceptions to the general provisions. Article 15(4), provides that nothing in Article 15 or in clause (2) of Article 29 shall prevent the state from making any special provision for the advancement of any socially and educationally backward classes of citizens or for the Scheduled Castes and Scheduled Tribes and Article 16(4) provides for that nothing in Article 16 shall prevent the state from making any provision for the reservation of appointments or post in favour of any backward class of citizens which, in the opinion of the state, is not adequately represented in the services under the State.

The Consititution ordained objectives means enjoined for the attained of the objectives and short-term deviations permitted from those means are clear in so far as they go; however, in actual practice it becomes a difficult question to decide as to what extent deviations can be practiced (without destroying the rule) and what can be the pace at which society can comfortably march toward its goal without forgetting the ultimate goal in the process. These are the matters with which the Governments have to wrestle every day. As they are popularly accountable, public opinion, popular pressures and considerations of electoral politics also play their role. Within the limits permissible under the Constitution the Governments exercise liberty to decide about the extent of deviation and pace of the march. But as we are committed to the principles of constitutionalism, every legislative or administrative action of the Government is subject to judicial scrutiny. Judiciary plays a vital role in balancing the conflicting interests and demands.

Scheduled Castes and Scheduled Tribes constitutes the most disadvantaged group among the weaker sections of the society. The Constitution specifically speaks of positive discrimination in favour of Scheduled Castes and Scheduled Tribes. Our judiciary has also played a significant role by deciding matters in favour of positive discrimination, and by and large it has upheld the provisions made in favour of Scheduled Castes and Scheduled Tribes. Declaring those Constitutionally valid, this remarkable positive trends has benefited a lot of Scheduled Castes and Scheduled Tribes. So that they have been also to reap the fruits of Constitutional provisions.

3

Historical Perspective and Origin of Scheduled Castes and Scheduled Tribes

India has a composite population having a number of groups based on religion, language, caste or creed and the Indian social system has for centuries perpetrated social and economic injustices by the so called higher castes on the lower castes who have been systematically denied equal chance in the opportunities and facilities of the larger society. There has been a considerable controversy over the origin of caste system in India. The origin of caste system is in the Varnashrama Dharma, the division of society into four Varnas[1] (four castes) viz., Brahmin, Kshatriya, Vaishya and Sudra. It was believed and preached that for the prosperity of the world the creater created the four Varnas. The creater created these Varnas from different parts of his body, i.e., the Brahmin was born from his mouth; the Kshatriya from his arms; the Vaishya from his thighs and the

1. Manu Smirti, Chapter-1, verse 31.

Sudra from his feet. He created Brahmins with Gayatri (metre); the Kshatriyas with Trishtubb; the Vaishyas with jagati and the Sudras without any metre.[2]

The first three Varnas are twice born (Dwija), the first birth being from the mother and the second from the investiture with the sacred girdle. In the second birth Savitri is the mother and the teacher is the father because he gives instruction in the Vedas.[3] Therefore, the first three Varnas are born twice while the Sudra is born only once.[4] Among the Brahmin, the Kshatriya, the Vaishya and the Sudra Varnas, each preceding Varna (caste) is superior by birth to the one following. It is popularly held that in the beginning there were only three Varnas and the fourth Varna of the Sudra is an outcome of the fight between Brahmins and Kshatriyas for the supremacy in the Varna (caste) hierarchy.[5]

It is the Untouchables and Sudras who has been have officially described as Scheduled Castes.[6] These are the lower caste who have suffered from the social disabilities. In contrast to the Scheduled Castes, the Scheduled Tribes or Adivasis live in exclusive territorial communities. Their basic disability is due to their physical isolation from the society and their exploitation by non-tribals. They are supposed to be the aboriginal denizens of any specific area who have their own socio-cultural environment.

To make the discussion more clear the origin of Scheduled Castes would be dealt under two heads.

(I) ORIGIN OF SCHEDULED CASTES

(A) Origin of Sudras
(B) Origin of Untouchables

2. Vasistha Dharma Sutras, Chapter IV.
3. *Ibid.*, Chapter-II, verses 1-4 and Chapter IV, verse 3.
4. Manu Smriti, Chapter X, verse 4.
5. B.R. Ambedkar, who were the Sudras (Bombay : Thacker and Company Ltd., 1946, pp. 119-20).
6. Parmanand Singh, Social Justice for the Harijans : Some Socio-legal Problems of Identification, *Conversion and Judical Review*, JILI 1978 p. 335.

(A) Origin of Sudras

The first reference about the origin of Sudras as a social class is found in Purushsukta passage[7] which recurs in nineteenth book of the Arthava Veda.[8] The other reference relevant to the present study may be traced back to the early period of Artharva Veda which mentions Brahmana, Rajana and Vaishya,[9] but leaves out the Sudras. It is clear that the Sudras appear as a social class only towards the end of the period of Artharva Veda, when the Purushsukta version of their origin might have been inserted into the tenth book of Rig Veda. In this way Sudras either appeared in the later Rig Vedic period or in the later period of Artharva Veda.

Regarding the manner of origin of Sudras, the scholars are not in accord. The Sudras, according to *Dr. Ambedkar,*[10] were Kshatriyas who were reduced to the position of Sudras as a result of long struggle with the Brahmins, who ultimately deprived their adversaries of the rights of Upanayana. On the basis of a solitary example occurring in the Santi Parvan of Mahabharata that Paijvana was a Sudra King, it is claimed that the Sudras were Kshatriyas in the beginning[11] as only the Kshatriyas could be the king. But such a view does not hold good as Kshatriyas as a well defined Varna with their rights and duties did not exist in the Rig Vedic period. Nor the loss of Upanayana was the decisive test of the Sudras.

Another theory regarding the origin of Sudras is the racial theory which is more convincing. The proponents of this theory claim the large section of people Aryans and non-Aryans, were reduced to the position of Sudras, partly through external and partly through internal conflicts.[12] As regards external conflict the Aryans were in conflict with Dasas and Dasyus which is clear from the recurring themes of the prayer to Indra for

7. Brahmanoasya mukhamaseda bahu rajanyha kritah uru tadasya yadyasyoh padmyam sudro ajayatah.—R.V.X, 90.12.
8. Brahmanoasya mukhamasida bahu rajanyo abhavatu moathyam yada vaishyah padmyam sudor ajayat.—A.V., XIX, 6.6.
9. Brahmaneva patirna rajanyo na vaishyah tat suryah prabruusnneti panchabhyo no manvehyah.—A.V., V, 17.9.
10. B.R. Ambedkar, who were the Sudras? p. 139.
11. *Ibid.*, pp. 139-42.
12. R.S. Sharma, Sudras in Ancient India, pp. 8-40.

overthrow of Dasa tribes.[13] And the main issue in the war between the forms of wealth, whereas differences in race, religion and mode of speech also served to exacerbate the relations. Such a conflict against Dasas was attended with much blood shed.

Alongside the conflict between Aryans and their enemies there went on an internal conflict in the Aryan tribal society.[14] And help of Indra and Varuna was taken to destroy Dasas and Aryans.[15] In response to such prayers, Indra and Varuna killed the Dasas and Aryans who were adversaries of Sudras[16] and thus protected them.[17] At the end of conflict those who remained after the conflict were absorbed in the Varna system. Since the conflicts centered mainly around the possession of cattle, and of land, those Aryans and non-Aryans who were disposed of these and impoverished came to be reckoned as the fourth class in the new society.

The next theory regarding the origin of Sudras is the occupational theory.[18] The proponents of this theory state that different kinds of jobs were entrusted to different groups of people in early Indian society. And those who came to be traditionally entrusted with the task of doing such odd jobs as menial service, removing unconsumed food, rubbish, ordure or dead animals, cleaning the privy, public scavenging, flaying carcasses and manufacturing leather articles from skin and hides formed the fourth, the Sudra Varna.

13. R.V., II, 11.4, VI. 25.2; and X.148.2.
14. R.S. Sharma, *op. cit.*, pp. 14-15.
15. Sahyama dasamaryam traya yuja sahashretna sahasa sadhasa sahasvata R.V., X 83.1.
16. Sudras was the head of the Bharata tribe. The internal conflict was known as Battle of Ten kings which was a conflict between two main branches of Rig. vedic Aryans, namely Purus and Bharatas. The Purus were led by ten kings whereas Bharata were led by the Sudras assisted by the priest Vasistha.
17. dasa ca vrtra hatamaryanica sudasam indravarunavasava tam. —R.V., VII, 83.1.
18. Legal Protection of Scheduled Castes and Tribes, Denzil Ibfeston and John C. Nesfield developed this theory. Olive C. Cox Caste, Class and Race, p. 96.

(B) Origin of Untouchables

In the beginning there was a difference between Sudra and Untouchables from the historical point of view although later such distinctions faded. The Untouchables have later origin than the Sudras and they suffered more severe disability than the Sudras in earlier times because the Untouchables had been set part outside and below the four main divisions of the Hindu society, i.e., Brahmin, Kshatriya, Vaisyas and Sudras. Collectively the Untouchables are known as Antyas or Bahyas, i.e. people living outside of the villages and towns.[19] In the Apastamba Dharma Sutra, the word 'Antah' is used in relation to Chandalas and shows that they lived at the end of the village.[20] In same tent the Bahayas, among whom the recitation of Veda was forbidden, are explained by Haradatta as the Ugras and the Nishadas. [21]

Buddhists were regarded as Mlechas.[22] They resided beyond three Aryan countries[23] i.e., Brahmanarto,[24] Brahmarshi land next to Brahmavarta[25] central land.[26] They spoke a barbarian language[27] which was different from the Aryan[28] and opposed the Varna system[29] and the Ashram system[30] and did

19. There is still there is a definite location of Harijan bustees. Usually they reside in the south of the village and it is believed by the villagers that the settlement is to avoid the polluted air because the south wind rerely blows.
20. I.3.9.15.
21. I.3.9.18.
22. During Andhra-Dushana period (30 B.C.-150 A.D.) Sakas, Kushanas and others who spoke different languages came from Central Asia to India through North-Western passages and accepted Buddhism as their religion and so the Brahmins always regarded them as foreigners or Mlechas. For details see: Naramdeshwar Prasad, The Myth of Caste System (Patna, Samjna Prakashan, 1957), pp. 72-73.
23. Manu Smriti, Chapter II, verse 23.
24. *Ibid.*, Chapter II, verse 17.
25. *Ibid.*, Chapter II, verse 19.
26. *Ibid.*, Chapter II, verse 21.
27. *Ibid.*, Chapter X, verse 45.
28. *Ibid.*, Chapter II, verse 25.
29. P.V. Kane, History of Dharma Shastras, 1974, Vol. II, Part I, p. 15.
30. P.V. Kane, *op. cit.*, Vol. II, 9, 378. See also Narmadeshwar Prasad, *op. cit.*, p. 73.

not believe in the Vedas.[31] They were branded as impure[32] and referred to as foreigners.[33] Those Mechas who accepted the caste system became Hindus.[34] They resided beyond the Vindhya mountain ranges (beyond Aryan culture) in Andhra, Anga, Vanga and Kalinga. Countries like Arattak, Karaskara, Pundra, Sauvira and Pranuna were also known as Mlecha countries.[35] After they were conquered, they were given position similar to that of the Chandlas in Aryavarta.[36] Greeks and Romans were treated as Mlechas and were reduced to slavery by Kautilya.[37] This was natural as *John Locks* states that the conqueror uses one of the following four methods to rule the conquered people.

1. He continues to rule them according to their own laws and assumes himself only the exercise of the political and civil government; or
2. Gives them a new government; or
3. Destroys and disperses their society; or
4. In fire, exterminates the people.[38]

The Kushans were foreigners or Mlechas whose kingdom extended upto the Bay of Bengal. They accepted Buddhism. King Julyaina destroyed many Sarglasrons (Buddhist monasteries) and killed Bhikus (Buddhist priests) in 2 B.C. Mlhlrokulc, a worshipper of Shiva, slaughtered countless Buddhists. Sashanka, king of Bengal, in the middle of 7 A.D. endeavoured many times to uproot the Bodhi tree (Buddhism). In Kashmir, Kshemagupta and Shri Harasha dealt ruthlessly with the Buddhists. At the instance of Kumaril Bhatt the Buddhists were driven out of Kerala. King Sudhanvan issued an injunction that from the Bridge of Ram in Sri Lanka to the Himalayas, one who does not slay a Buddhist, both old and

31. *Ibid.*
32. Manu Smriti, Chapter VII, Verse 149.
33. Naramdeshwar Prasad, *op. cit.*, p 87.
34. P.L. Narsu, The Essence of Buddhism (1948), p. 99.
35. P.V. Kane, *op. cit.*, Vol. II, Part I, pp. 15-16.
36. *Ibid.*
37. K.M. Saran, Labour in Ancient India (1957), pp. 27-28. See also Narmadeshwar Prasad, *op. cit.*, p. 9.
38. Morris, Clarence, The Great Legal Philosophers (1959), p. 167.

young, shall be slain.[39] Thus, many Buddhist countries were destroyed because of their not believing in the Vedas and the Varna system. After their conquest they were made slaves and were not given the position of even Shudras but Chandalas – the untouchables. Therefore, they were kept outside the Varna system whereas the Jains who not only accepted[40] the Varna system but also the superiority of Brahmins and Brahmins were made the priests of Jaina temples.[41] They had no alternative but to surrender to Brahminism. As a reward the Jains were not regarded as Mlechas or Panchamas. This was a theological distinction and not a racial one. The Aryas even surrendered Mlechhas for food.[42] The Brahmins were the enemies of Buddhism as they imposed untouchability on broken men when they refused to leave Buddhism.[43] The defeated tribes became broken wanderers to settle themselves along with the settled tribes. They accepted to stay outside the village settlements.[44] Untouchability was born out of the struggle for supremacy between Buddhism and Brahminism which has contributed a great deal to the moulding of the history of India.[45] The Panchamas were defeated Buddhist who were made untouchables without any rights whatsoever, under the law of Brahmin countries.[46]

Regarding the manner of origin of Untouchables, scholars are also not in accord. Untouchables were, according to *Dr. Ambedkar,* originally "broken men", i.e., persons who had left their own tribes and sought shelter with the people who had already been settled in the villages. The "broken men", however, lived outside the village. When Buddhism was spreading far and wide they embraced Buddhism. The Brahmins had reasons

39. P.L. Narsu, The Essence of Buddhism (1948), p. 39.
40. B.R. Ambedkar, *op. cit.*, p. 153.
41. Gopalchandra Sarkar Sastry, The Hindu Law of Adoption; quoted in P.V. Borale, Problem of Untouchablity and Former Untouchables, p. 58.
42. S.A. Dange, India from Primitive Communism to Slavery (1949), p. 174.
43. B.R. Ambedkar, *op. cit.*, p. 78.
44. B.R. Ambedkar, *op. cit.*, p. 29.
45. B.R. Ambedkar, *op. cit.*, p. 154.
46. P.T. Borale, *op. cit.*, p. 64.

to hate Buddhists, imposed servere restrictions on the "broken men" who used to eat beef. These restrictions in course of time amounted to what we know as the practice of Untouchablility.[47] But such a view is untenable, for this social phenomenon appears in the Pre-mauryan period which witnessed the rise and growth of Buddhism.

Another theory states that the origin of Untouchables is the result of intermixture of castes.[48] Early law texts trace the origin of about a dozen mixed castes. For example, the issue begotten by a Sudra on women of Kshatriya Varna was known as a Ksatr, and the one begotten on a female of the Vaishya caste as a Magadha. The son of a Sudra by a Brahmin woman was branded as Chandals. Similarly, other Untouchables, according to this theory, were produced as a result of various combinations.[49] However, it is very difficult to imagine that persons born out of forbidden sex contacts were numerous enough to form a separate caste group, since they are to be found particularly in all the villages of India. *Kuppuswamy* points out:

> "It is possible that because they were following occupations which were dispised, they were characterised by the Upanishads and Dharmshastras as equivalent to the despicable progeny of forbidden sex."[50]

The above view seems to be reasonable. Untouchables might have originated as a result of inter-mixture of castes; but later those who continued to practice the despised occupations were also degraded to the position of Untouchables. This view also explains the wide prevalence of Untouchables in village India.

---

47. B.R. Ambedkar, The Untouchables (Who were they ? And Why They Became Untouchables ?) Ch. X.
48. Most of Dharmsutras, i.e. Ancient Law texts attribute the origin of untouchables to the inter-mixture of castes.
49. Other mixed castes orginating as a result of inter-mixure of castes are the nisada, the parasava, the urga, the ayogava, the puhhase, the hukkutaka, the svapaka, and the vena. Manu. X 8-9, 12, 16, 18, 19.
50. B. Kuppuswamy, Social Change in India, 1972, Vikas Publication, New Delhi, p. 138.

(II) MEANING OF SCHEDULED CASTES

The origin of the term "Scheduled Castes," as it is understood today, can be traced back to the latter part of the eighteenth century. Since then the term has undergone great changes both in its definition as well as constitutional import. The meaning and definition of the term was discussed in the Legislative councils, Franchise committee, Statutory commission, and Indian central committee. The term coined by the several committees to denote "Scheduled Castes" were, "Depressed classes", "Exterior castes", "Excluded castes" and "Backward classes". The term Scheduled Castes came in vogue only with the Government of India Act, 1935 and this term is retained in our Constitution also.

It is expedient here to examine the legal and constitutional meaning of the term "Scheduled Caste" as understood at the various phases of transformation.

The definition of the term "Depressed classes" was discussed in the Indian Legislative Council as far back as 1916. It was decided in the Council that the term "Depressed classes" should include:

(a) Criminal and wandering tribes,
(b) Aboriginal tribes, and
(c) Untouchables.

In 1971, Sir Henry Sharp, Educational Commissioner for Government of India, prepared a list of Depressed classes in which he included:

(a) Aboriginal or hill tribes,
(b) Depressed classes, and
(c) Criminal tribes.

The explanation of the term "Depressed Classes" according to Educational Commissioner of Government of India, reads:

> . . . the depressed classes from the unclean castes whose touch or even shadow is polluting. But a wider significance is often attached to the expression, so that it includes

communities which though not absolutely outside the pale of caste, are backward and educationally poor and dispised and also certain classes of Mohammedans, some have interpreted it as simply educationally backward. The task of defining Scheduled Caste is made difficult by doubt as to where the line should be drawn and the elastic difference of such classes dwell on the borderland of respectability. Sometimes the whole community declares itself to be depressed with a view to reaping special concessions of education or appointment.[51]

In the above explanation, we find that diverse groups, aborigines, depressed classes, and criminal tribes were grouped under one head "Depressed classes", the term was rather vague, dealing with all sections of society who were downtrodden socially, educationally and economically. However, the criterion for classifying the "Depressed classes" is hinted in the explanation that those who pursue "Unclean profession" or those who belong to "Unclean caste" whose touch or even shadow is supposed to be polluting. But the main drawback was the combining of other two classes in the same terminology without precise definition.

The South Borough Committee, 1919, the Statutary Commission and the Indian Central Committee, however took a different stand from that of Sir Henry Sharp. They accepted the test of "Untouchability" as the criterion for classifying "Depressed classes". The Indian Franchise Committee stated that the term "Depressed classes" should not include those Hindus who are only economically poor and in other ways backward but are not regarded as Untouchables.[52]

The test of "Untouchability" to classify "Depressed classes" was accepted by the census of 1911. Only those who were Untouchables and who were denied access to the interior of ordinary Hindu temples; cause pollution (a) by touch, and (b) within a certain distance were included in the term "Depressed Classes."

---

51. Quoted in the Report of the Indian Franchise Committee, Vol. 1, 1932, Para 279, p. 109.
52. *Ibid.*, Vol. 1, Para 282, p. 109.

But later on the 1921 census did not specify any criterion for classifying "Depressed Classes."

Later, *Dr. B.R. Ambedkar* found the need for substituting the term "Depressed classes", by some other term like "Exterior castes" or "Excluded castes", until a better term was coined. In his note of dissent in the report of the Indian Franchise Committee he observed:

> "This designation has many advantages. It defines exactly the position of the Untouchables who are within the Hindu religion but outside the Hindu society, and distinguishes it from Hindus who are economically and educationally depressed but who are both within the pale of Hindu religion and Hindu society."[53]

Commenting on the precise definition of Untouchables by the term "Exterior castes," he further remarked: The term has two other advantages. It avoids all the confusion that is now caused by use of the vague term "Depressed classes" and at the same time is not offensive.

Dr. Ambedkar's suggestion found expression in the 1931 census. The reason for substituting the term "exterior" for out-castes was given by the census commissioner for India thus:

> Outcaste correctly interpreted seems to mean no more than one who is outside the caste system and is therefore not admitted to Hindu society, but since in practice the "Exterior caste" also contained those who had been cast out from the Hindu social body for such breach of caste rules, "outcaste" and "outcast" were in some cases synonymous and the derogatory implications of obliquity attaching to the latter term have unjustly coloured the former, a taint which is not conveyed by the substitution of the word "Exterior" which may connote exclusion but not extrusion.

The term "Exterior castes" was further defined by the Provincial Superintendent of Assam as follow :

53. *Ibid.*, Vol. 1, Para-14, p. 211.

By this expression, I mean castes recognised definitely as Hindu castes. whose water is not acceptable and who in addition, are so deficient as castes in education, wealth and influence, or for some reason connected with their traditional occupations are so looked down upon that there seems little hope of there being allowed by Hindu society to acquire any further social privileges within at any rate the next decade.

The tests applied in classifying Untouchables for purpose of census enumeration of 1931 were :

(a) Whether the caste or class in question can be served by clean Brahmins or not.
(b) Whether the caste or class in question can be served by the barbers, water carriers, tailors, etc. who serve the caste Hindus.
(c) Whether the caste in question pollutes a high caste Hindu by contact or by proximity.
(d) Whether the caste or class in question is one form whose hands a caste Hindu can take water.
(e) Whether the caste or class in question is debarred from using public conveniences such as roads, ferries, wells or schools.
(f) Whether the caste or class in question is debarred from the use of Hindu temples.
(g) Whether in ordinary social intercourse a well educated member of the caste or class in question will be treated as an equal by high caste men of the educational qualifications.
(h) Whether the caste or class in question is merely depressed on account of its own ignorance, illiteracy or poverty and but for that occupation it would be subject to no social disability.
(i) Whether it is depressed on account of the occupation followed and whether but for that occupation it would be subject to no social disability.[54]

54. Census Report 1931, Vol. 1, p. 472.

Thus, the term "Exterior castes" was suggested as the satisfactory substitute for connoting the Depressed classes. "Untouchability" was the chief test for classifying Depressed classes. Socio-religious disabilities thrust on certain sections of society, as a consequence of which they suffered social exclusiveness and separateness, were given prime importance in any classification of Depressed classes.

Ultimately, the term "Scheduled Castes" to connote Depressed classes was coined by the Government of India Act, 1935. The term was defined as follows :

> "The 'Scheduled Castes' means such castes, races and tribe, corresponding to the classes of persons formerly known as the 'depressed classes' as His Majesty in Council may specify."[55]

The Indian Independence Act 1947, defined the term as :

> The "Scheduled Castes" means such castes, races or tribe or parts or groups within castes, races or tribes, being castes, races, tribes, parts or groups which appear to the Governer-General to correspond to the classes of persons formerly known as the "Depressed classes" as the Governer-General may by order specify.

After Independence, the term "Scheduled Caste" is used in the Constitution to specify the Untouchables and Sudras. Article 341 reads.

> (1) The President may with respect to any State or Union territory, and where it is a State, after consultation with the Governer thereof, by public notification specify the castes, races or tribes or parts of or groups within castes, races or tribes which shall for the purposes of this Constitution be deemed to be Scheduled Castes in relation to that State or Union territory, as the case may be.
>
> (2) Parliament may by law include or exclude from the

55. Government of India Act, 1935, Sec. 24 of First Schedule, part-1.

> list of Scheduled Castes specified in a notification issued under clause (1) any caste, race or tribe or part of a group within any caste, race or tribe, but save as aforesaid a notification issued under the said clause shall not be varied by any subsequent notification.

The term "Scheduled Castes" is defined in Article 366(24) as follows :

> "Scheduled Castes means such castes, races or tribes as are deemed under Article 341 to be Scheduled Castes for the purposes of this Constitution."

The effect of Article 366(24) read with Article 341 is that Scheduled Castes are those castes, races or tribes or parts thereof, as the President may notify. According to Article 341(1) the President may by public notification specify what castes, races or tribes, or groups thereof in each State and Union territory would be regarded as Scheduled Castes for the purpose of the Constitution. Thus, the list of Scheduled Castes may vary from State to State and Territory to Territory. As regards the States, the President issues the notification after consultation with the Governor of the State concerned. The purpose of this provision is to avoid disputes as to whether a particular caste should be specified as a Scheduled Castes or not. Only those castes can be characterised as Scheduled Castes which are notified in the Presidential order under Article 341. To determine whether or not a particular caste is a Scheduled Caste, one has to look at the notification issued by the President under Article 341.[56]

Under Article 341(2), however, once the notification is issued by the President, any modifications therein, by way either of including or excluding from the list any caste, race or tribe or a part or a group thereof, can be made by Parliament by law and not by the Presidential notification. The Presidential notification is thus final unless altered by Parliament by law.[57]

56. K. Adhikanda Parta *v.* Gandua, AIR 1983 Orissa 89.
57. B. Basavalinggappa *v.* D. Munichinappa, AIR 1965 S.C. 1269.

The criterion for specifying "Scheduled Castes" is precise and simple. The stigma of Untouchability or socio-religious disabilities associated with the caste system have been made the basis for classifying Scheduled Castes. Accordingly, the Constitution (Scheduled Castes) Order, 1950 and the Constitution (Scheduled Castes) (Union Territories) Order, 1951 were passed, which specifies Scheduled Castes with relation to each State and Union territory.

In *Parsram* v. *Shivchand*[58] it was held that in order to determine whether a particular caste is a Scheduled Caste within the meaning of Article 341, one has to look at the public notification issued by the President in that behalf, it is not open to the court to scrutinise by evidence whether a person described as Mochi in Punjab does not fall within the caste of "Chamar" as included in the said order of 1950 issued by the President. . . . The Courts, it was explained, would not scrutinise the gazetteers and the glossaries on the Punjab castes for this purpose.

The members of a Scheduled Caste can be such persons who are Hindus or Sikhs although they may not be Hindu or Sikh by birth. They are such castes, races or tribes as are deemed to be Scheduled Castes. Their religion is either Hinduism or Sikhism. Persons professing any other religion are not Scheduled Caste men.[59] The declaration ascribing the character of Scheduled Caste to Hindus and Sikhs only is not discriminatory against members of say, Christian religion.[60] Those member of a Scheduled Castes, who embrace, Buddhism, Jainism, Islam or Christianity may cease to be members of their caste to which they belonged by birth.[61] However if the structure of the caste and its rules and regulation do not forbid. The converts may not cease to be Scheduled Castes. The Supreme Court has found that the presumption of loss of caste membership on conversion is not generally invariable.[62] It found that a member belonging to any of the certain Scheduled

58. AIR 1969 S.C. 597.
59. Para-3, Scheduled Caste 1950 (Order) as amended.
60. Soosain *v.* Union of India, AIR 1986 S.C. 733.
61. The Scheduled Castes and Scheduled Tribes (Amendment) Act, 1956.
62. C.M. Arumugam *v.* S. Rajgopal, AIR 1979 S.C. 939.

Castes in South India, on conversion does not cease to belong to his castes, although their children born subsequent to conversion may not. The converts may cease to be the Scheduled Caste men, unless it is established that the disabilities and handicaps suffered from the Caste membership in the Hindu social order continue in their oppressive severity in the newer environment of the converting community.[63] The latter may, however, on reconversion back to the Hindu fold may get to the original caste of their parents, if the members of the caste welcome them.[64] Only those castes which are there in Presidential notification are treated as Scheduled Caste and the Presidential notification is conclusive; and any alteration in the notification can be made by Parliament only. In *Bhaiyalal* v. *Harikishan Singh*[65] election to State legislature was challenged on the ground that the successful candidate belonged to Dohar Caste which was not recognised as Scheduled Caste for the district in question. The notification issued by the President under Article 341 referred to Chamar, Jatav and Mochi. It was held by the Supreme Court that the successful candidate was not a Chamar and as such, he could not claim the status of a Chamar on the plea that he belonged to Dohar Caste, which is a sub-caste of Chamar caste and that an enquiry of the kind should not be permissible having regard to the provisions of Article 341. It was urged that Chamars were recognised as a Scheduled Caste but not the Dohars. The successful candidate was a Dohar and not a Chamar. The Court declined to allow a plea to be raised that Dohars were in some areas recognised as a sub-caste of Chamars. This is so because the President can specify castes, races or tribes or parts thereof even in relation to the parts of the state where he is satisfied that such specification is justified. It was held that as to the categories of the Scheduled Castes, the President's order is conclusive.

(III) ORIGIN OF SCHEDULED TRIBES

We can trace back the origin of Scheduled Tribes in our caste ridden Hindu social system. Although stones implements

63. Soosain *v.* Union of India, AIR 1986 S.C. 733.
64. Guntur Medical College *v.* Mohan Rao, AIR 1976 S.C. 1904.
65. AIR 1965 S.C. (1557-60).

of prehistoric man have been found in various sites dating back to the Lower Paleolithic period, so far no skeletal finds have been made of these earlier times. And the human fossil finds of later periods are too few and insignificant to enable us to draw any definite conclusion as to the racial history of India in prehistoric times. But it has now become an established fact that the aboriginal tribes in India are, in most cases, survivals from the later prehistoric groups. Some tribes may even have degenerated from a higher technological level due to adverse circumstances.[66]

The aborigines of the Indian sub-continent do not form a uniform race. Entering India from various directions and from various regions of Asia, they also belong to different races. It has not yet been possible to arrange the aboriginal tribes of India into definite racial groups. Hence, more anthropological research is necessary before racial and cultural history of Indian aboriginal population can be presented in a definite perspective. Though our knowledge is vague about the origin and subsequent history of the numerous aboriginal tribes of India in the absence of sufficient archaeological and palaentological data, yet a story of their glory and decline may be arranged as far as the historic period is concerned. The historical data do shed some light on their life and we start picking up threads of reliable proofs instead of clinging to the conjectural schemes of things. This has become possible only due to the invention of script and commencement of written records.[67]

Let me first briefly review the rise and fall of Indus valley civilization and advent of Aryans on the Indian soil as background to ascertain the role of earliest known aboriginal tribes of India. The Indus Valley civilization is most probably a genuine gradual growth on Indian soil, but an importation by immigrant foreigners establishing a colony in India. The sudden, almost explosive rise of this civilization and its spontaneous growth may have several causes. One of them was the highly favourable ecological situation of the Indus valley. The great fertility of the soil caused the population to increase

66. Encyclopedia : Scheduled Tribes issue and challenges by R.S. Sharma, p. 1.
67. *Ibid.*, pp. 1-2.

rapidly. Though initially the population of the Indus valley civilization may have been a uniform race, it did not remain so, for the skeletons found in the cemeteries of the sites show a mixed racial composition. The reasons for its decline and final disappearance cannot yet be definitely stated. One cause might have been a disastrous alteration of the course of the Indus river resulting in destructive flooding of settlements and silting of fields. "Since the chronology has been revised and the end of the civilization fixed at about 1750 B.C., the old hypothesis has been revived that the Aryan invaders, the early forerunners of the Rigvedic Aryans—might have destroyed the centres of Harrapan civilization and killed or dispersed its population. The discovery of unburied skeletons on the steps of a building in Mohenjodaro seem to support such an assumption."[68]

The racial immigration took place in the last phase of prehistoric times and caused the most profound change in shaping the cultures and history of India was that of the Aryans, somewhere in the second millennium B.C. When exactly the first Aryans appeared on the border of India is still unknown. Prehistoric evidence for the early phase of Aryan immigration and conquest is very scanty and some important questions still demand convincing answers. Were the conquered peoples those of the Indus valley civilization? Did they speak Dravidian language?

The Rigvedic period (2000 to 1000 B.C.) witnessed wild Aryan tribes pouring into the north-western parts of the country, fighting not only among themselves but waging a war unto death against non-Aryan tribes. Indra, the thunder-wielder armed with his bolt, is invoked to shatter the forts of Dasas, cast his dart of Dasyus and increase the Arya's might and glory. He slays both Dasyus and Samyus. Saraswati kills the Parvatas, a hostile tribe who dwelt on the banks of the Parushni; Vishnu conquers in his battles the bull-jawed Dasyus and together with Indra destroys Sambara's castles. The Asuras who captured an Aryan sage Dabhiti's city, were defeated by Indra and dispossessed of their body. "Indian tribes have not lain 'torpid' on the fringe of civilization but have responded to 'static and

68. Fuch 1973, as quoted in R.S. Sharma's Scheduled Tribes Issue and Challenges, p. 2.

dynamic' rhythms of history. Their role is limited not merely to references to such of them as Saoras, Kinnaras and Kiratas. (historical Nagas) in ancient texts. It is part of the process of the fusion of races and cultures in the sub-continent, of the growth of Hinduism and its amorphous mass of myths and legends, magic and religion, traditions and customs. Tribal contents in Indian life may be compared to an ice-berg in an ocean and these can be identified as much as the Aryan or the Dravidian. The erosion of tribal mass, ethnic and cultural, and its absorption in the dominant society is a process working even today."[69] The thread of this story is to be carefully picked through ancient literary texts, archaeological and epigraphic evidence, medieval historical works and British records and documents.

The process of fusion of Aryan and non-Aryan tribes continued. The later Vedic period (1000 to 600 B.C.) is marked by further working of the twin processes of emerging Hinduism, Aryanisation of the tribals and the tribalisation of the Aryans. The two great epics, the Ramayan and the Mahabharat, whatever their historical value, refer to tribals such as the Sudras, Abhiras, Dravidas, Pulindas and Sabaras or Saoras. Of these "Sabaras are the most familiar and they are probably the only tribe existing today whose earliest references could be traced to Aitareya Brahman." Sabari, who offered fruits to Rama, has become "a symbol of the contributions that tribes can and will make to the life of India.[70] Most of the then known tribes claimed to have participated in the Mahabharat and its innumberable episodes. Eklavya, a Bhil, has gone down in legends as an ideal disciple who offered his thumb to Guru Dronacharya. Munda and Naga claimed to have fought on the side of the Kurus against the five brothers. Bhima's son Ghatotkacha who performs prodigies of valour in the war, is born of his tribal wife; Arjuna marries Chitrangada, a Naga princess.

The Nagas derserve comprehensive study in view of their significant contribution and participation in the Indian

69. Suresh Singh, 1964, as quoted in R.S. Sharma's Scheduled Tribes Issue and Challenges pp. 2-3.
70. Verrier Elwin, *Ibid.*, p. 4.

mainstream of earliest historical period. The historical or mythical Nagas have been absorbed so completely into the Hindu society that no trace of theirs is left today. Significantly the Nagas of Nagaland have no relation with their celebrated namesakes. The extent of the Naga influence may be measured by the observance of Naga Panchami, the influence of the snake-cult on the Vishnu creed (Vishnu's make bed) and Shaivism, Naga motifs in sculptures at Mahabalipuram and Rajgriha and such lace names as Takshila, Anant Nag, Nalanda, Nagpur and Chhota Nagpur. The Mahabharat is, in a way, an essentially Naga-story. Buddha converted a few Nagas. Naga cult survived in the abundance of names with a Naga prefix—Nagdatta, Nagsena, Nagdeva, etc., further testifies to their influence.

During the earliest phase of historical period small tribals pockets were subjugated by invaders or indigenous imperial powers. Ajatsatru destroyed the tribal republic of Vaisali, Alexander wiped out tribal pockets on the north-western border. The Arthasastra refers to Atvikas who are looked upon as potential trouble shooters. Ashoka threatens north-western tribes with dire consequences if they rise in revolt, while assuring forest tribes, in his dominion, of his compassion.

Sharma (1961)[71] dwells at length about the social structure of this period. He states that the Dhamasutra (600 to 300 B.C.) and the Manusmriti (200 BC to 200 AD) continued the old process of fusion and assimilation. The concept of mixed castes is only a fanciful and convenient Brahminical way of explaining this trend. These so-called mixed castes were the supposed progeny of male or begotten on the woman of another caste. A few of these, probably Brahmanised tribes labelled as mixed castes were Nishadas who lost during this period their earlier position and lived by hunting; Medas, Andhras, Madgas and Chenchus hunted wild animals; Ksahlas, Urgas and Pukkasas who caught animals and birds; Ayogavas worked in wood; Dhigvana and Karauras in leather; Pandusopake in cane; Margavas were boatmen; Veras played on drums and Sarendhas acted as servants and skilled dressers. The Chandalas, a tribes, were absorbed in Hindu society and assigned the task of removing dead bodies of animals and human beings, whipping

71. *Ibid*, pp. 3-4.

and chopping-off the limbs of criminals. Thus the process of downgrading of tribals continued.

That the tribes were not leading an isolated and alienated existence in borne out by the fact that many of them participated in the sub-Puranic and epic traditions of myths and folklores. The impact of epic heroes like Rama, Sita, Lakshmana, Ravan, Bhima, etc., on some of the tribes in central India is evident from their treasures of myths and lores. Gonds call themselves children of Ravan. Manu is another Puranic figure who has deeply exercised the tribes, and Mundas call themselves Manoako after him.

Ancient Sanskrit literature is replete with their descriptions. Panchatantra and Kathasarit Sagar present them in a romantic and friendly perspective. Vishnu Purana describes them as "dwarfish with flat nose". In Kadambari and Harsha-Charita, Bana presented detailed description of the Soara chief.

The feudal period (400-100 A.D.) saw a greater opening of tribal areas and Hindustan of tribal chiefs. The Brahmin priests prepared suitable Puranic geneologies for them and the ruling Brahmin class spearheaded the process of Sanskritisation or Brahminisation of tribals. Subsequently in the wake of Muslim invasion in the 11th and 12th centuries, there followed the influx of Rajputs who did not submit, into the tribal areas and the destruction of tribals pockets. Thus, Parmar Rajputs expelled Cheros from Shahabad and the Chandels replaced Bhuinya in South Monghyr district of Bihar.

The Muslim rule (12th to 18th century) witnessed a new phenomenon. The Turko Afghan and Mughal rulers mostly secured a mere formal allegiance of tribal chiefs or of Hindu rulers in tribal areas of Central India and Bihar. In 1585 and 1616 A.D., Muslim armies marched into Chotanagpur and subjugated the Raja of Khukra. Similarly the tribal areas of Assam were also subjugated by another Muslim general.

One, Daud Khan subjugated the Cheros of Palamau around 1661 A.D. During this period the conversion of tribals in the north-west frontier region to Islam took place. Some Muslim saints worked and preached on the fringes of tribal areas, like Pir Syed Shah Kamal who worked among the Nats and Pir Syed Mohammad who worked among the Kols.

Some streams of Hinduism like Bhakti movement also affected the tribals such as Munda, Oraon, etc. Chaitanya Mahaprabhu passed through Jharkhand and Vaishnava preachers like Binand Das working in Munda area converted many tribals. The Bhuinyas were completely Hinduised and lost all their tribal traits. "The roots of subsequent Bhagat movements among the tribals could be traced to the Vaishnava influence. Nothing illustrates more eloquently than the conversion of the Ahoms in Assam".[72]

Now appear the British colonialists with modern technology, new approach and vested interests. The advent of British rule meant opening up of tribal areas along the sea coast and in Bihar and Bengal. The construction of Grand Trunk Road through tribal pockets accelerated the influx of aliens such as merchants, moneylenders and land grabbers from outside. Furthermore, the pressure of growing population and the ruthless exploitation and oppression by Zamindars facilitated migration of peasants and artisans to inaccessible tribal areas. The Christian missions also got their pound of flesh.

The monumental endurance and patience of the tribals exhausted in the wake of the breakdown of tribal order in tribal areas in the 18th century. Paharia uprising towards the end of the 18th century, Munda uprising (1789-1901), the Santhal insurrection (1855-56), the Bhil rebellion (1879-80), Bastar uprising (1901-11) and Gond rebellion (1940) are some of the examples of the new awakening among the tribals of India.

Another very significant point to be noted in this historical journey of the Indian tribals is the status of the three major religions of India. While Hinduism and Islam had stopped short at the fringes (in most of the cases), Christianity penetrated deep into the tribal areas under the patronage of British rulers. This led to revitalization of movements among the tribals like Kherwar movement (1871-80), Sardari movement (1881-95), Birsa movement (1895-1901), Tana Bhagat movement (1920-35) and a host of others. The agrarian-*cum*-cultural movement threw up politico-religious leaders of stature who deeply influenced the tribal's thinking for decades to come.

---

72. Suresh Singh, 1964 as quoted in R.S. Sharma's Scheduled Tribes Issue and Challenges, p. 4.

It is the Constitution of India, which coined the term Scheduled Tribes for these Adivasis and made some specific beneficial provisions relating to them.

(IV) MEANING OF SCHEDULED TRIBES

The problem of Scheduled Tribes is peculiar, as they were subjected not only to social ostracism but also segregation from the rest of the population. As it is supposed that Scheduled Tribes are those who generally live far away from the cultured society in Jungles and hilly areas, and there too at such places which are quite aloof from the populated areas and the inhabitants of that place may not like to mix up with the cultured society. Interestingly but sadly the anthropologists, sociologists, social workers, administrators and such other people who have been involved with the tribes and their problems either on theoretical plane or on practical grounds are still not on the same wave length regarding the meaning and the definition of their subject matter. *Arthur Wilke*, puts the problem in proper perspective by stating that for years ambiguity has stalked India's official portrait of tribal people.[73]

No doubt, with the passage of time, the differences on the meaning and definition of a tribe have certainly narrowed down to an appreciable extent, but a theoretical discussion seems imperative to understand this problem in its proper perspective.

Here are a few definitions of 'tribe' being used as the basis of discussion in the present chapter :

> A tribe is a collection of families bearing a common name, speaking a common dialect, occupying or professing to occupy a common territory and is not usually endogamous, though originally it might have been so.
>
> —*Imperial Gazeteer of India*
>
> A tribe is a group of people in a primitive or barbarous stage of development acknowledging the authority of a chief and usually regarding themselves as having a common ancestor.
>
> —*Oxford Dictionary*

73. R.S. Sharma, Problems with the Concept and Definition of Tribe, p. 6.

> In its simplest form the tribe is a group of bands occupying a contiguous territory or territories and having a feeling of unity deriving from numerous similarities in culture frequent contacts, and a certain community of interest.
>
> —*Ralph Linton*

> A tribe is an independent political division of a population with a common culture.
>
> —*Lucy Mair*

> A tribe is a group united by a common name in which the members take a pride by a common language, by a common territory, and by a feeling that all who do not share this name are outsiders, 'enemies' in fact.
>
> —*G.W.B. Huntingford*

> A tribe is a social group with territorial affiliation, endogamous, with no specialization of functions, ruled by tribal officers, hereditary or otherwise, united in language or dialect, recognising social distance with other tribes or castes, without any social obloquy attaching to them, as it does in the caste structure, following tribal traditions, beliefs and customs, illiberal of naturalisation of ideas from alien sources, above all conscious of homogenity of ethnic and territorial integration.
>
> —*D.N. Majumdar*

> Ideally, tribal societies are small in scale, are restricted in the spatial and temporal range of their social, legal, and political relations, and possess a morality, a religion, and world-view of corresponding dimensions. Characteristically too, tribal languages are unwritten, and hence, the extent of communication both in time and space is inevitably narrow. At the same time, tribal societies exihibit a remarkable economy of design and have a compactness and self-sufficiency lacking in modern society.
>
> —*L.M. Lewis*

A major hurdle of defining a tribe is that related with the problem of distinguishing the tribe from peasantry. "It is no doubt possible to use the labels 'tribal' and 'peasant' for this type of social organisation and to characterise one by contrasting it with the other. But in spite of all the effort's invested by anthropologists in the study of primitive societies, there really is no satisfactory way of defining a tribal society. What this amounts to in the Indian context is that anthropologists have tried to characterise a somewhat nebulous sociological type by contrasting it with another which is almost equally nebulous. Earlier anthropologists had not paid sufficient attention to the definition of tribal society, but tacitly assumed that what they were studying in Australia, Malaysia and Africa were various forms of tribal society. The tribe was somewhat vaguely assumed to be a more or less homogeneous society having a common government, a common dialect and a common culture".[74]

The above discussion shows that it is not easy to define a tribe or a tribal society conclusively and any standardisation in this regard is very difficult to obtain. Hence the regional connotation of the concept of tribe focus on gaining standardisation within the Indian universe to solve our own problems. This seems to be quite sensible in the situation when definitions of universal applicability are either very broad and loose or very narrow and restricted. *Bailey* is perhaps the only anthropologist working in the Indian field who has tried to characterise tribes in terms of segmentary principles, but the contrast in which he is interested is not between 'tribe' and 'peasant' but between 'tribe' and 'caste'.

In 1917, *Sir Henary Sharp,* Educational Commissioner, Government of India prepared a list of Depressed classes, wherein he included aboriginal or hill tribes, depressed classes, and criminal tribes all in one. The need for separating "Aboriginal Tribes" from "Depressed classes" was felt by the Franchise Committee in 1919. Since then, the tribals were accorded a separate nomenclature.

In the 1931 census, we come across the term "Primitive Tribes" to specify the tribal population of India who were till then termed as "Forest Tribes" or "Hill Tribes".

74. *Ibid.*, p. 9.

The 1941 Census just mentioned "Tribes" and all adjectives for the first time were dropped to qualify the tribes. Today, under the Constitution of India, the tribals are Scheduled and are popularly termed as "Scheduled Tribes", Article 342 of the Constitution has provisions regarding Scheduled Tribes. It run as follows :

(1) The President may with respect to any State or Union Territory and where it is a State after consultation with the Governor thereof by public notification specify the tribes or tribal communities of parts of or groups within tribes or tribal communities which shall for the purposes of the Constitution be deemed to be Scheduled Tribes in relation to that State or Union Territory, as the case may be.

(2) Parliament may by law include in or exclude from the list Scheduled Tribes specified in a notification issued under clause (1) any tribe or tribal community or part of or group within any tribe or tribal community, but save as aforesaid a notification issued under the said clause shall not be varied by any subsequent notification.

The term Scheduled Tribes is defined under Article 366(25) as :

"Scheduled Tribes means such tribes or tribal communities or parts of a groups within such tribes or tribal communities as are deemed under Article 342 to be Scheduled Tribes for the purpose of this Constitution."

The effect of Article 366(25) read with Article 342 is that Scheduled Tribes are those tribes or tribal communities, or parts or groups thereof, as the President may notify. The President may specify under Article 342(1) by public notification what tribes or tribal communities are to be treated as the Scheduled Tribes with respect to each State and Union territory. In case of the States, the President issues the notification after consulting the Governor of the State concerned.

Once these lists have been issued by the President any later additions or substractions can be made their in only by a law of Parliament and not by a Presidential notification.

There is no uniform test for classifying the tribes as the Scheduled Tribes and therefore, there exist difficulties in determining which tribes can rightly be included in or excluded from the Schedule of tribes.

T.B. Naik[75] raises the problem in proper perspective by talking of the criteria an indices of the tribal life in specifically Indian setting. What should be the criteria and indices of the tribal life in specifically Indian setting. What should be the criteria and indices of tribal life ? Living in forest ? The Dublas of Surat and a host of others do not live in forests. They live in fertile plains, nevertheless they are included in the schedule. Primitive religion? But you do not know what primitive religion is in India, there being a continuance from the most abstruse philosophy to the tribal gods and superstitious beliefs in the religion of most of the advanced communities of India. This index being very fluid and not exact will not do. Geographical isolation? There are hundreds of tribal groups who are not living an isolated life. Primitive economic system? There are many peasant groups who are living by equally primitive economic system. Thus, Naik goes on to present his own criteria for a tribe which are as follows :

1. A tribe to be a 'tribe' should have the least functional interdependence within the community (the Hindu caste system is an example of high interdependence).
2. It should be economically backward, which means :
   - (i) the full import of monetary economics should not be understood by its members;
   - (ii) primitive means of exploiting natural resources should be used;
   - (iii) the tribes economy should be at an underdeveloped stage; and
   - (iv) it should have multifarious economic pursuits.
3. There should be a comparative geopraphic isolation of its people from others.

75. *Ibid.*, p. 8.

4. Culturally, members of a tribe should have a common dialect which may be subject to regional variations.
5. A tribe should be politically organized and its community Panchayat should be an influential institution.
6. The tribe's members should have the least desire to change. They should have a sort of psychological conservatism making them stick to their old customs.
7. A tribe should have customary laws and its members might have to suffer in a law court because of these laws.

Naik further elaborates that a community to be a 'tribe' must have all these attributes. It might be undergoing acculturation, but the degree of acculturation will have to be determined in the context of its customs, gods, language, etc. A very high degree of acculturation will automatically debar it from being a tribe. *Ehrenfels*[76] elaborates some of the points already discussed by saying:

1. A community, however small it may be remain in isolation from the other communites within a geographical region. This applies to a caste as well as to a tribe. The members of a true tribes, however, are generally not included into the traditional Hindu caste hierarchy and frequently speak also a common dialect, entertain common beliefs, follow common occupational practices and (most important) consider themselves as members of a small but semi-national unit.
2. We would delete in the above definition the words "economically backward", "primitive means" and "under-developed stage" and substitute them by the words "self-sufficent" (of Khasi, Gond, Bhil, Agaria and others who are in part more specialized economically, even then their non-tribal neighbours). Though each individual of a tribe may work for his

76. R.S. Sharma, Problems with the concept and definition of Tribes, p. 9.

family group and thus may remain functionally dependent on the other tribal members, it is to be seen how far every individual lives in solidarity with the tribes as a whole, rather than as a co-partner in the caste hierarchy of non-tribal Hindus.

3. We agree with the definition of geopraphical isolation though not every tribe is an isolated unit of people (e.g., Bhil, Santhals, Irula, etc.). But if a tribe has its own system of economy, its solidarity will no doubt be more stable.
4. Common dialects or languages are typical for tribes in Assam and the Central areas, but not in the Southern and Western State of India. Community of language stresses that, but is not imperative for building up tribal consciousness. The original religious concepts of most tribe in pre-acculturation days were different from their Hindu, Buddhist, Muslim or Christian neighbours, but are not always so now.
5. A tribe need only always be politically organized nor have a community panchayat. It may, or may not, have a single chief or a few elders who may wield more or less power within the community.
6. We would delete the relevant para of the above and substitute it with the words, "The members of a tribe have a feeling of belonging to a group the existence of which is valuable."
7. Almost all tribes have customary laws and practices, more or less different from their non-tribal neighbours. Very often they are indeed made to suffer on this account in law courts and in other contact situations with non-tribals.

The Tata Institute of Social Sciences in its report on the Indian Tribes has also joined those who have been criticising the anthropologist's approach of the problem. It says that the (anthropological) criteria apply to ideal typical tribal communities as conceived by the anthropologists for theoretical purpose. These do not appear to be empirically related to communities that have been included in the list of the Scheduled Tribes. The logical implication seems to be that communities which do not satisfy the above criteria should not be considered as tribes even though they are included in the list of the Scheduled Tribes. Arthur Wilke *et. al.* too, like some others, opine that some measure, if not a substantial measure, of the difficulty is inherent in the intellectual legacy of the discipline of anthropology. Aiyappan, provoked by such statements remarks rather skeptically, reminding us of the well-known definition given by Tate Regan of 'species.' Adopting the definition he (Aiyappan) said that a tribe is a group which a competent anthropologist considers to be a tribe. If the administrator wants a clear-cut definition which he can apply blindly and get along with, he says, we should tell him that we don't have it, just as the zoologist is not in a position to give a clear-cut all-purpose definition of 'species.'

Despite such rhetoric and academic polemics on the problem of definition of 'tribe' quite a substantial measure of standardization has been accomplished in designating which people are or are not entitled to particular protection and privilege. This could become possible only due to vigorous academic efforts of the much maligned and misunderstood anthropologists who, with the help of rigorous and painstaking empirical research, ultimately came out with definite and empirically verifiable ethnographic data to clear the cobwebs of misgiving regarding Indian tribes. Majumdar demonstrates this new mood by emphatically stating the following facts :

1. In Tribal India and Tribe is definitely a territorial group; a tribe has a traditional territory, and emigrants always refer to it as their home. The Santhals working in the Assam tea gardens refer to particular regions of Bihar or Bengal as their home.
2. All members of a tribe are not kin of each other, but within every Indian tribe kinship operates as a strong, associatives regulative and integrating principle. The consequesnces is tribal endogamy and the division of a tribe in to clans and sub-clans and so on. These clans, etc. being kin groups, are exogamous.
3. Members of an Indian tribe speak one common language, their own or/and that of their neighbours. Intra-tribal conflict on a group scale is not a feature of

Indian Tribes. Joint ownership of property, wherever present, as for instance among the Hos, is not exclusive. Politically, Indian tribes are under the control of the State Governments, but within a tribe there may be number of Panchayats correspondings to the heterogeneity, racial and cultural, of the constituent population in a village or in adjacent villages.

4. There are other distinguishing features of Indian tribes. Thus, there are their dormitory institutions, the absence of institutional schooling for boys and girls, distinctive customs regarding birth, marriage, and death; a moral code different from that of Hindus and Muslims; peculiarities of religious beliefs and rituals which may distinguish tribesmen even from low caste Hindus.

The courts also try to define and interpret the meaning of scheduled Tribes. In *Bhaiya Ram Munda* v. *Anirudh Patar,*[77] in the context of an election petition a question was raised whether the respondent, a Patar, belonged to a Scheduled Tribe designated as a Munda as recognised in the Presidential Order. It was argued that Patars are not Mundas, and even if Patars are Mundas, since Patars have not been included in the Presidential Order, the respondent could not be elected from the reserved constituency. The Supreme Court held that whether a particular person is a member of Scheduled Tribe so declared by the President under Article 342 is essentially a question of law. Though an admission made by him expressly, or by implication, that he is not a member of a Scheduled Tribe is evidence against him in an election petition, the evidence is not conclusive however on a consideration of all the evidences the Court concluded that Patars are a sub-tribes Munda and that they are not different form Mundas. Because some sub-tribes of Mundas are enumerated in the Order and others are not, no inference will arise that those not enumerated are not Mundas. The Court did not accept the plea that because Patars are not specifically

77. AIR 1970 S.C. 2533.

mentioned in the Order. They can not been included in the general heading Munda.

However in *Srish Kumar Chaudhary* v. *State of Tripura,*[78] The Court could not help the petitioner belonging to the Laskars tribe falling within the description of Deshi Tripura tribe because neither of these tribes was specifically mentioned in the Presidential order. Though the Court was convinced that the Laskars tribes had been traditionally availing special favours, it expressed its inability to go behind the Presidential order which it considered to be final in the respect.

In *N.E. Horo* v. *Jahanara Jaipal Singh*[79] as issue was raised out of rejection of the nomination papers of the respondent by the Returning Officer on the ground that she was not a member of Scheduled Tribe and therefore, was not eligible to contest for the parliamentary constituency in question. The Supreme Court held that she acquired the membership of Munda tribe through her marriage with the deceased Jaipal Singh of that tribe. Article 342 shows that wide import and meaning should be given to the expression "tribal community", and even if a person is not a member of the Munda tribe by virtue of birth, she being married to a Munda, after due observance of all formalities and after obtaining the .approval of the elders of the tribe, a woman would belong to the tribal community which her husband belongs on the analogy of the wife taking the husband's domicile.[80]

In *Marri Chandra* v. *Dean, S.G.S. Medical College*[81] a Constitution bench of the Supreme Court through Mukharjee, C.J. has unanimously held that a member of any Scheduled Tribe in one State does not carry that status if he moves to a State where that Tribe is not recognised as Scheduled Tribe. Therefore, he can not claim the benefits available to the Scheduled Tribes in the latter State. In this case the Petitioner's father, belonging to a Scheduled Tribe in Andhra Pradesh availing benefit of the status he moved to Maharashtra as a Central Government employee. The Petitioner grew and studied

78. SCC 1990 (supp) 230.
79. AIR 1972 S.C. 1840.
80. N.E. Horo *v.* Jahanara Jaipal Singh, AIR 1972 S.C. 1840.
81. SCC (3) 1990 130.

in Maharashtra for about ten years when after the completion of twelfth class he applied for admission to medical colleges in that State as Scheduled Tribe. He, however, could not be treated a Scheduled Tribe because the tribe to which he beonged in Andhra Pradesh was not included among the Scheduled Tribes are specified in relation to each State and Union Territory and therefore a Scheduled Tribe in one State or Union Territory does not carry that status in another State or Union Territory as a matter of course. The Court justified its interpretation by saying that a member of Scheduled Tribe does not suffer the same handicap and disadvantage in a State where his tribe is not specified as Scheduled Tribe as be suffers in a State where it is so specified and that among the tribes also the ones which need protection in a particular state must have preference over those which do not require such preference in that State.

The Supreme Court decisions during the last decade of 20th century and the first decade of 21st century have preferred restrictive interpretation of Articles 341 and 342 read with 366(24) and 366(25). The judicial approach in *Bhaiya Ram Munda* v. *Anirudh Patar*[82] and in *Dina* v. *Narain Singh*[83] have been departed and finality has been attached to the Presidential order without any liberal interpretation in *Srish Kumar Chaudhary* v. *State of Tripura*[84] the Supreme Court denied lasker's tribes the benefit of Desi Tripura tribe because, they were not mentioned in Presidential order. This view was taken in spite of the fact that the Court was convinced that the lasker's tribes had been traditionally availing traditional affairs. The court was strict on the point of any inclusion or exclusion to be made in Presidential order. The court has also given restrictive interpretation and excluded the benefit of reservation to those who have acquired the tribal status by marriage. In *Valasamma Pal* v. *Cochin University*[85] the Supreme Court held that the benefits of reservation can't be given to those who claim such benefit on the basis of marriage, adoption and conversion. The

82. (1970) 2 SCC 825.
83. 38 ELR 212.
84. 1990 Supp SCC 220.
85. (1996) 3 SCC 545.

same view was reiterated in *Sobha Hymawathi Devi* v. *Setti Ganga Dhar Swamy*.[86]

The judicial pronouncements have tried to balance between the different interests, i.e. interest of the Scheduled Castes and Scheduled Tribes and the society at large. So for as disallowing the inclusion of some sub-caste or tribes from the Scheduled Castes and Scheduled Tribes category beyond the Presidential order is concerned. The issue involved in relates to *Scheduled Castes* v. *Scheduled Castes* and *Scheduled Tribes* v. *Scheduled Tribes* and it may be possible that Presidential order may not be conclusive. There may be likelihood of certain sub-castes and sub-tribes of castes and tribes included in Presidential order. And in this respect the court may adopt the liberal approach so as to provide benefits of reservations to the Scheduled Castes and Scheduled Tribes people as the court had done in *Bhaiya Ram Munda* v. *Anirudh Patar*.[87]

The Supreme Court has denied the benefit of the Scheduled Castes and Scheduled Tribes to such candidates in States other than the State which includes their name in the Presidential order. Thus in *Marri Chander* v. *Dean Seth G.S. Medical College*[88] the Supreme Court denied the benefit of reservation to the petitioner whose father belongs to Scheduled Tribes in Andhra Pradesh but who was claiming such benefit in Maharashtra as a central government employee. Though on the facts of the case is appreciable and does not affect the claimant much as he had got his education in Maharashtra but in some cases where the initial schooling of the candidate has been in the State where his caste or tribe is included in Presidential order but he claims the benefit of reservation in some other State. To deny the benefit to such candidate is bound to ignore the stresses and strength through which they have gone through during their schooling.

The denial of the benefit of Scheduled Castes and Scheduled Tribes to those who have acquired new status on the basis of adoption marriage or conversion involves the interest of reserved category people *vis-a-vis* the rest of the society and

86. (2005) 2 SCC 244.
87. (1970) 2 SCC 825.
88. (1990) 3 SCC 130.

perhaps the courts appears to alive the problem of the misuse of the adoption, marriage and conversion for ulterior purposes but discouragement of such benefit may be impediment in the way of serving the social cause of desegregation and assimilation of different segment of society more particularly the upper caste girls getting married to the Scheduled Castes and Scheduled Tribes any way the misuse of adoption can't be ruled out the case of conversion may also sail on the same boat.

4

Causes for Degradation of Scheduled Castes and Scheduled Tribes

In the previous chapter the historical perspective and origin of Scheduled Castes and Scheduled Tribes have been discussed. As has been told in last chapter in older times, Scheduled Castes and Scheduled Tribes were known as Sudras, Untouchables, Weaker section of society, Depressed classes and Adivasis, etc. These terms vividly show that their condition was not humane and they were not at par with rest of the society.

In the present chapter the causes for degradation of Scheduled Castes and Scheduled Tribes has been dealt with. I have elaborated the factors and circumstances which have made their lives miserable. There were numerous reasons which were prevailing in the then society which led to their degraded condition.

(I) GENERAL

The Hindu social order was immemorially established on foundations of a four-tired Varna (caste) system. The Varna (caste) were as follows, namely :

(1) Brahmin
(2) Kshatriya .
(3) Vaisya; and
(4) Sudra

This four fold division of Varna by certain Brahmin rishis, deemed as of divine origin, having been established by Brahma, the God of creation, to ensure progress of the society.[1]

The lord declared the assigned roles, functions and obligations of men belonging to different Varnas.[2] The Varnas karma order was thus a rank order of social status.

Brahmin was ordained to study, to teach, to do yajna, and to defend Dharma. Kshatriya was ordained to protect and defend the realm, to rule and to make donations. Vaisya was asked to do cultivation, to protect the cattle, to trade and establish industry, to lend money and to make donations. Sudra was obliged to show respect to those who were his superior by caste; and to serve men of those higher castes.

The Brahmin was placed at the apex in the pyramidal Varna (caste) hierarchy and the Sudra at the base. The Brahmin read Vedas. He inherited 'Sacred learning' and Sacred Science could be learned under him. Subject to his not falling off from the ordinance of law he could be a teacher and a preacher; and would command respect and reverence from persons of other castes. He was the intellectual leader, may be claimed the distinction of being the only one endowed with learning and intellect. He could deny knowledge to a Sudra. The great guru of the times of Mahabharata "Dronacharya" refused to admit "Eklavya" as his student, because of his lower origin and, thus,

---

1. Lokanam tu vivridth yarth mukh bahu rupadtah; Brahmanan Kshatriya Vaishaya shudram cha Nikhartayat.
2. Chaturvarna Maya Srishtam Guna karma vivhagayah.

denied him the opportunity to learn and practice archery in his ashram.[3] Not only this was taken away as Gurudakshina.

The Brahmin person was supposed to be sacred. He was deemed worth more than what could be compensated. One who killed him would commit most reprehensive crime. No amount· of head money would atone the sin. A sacred law text of that period,[4] provided that the Brahmin would not intercourse, interdine and intermarry with non-Brahmin more so with Sudras. He would not eat food offered by a Sudra or "which has been brought (being touched or not) by an impure Sudra. He would not eat in the same row with a Sudra. If a Sudra touched him while eating, he would leave off. He would keep the prescribed minimum distance between himself and Untouchables.

Next in the order was Kshatriya. He was the ruler, and belonged to the warrior class. He showed respect to a Brahmina. He held political power and bore arms. His duties included defence of the territory, protection of the subjects, organisation of the Government and administration of justice. He was worthy more then the ruled. The killer of a Kshatriya was to give thousand cows for expiations of his sin.

The Vaishya along with Brahmin and Kshatriya was included in the so-called dwija, and thus was also entitled to undergo thread ceremony (upnayan samaskar) and study of Veda, cultivated land, established industry. He controlled economic power; and cooperated with the Kshatriya, to maintain his hold on means of production and land ownership. One who killed him gave one hundred cows to earn expiation of his sin.

The lowest and the last in the caste hierarchy was the Sudras. He showed respect to those superior by caste and derived the highest bliss by doing his assigned duties. He was not allowed to withhold labour or strike work. His duty was to serve only, and not to ask reason. He could not pass a learned Brahmin without addressing him. He was an unskilled manual labourer and more often than not received less than the cost of

3. M.C.J. Kagzi, Segregation and Untouchability Abolition, New Delhi, Metropolitan Book Co., 1976.
4. Apastamba Dharmasutra.

his labour. He was for that reason, most exploited, landless poor and afflicted with dependence upon the higher caste men. One who killed him gave only ten cows for expiation. He was not entitled to study Vedas; and would not kindle sacred fire or do works "Productive of rewards". Neither a teacher would initiated him, nor would permit him to reside in ashram. A Brahmin would avoid him and would interrupt recitation of Veda, if he was around. The latter was segregated from men of the higher caste in matters of residence, food, education and not only he lived separately but also did not frequent the areas inhabited by the higher castes, except while on work. He was so to say, an Untouchable. The stigma of Untouchability could not be shed or washed-off. Born an Untouchable, he would die as such. According to his jati (sub-caste) and avocation, he would be a Bhangi, Jamadar (Sweeper), Chamar (Shoe-maker), Dhobi (washerman), Kahar (Waterman), Kasai (butcher) or dome. Certain of the occupations as swine herding, leather tanning and shoe-making, toddy tapping which were often considered defiling were associated with the low caste man. He was a servant or an unskilled landless labourer if not carrying his traditional avocation. So his head price was very low.[5]

There are numerous examples which shows the humiliating situation of Untouchable. It was supposed that even their shadows could pollute other higher Caste. Certain examples from different part of India throws light on their down-trodden condition.

In the Maratha country the shadow of an Untouchable was sufficient if it falls on a member of the higher caste to pollute him. In Madras and specifically in Malabar this doctrine was still further elaborated so that certain lower castes have always to maintain a stated distinction between themselves and the Brahmins and other higher castes so as not to defile the latter. Among the people of Kerala a Nayar may approach a Namboodari Brahmin but must not touch him, while a Tiyan must keep himself at a distance of thirty-six steps from the Brahmin and a Pulayan may not approach him within ninety-six Paces.[6] Even a modern Brahmin doctor when feeling the pulse

5. M.C.J. Kagzi, Segregation and Untouchability Abolition, p. 197.
6. Rao, M.S.A., Social Change in Malabar. 1957, p. 21.

of a Sudra first wraps up the patient's wrist with a small piece of silk so that he may not be defiled by touching his skin.[7]

One will be wonderstruck to note that "In Trichinopoly district the village have the houses arranged in streets. The Brahmin, Sudras and Panchnama quarters are separate and in the last of these Pallans, Paraiyans and Chakkiliyans live in separate streets".[8]

It is recorded that under the rule of Marathas and Peshawas the Mahars and Mongs were not allowed within the gates of Poona after 3 P.M. and before 9 P.M. because after 3 P.M. and before 9 P.M. their bodies cast too long a shadow which falling upon a member of a higher castes especially Brahmin defiles him.[9] This extended to an unduly intolerable length so much so that in Maratha country a Mahar, one of the Untouchable, might not spit on the road lest a pure caste Hindu should be polluted.[10]

The Varna caused rigid social divisions, class hierarchies and status stratification sanctioned by dharma, and law. To abide by, and conformity with approved social behaviour in accordance to Varna Samskar was a virtue and in accordance with dharma. Law also recognised and enforced caste in inequalities and provided for discrimination and segregation at caste levels. The legal rules derived from the written texts and also customs and usages having force of law provided negative sanctions from violations of caste injunctions in respect of marriage, inheritance, adoption, maintenance, property relations, law, administration and state services. The penal law and procedure for trial varied with the caste of the accused. The protection of the law too was unequal. The punishment for similar offences was dissimilar, was fixed variously for men of various castes. People were treated unequally before the law, because, the law was the caste law, and there was no general law of the land, there were no general equal laws for all. The following table is an illustrative example of discriminative justice in ancient India.

7. Ghuriya, G.S., Caste and Race in India, p. 9, Encyclopaedia of R and E, Vol. X, p. 491.
8. *Ibid.*, p. 10, Trichinopoly Distt. Gazette, Vol. I, p. 81.
9. Encyclopaedia of Russel, Vol. IV, p. 189.
10. *Ibid.*, Vol. 1, p. 72.

Discriminative Justice in Ancient India

Offence	*Offender*	*Victim*	*Punishment of Offender*
(1)	*(2)*	*(3)*	*(4)*
Killing[11]	Anyone	Kshatriya	Giving 100 cows to Brahmin
Killing[11]	Anyone	Vaishya	Giving 100 cows to Brahmin
Killing[11]	Anyone	Shudra	Giving 10 cows to Brahmin
Abusing[12]	Kshatriya	Brahmin	100 (Karshapanas)
Abusing[12]	Kshatriya	Brahmin	200 (Karshapanas)
Abusing[12]	Vaishya	Brahmin	150 (Karshapanas)
Abusing[12]	Brahmin	Vaishya	50 (Karshapanas)
Abusing[12]	Brahmin	Vaishya	25 (Karshapanas)
Abusing[12]	Brahmin	Shudra	Nil
Reviling[13]	Vaishya	Kshatriya	100 panas
Reviling[13]	Kshatriya	Vaishya	50 panas

11. Apasthamba Dharma Sutras, Verses 1-3.
12. Apasthamba Dharma Sutras, Chapter XII, Sutras 8-13; same points are mentioned in Brihaspati's Dharma Sastras.
13. Brihaspati's Dharma Sastras, Chapter XX, Verses 7-11.

Reviling[13]	Kshatriya	Shudra	20 panas
Abusing[13]	Shudra	Vaishya	Compelled to pay fine
Abusing[13]	Shudra	Kshatriya	Payment of fine doubled that of Vaishya
Abusing[13]	Shudra	Brahmin	The highest fine
Reviling[14]	Kshatriya	Brahmin	100 panas
Reviling[14]	Vaishya	Brahmin	150-200 panas
Reviling[14]	Shudra	Brahmin	Corporal punishment
Insult[14]	Brahmin	Kshatriya	50 panas
Insult[15]	Brahmin	Vaishya	25 panas
Insult[15]	Brahmin	Shudra	12 panas
Murder[16]	Any one	Brahmin	Penance
Murder[16]	Any one	Kshatriya	1/4 of the penance prescribed for slaying a Brahmin.
Murder[16]	Any one	Vaishya	1/8 of the penance prescribed for slaying a Brahmin.

14. Manu Smriti, *op. cit*.
15. Manu Smriti, Chapter VIII, Verses 267-68.
16. *Ibid*., Chapter XI, Verses 127-31.

Murder[16]	Any one	Shudras (Virtuous)	1/16 of the penance prescribed for slaying a Brahmin.
Slaying [16]	Brahmin	Kshatriya	1000 cows and bulls or three years (with senses subdued and locks braided, follow the obrservances of one who has slain a Brahmin living in a place far from town, his dwelling place shall be the foot of a tree.
Slaying[16] (Involuntary)	Brahmin	Vaishya (Virtuous)	Punishment for one year as above and giving of 10 cattle (heads of cattle) to Brahmin
Slaying[16] (Involuntary)	Any one	Shudra	Some observance for six months or giving of 10 white cows and bull to a priest (Brahmin)
Insulting[17] Superior caste by limbs	Any one (except Brahmin)	Superior Caste	King shall cut-off the limb
(a) Seating on a seat of superior	Any one (except Brahmin)	Superior Caste	Banishing with a mark on buttocks.
(b) Spit on superior caste	Any one (except Brahmin)	Superior Caste	Lose both lips

17. Vishnu Smriti, Chapter V, Sutras 19-25.

(c) Breaking wind against superior caste	Any one (except Brahmin)	Superior Caste	Lose his hind parts
(d) Abusive language	Any one (except Brahmin)	Superior Caste	Lose tongue
(e) Instructing about duties with pride to higher caste	Any one (except Brahmin)	Superior Caste	Hot oil be dropped into his mouth
(f) Mentioning the name of superior revitingly	Any one (except Brahmin)	Superior Caste	Ten fingers long (hot red) iron pin shall be thrust into his mouth
(g) Teching the precepts of religion or uttering Vedas Insulting a Brahmin[18]	Shudra	Nil	Cutting-off his tongue

18. Brihaspati Smriti, Chapter XII, Verse 12.

(i) Listening[19] intentionally to the Vedas	Shudra	Nil	(i) Ear shall be filled with (molten tinlac)
(ii) Reciting[19] Veda	Shudra	Nil	(ii) Tongue shall be cut-off
Prohibitions			
(i) Teaching Shudra[20] or learning from Shudra	Dwija	Nil	Unfit for being invited at the performance in honour of Devas and Pitris
(ii) Advising, giving food or butter to Shudra that has been offence[21]	Dwija	Nil	Together with Shudra shall sink in the darkness of hell called Assamvrita.
(iii) Teaching of law of Shudra[21]	Dwija	Nil	Together with Shudra shall sink in the darkness of hell called Assamvrita.

19. Gautam Dharma Sutras, Chapter XX, Sutras 4-6.
20. Manu Smriti, Chapter III, Verse 156.
21. *Ibid.*, Chapter IV, Verses 78-81.

(iv) Giving instructions on religious matters[21]	Dwija	Nil	Together with Shudra shall sink in the darkness of hell called Assamvrita.
Adultery [22]	Dwija	Shudra woman	Shall be banished
Adultery	Shudra	Dwija woman	Capital punishment
Criminal intercourse[23]	Shudra	Any woman	Organ (penis) shall be cut-off and property to confiscated. If the woman has a protector (i.e., under guardianship of somebody) Shudra shall be executed after having undergone above prescribed punishment.
Loving a girl[24] of Dwijas	Shudra	Dwija woman	Corporal punishment
Cohabiting with Dwija women[25]	Shudra	Dwija woman	If she is not guarded,deprive his members and all his property and of anything if she is guarded.

22. Apasthamba Dharma Sutras, Prasana 11, Patala 10.
23. Gautam Dharma Sutras, Chapter XII, Sutras 2-3.
24. Manu Smriti, Chapter VIII, Verse 366.
25. *Ibid.*, Verse 374.

Intentionally reviling by criminal abuse or assault[26]	Shudra	Dwija woman	Shall be deprived of the limb with which he offends
Assuming equal position with twice born in laying down in conversation or on the road[27]	Shudra	Dwija woman	Corporal punishment
Assault with virulent words[28]	Shudra	Dwija	Cut-off his tongue
Mentioning names in insulting manner[28]	Shudra	Dwija	Red hot iron rod ten fingers long should be thrust into his mouth.
Instructing priest regarding his duties[28]	Shudra	Brahmin	Boiling hot oil be poured into his mouth and ear.

26. Gautam Dharma Sutras, Chapter X, Sutras 50, 56-59.
27. *Ibid.*, Chapter IV, Sutras 1-7.
28. Manu Smriti, Chapter VIII, Verses 270-72.

Lifting up hand or staff[29]	Shudra	Dwija	Cut-off his hands
Smites with feet in anger[29]	Shudra	Dwija	Cut-off his feet.
Sits down by the side of high born[29]	Shudra	Dwija	To be banished after being branded on his hip or his backside be cut-off.
Spitting [29]	Shudra	Dwija	Cut-off lips
Making water[29]	Shudra	Dwija	Cut-off penis
Breaking wind[29]	Shudra	Dwija	Cut-off anus
If he seizes by the locks[29]	Shudra	Dwija	Cut-off both his hands also (if he seize by feet) hand, neck testicles.
False accusation[29]	Shudra	Dwija	Split tongue and put on stakes
Insulting referring with contempt[30]	Shudra	Dwija	Cut-off tongue, ten fingers long red hot iron rod should be thrust into his mouth.
Giving lessons to Brahmins about their duty [30]	Shudra	Brahmin	Hot oil be poured into his mouth and ear.

29. *Ibid.*, Chapter VIII, Verses 279-84.
30. Narada Smriti, Chapter XV, Verses 22-27.

Offending[30]	Shudra	Dwija	The concerned limb should be cut-off
Seating with high caste[30]	Shudra	Dwija	To be branded on hip banished or backside be gashed
Arrogance spit[30]	Shudra	Dwija	Cut-off both lips
Making water[30]	Shudra	Dwija	Cut-off penis
Breaking wind[30]	Shudra	Dwija	Cut-off buttocks.

A Brahmin may take the belongings of the Shudra[31] with perfect peace of mind as nothing belongs to the Shudra but to his master.[32] The mere sight of possession of wealth by the Shudra injures a Brahmin.[33] A Shudra giving judical decision would sink the kingdom into misfortune.[34] The region chiefly inhibited by the Shudras is bound to be oppressed by famine and disease.[35] Even if freed by his master, the Shudra, whether bought or not by the Brahmin, may be compelled to practise servitude as he was created merely to serve the Brahmin.[36]

Only two classes of Shudras were exempted from taxes[37] : (1) Those Shudras who used to like washing the feet of the Brahmins, and (2) those who were deaf and dumb or were suffering from diseases. In such a case the relaxation was to last till the infirmities continued.

To serve the upper three castes was ordained for the Shudra. The higher the caste he served the greater would be the merit.[38] If the Shudra pursues his duties without complaining against the system, then he gains in this as also the other world.[39] His mild speech, submissiveness to the Brahmins give him a higher birth.[40] He may serve the Kshatriya for subsistence, the Vaishya for support of life and the Brahmin for the heaven. However, food which was left over, old clothes, blighted part of grains and very old furniture could be given to the Shudras.[41] Protection was of the caste law which prescribed social injunctions, prohibitions and obligations ordained intra caste social intercourse, and prohibited violations of caste prohibitions, 'Manu' prescribed intra-caste Savarna and Sajatiya

31. Manu Smriti, Chapter I, Verses 87-91.
32. *Ibid.*, Chapter VIII, Verse 417.
33. *Ibid.*, Chapter X, Verse 129.
34. *Ibid.*, Chapter VIII, Verses 20-22.
35. *Ibid.*
36. *Ibid.*, Chapter VIII, Verses 412-14.
37. Apasthamba Dharma Sutras.
38. *Ibid.*, Prasana 1, Patala 1, Skanda 1, Sutras 7-8.
39. Manu Smriti, Chapter X, Verse 128.
40. *Ibid.*, Chapter IX, Verses 334-35.
41. *Ibid.*, Chapter X, Verses 121-25.

(endogamous) marriage between a higher caste men. Legally, the Shudra could marry only a Shudra woman,Vaishya could marry a Shudra and or a Vaishya woman, Kshatriya could marry a Shudra, a Vaishya and a Kshatriya woman, while a Brahmin woman could be a wife of only a Brahmin.[42] Twice born marrying a casteless (Hinayatt) woman would descend to the rank of Shudra.[43] A child born to a Brahmin by a Shudra woman was deprived of Brahminhood.[44] Then both Anuloma (higher caste male and lower caste female) and Pratiloma (lower caste male and higher caste female) marriages were prohibited. Dasi (slave) also included a Shudra woman kept as concubine.[45]

Shudra did not have the right of property.[46] The Dwijas took advantage of it and reduced the Shudra woman's position to that of a Dasi or concubine. The powerful Shudra married a Brahmin woman. In order to prevent such marriages, Pratiloma marriage was prohibited and persons concerned were regarded as Chandalas.[47] Their status was degraded, i.e., after the touch of a Chandala, one should plunge into water, after talk with a Chandala, one should converse with a Brahmin and after seeking a Chandala, one should look at either the sun or the moon or the stars for purification.

The offsprings of Anuloma marriage were given intermediate caste above the mother's caste and below the father's caste.[48] This law multiplied caste. Some examples can be cited as under.[49]

1. Brahmin man + Vaishya women = Ambustha
2. Brahmin man + Shudra women = Nishad
3. Kshatriya man + Shudra women = Urga
4. Kshatriya man + Brahmin women = Suta

---

42. Manu Smriti, Chapter III, Verse 13.
43. *Ibid.*, Chapter III, Verse 15.
44. *Ibid.*, Chapter III, Verse 17.
45. D.F. Mulla, Principles of Hindu Law, p. 704.
46. Manu Smriti, Chapter X, Verse 25.
47. P.V. Kane, History of Dharmashastras, Vol. II, Part 1, p. 171.
48. D.F. Mulla, *op. cit.* , p. 611.
49. Manu Smriti, Chapter X, Verse 25.

5.	Vaishya man	+ Kshatriya women	= Magadha
6.	Vaishya man	+ Brahmin women	= Vaideha
7.	Shudra man	+ Vaishya women	= Ayogara
8.	Shudra man	+ Kshatriya women	= Kahattar
9.	Shudra man	+ Brahmin women	= Chandala
10.	Brahmin man	+ Ugra women	= Awrita
11.	Brahmin man	+ Ambastha women	= Abhira
12.	Brahmin man	+ Ayogava	= Shigyana
13.	Nishada man	+ Shudra women	= Pukkasa
14.	Shudra man	+ Nishada women	= Kukkutta
15.	Kshattar man	+ Ugra women	= Sapaka
16.	Vaidehaka man	+ Ambastha women	= Vena

Krishna exhorted Arjuna to fight the religions war of Mahabharata for the reason among others protection of Kshatriya women because the clan and caste family status which would be lost, if the women became polluted with caste degradation. Even if prohibition of hypergamy intercaste marriage was directory in the beginning, it hardened later into a rule of a hard rigid custom. The Mitakshara and the Dayabhaga, the two works on the uncodified Hindu Law prohibited intercaste marriages between a man of a inferior caste and a woman of a higher caste.

It is clear that those who were at the bottom of the pyramid of caste hierarchy, used to live in suppressed condition. They were denied basic amenities such as drinking water, food and proper living.

Thus, the entire social system was governed by the Brahminical law which was regressive in its character and was used as an instrument by socially privileged Dwijas who were also economically and politically powerful to keep the Shudras and the Avarnas in subjection and perpetual poverty. An arrangement was made so that the subjected class could never rise even in future by way of depriving them of any chance of economic power. This has continued even today. As a result, the Avarnas, Panchamas or Scheduled Castes are deprived of the economic power or property.

(II) FACTORS RESPONSIBLE FOR DEGRADATION OF SCHEDULED CASTES AND SCHEDULED TRIBES

The writers of ancient law text have played an important role in the imposition of various kinds of disabilities upon the Sudras and Untouchables.[50]

The imposition of disabilities and practice of Untouchability have mainly contributed in the horrific living condition of Untouchables. The imposition of disabilities upon them has further degraded the condition of the Sudras and made them more vulnerable to humiliation and exploitation resulting into their down-trodden condition. Untouchability can be attributed as playing pivotal role in imposition of disabilities which has made their lives miserable; but there are certain other factors also.

(A) Idea of Pollution as a Factor

This is regarded as one of the most important factor responsible for the humiliating condition of Untouchables. Ghurye write:

> "Ideas of purity whether occupational or ceremonial, which are found to have been a factor in the genesis of caste are the very soul of the idea and practice of Untouchability."[51]

H.N.C. Stevenson has analysed the concept of pollution. According to him pollution indicates a mystical kind of belief regarding the purity or impurity of certain classes or things, phenomenon and person. Certain things such as birth, death, etc., bring about a temporary state of pollution which can be warded-off by bathing, giving alms, etc. or specific offerings made to God or Priest. On the other hand being born in a certain caste was supposed to bring a degree of pollution permanently associated with caste. In case of Untouchables it was believed to be so deep that not only no amount of purificatory ritual could

---

50. The worst thing for Scheduled Castes is the Practice of Untouchability. H.R. Isaacs, Indian's Ex-Untouchables 29, (1965).
51. Quoted in B. Kuppuswamy, Social Change in India, 1972, p. 138.

ward-off pollution ascribed to them, but their touch and proximity were believed to defile and pollute others. Such other people had to follow certain rituals to become free from the effect of pollution.[52]

It is the idea of pollution which was ascribed to Untouchables and it is this idea which governed higher castes Hindus relations towards the Untouchables.[53] It is on this ground on which many social and religious disabilities were imposed upon Untouchables.

(B) Support by Dharmashastra and Ancient Law Texts as a Factor

As has been told earlier, Untouchability has played a major role for the miserable condition of Untouchables, so it seems to be expedient to discuss the cause of Untouchability which had imposed restriction upon Untouchables and these restrictions had led to their down-trodden condition. The Ancient law texts and Dharmashatra have not only supported the practice of Untouchability but even, they did provide sanctions to positively enforce it. They provided the sanctions in the forms of *penances*.[54] If a Brahmin was touched by a Chandala he was

52. The pollution of Untouchables is so much that orthodox Hindus perform certain rituals to become free form the effect of pollution. Ruth and Benedict like such ritualistic pattern of behaviour as compulsive neurotic-a kind of mental disorder of functional nature in which the person feels compelled to perform certain action in certain circumstances.
53. Once the Hindus believed that the Untouchables were permanently polluted and touch or even prosiunity of them can pollute them, it seemed natural for them to avoid contact with Untouchables resulting in the practice of Untouchability if we analyse the psychological state of those who practice Untouchability there appears two sets of ideas which are controlling their responses towards Untouchables:
    (A) That person born in a low caste are polluted and cause pollution, and
    (B) By following certain kind of acts, the pollution can be avoided.
54. A kind of self-punishment for higher castes whereas the sanction in the form of punishment was provided for the castes in case they deviated from prescribed norms of behaviour.

required to take bath for purification.[55] On the other hand, if he was touched by a Chandala while passing urine or excreta he was purified by fasting for three nights.[56] In case a Vipra was touched by a degraded caste. He should bath in the night before the fire, with the water brought during the day time.[57] Similarly, by getting on the shadow of a low-caste person, one was required to drink clarified butter after bathing.[58] Not only this, he should also look at the sun in an impure state and recite mantram "Anindraja".

The restriction was not only regarding touch but it also extended to drinking water, accepting food, reciting Vedas in presence of degraded person, accepting articles and also mixing with them. If a Brahmin unknowingly drank water from a well or from the vessel belonging to a Chandala, he should perform "*Santapanam*"[59] distructive of sins.

Similarly, if a Brahmin drunk water touched by a Chandala, he could only became pure by fasting for three nights, or by taking the *Panchgavya*.[60] if a Brahmin took food prepared by a degraded Caste,[61] he should perform "*Taptakricha*".[62] A Brahmin who took boiled rice from a Chandala[63] should perform the penance of the "*Chandrayana*".[64] In the same way if a Brahmin accepted an article from an

55. Chandala sutinsuantaya narimanrajasvalam sprista chayasudhrth talsprishtan, shadacha ret. —Us' ana Samhita. IX 75.
56. Apichandala sparshva asprishte va virmutza ava chatzistatran vishudhih syanangishatah, shadacha ret. —Us' ana Samhita. IX 103.
57. Yama Samhita; 63.
58. Us' ana Samhita. IX.89.
59. By taking the panchgavya (Milk, curd, urine of a cow, cowdung, and clarified butter made of the milk of the cow), one should fast the next day. This is the regulation about "Santapana". –Arti Samhita. 116.
60. Us' ana Samhita. IX, 48.
61. Us' ana Samhita. IX, 40.
62. In a tapta-Kricha, one should drink hot water for three days, and hot milk for another three days. And drinking hot clarified butter for three days, one should live or air for the next three days.
63. Us' ana Samhita, IX. 41.
64. In the light fortnight, one should increase the number of morsels one by one and similarly decrease it in dark fortnight,one should not take meal on Amavasya. Such is the regulation about Chandrayana.

outcaste, he could become purified by throwing it away and by performing the penance.[65] And if, out of mistake one touched an article touched by a Chandala purification was obtained by bathing, rinsing the mouth and thereafter reciting the Gayatri.[66] If one recited the Vedas before the Chandala one was purified by "Chandrayana".[67]

On the other hand, punishment was provided for low caste person if they dared for violate the prescribed norms of behaviours. The king was authorised to kill the Sudras if he recited the Gayatri and offered oblation to the sacred fire, as such behaviour of Sudras was considered to be destroyer of kingdom.[68] Similarly, ancient text writer Gautama lays down that if a Sudra recited the vedic texts, his tongue should be cut off, if he remembered them, his body should be spilt in twain.[69] And if he arrogantly teached Brahmins, their duties, the king should cause hot oil to be poured into his (untouchable's) mouth and ears.[70]

The low born person was required to be banished after being branded on the hip or the king might cause his back side to be cut off, if the Sudras endeavoured to sit down by the side of a high born man.[71] Apastamba and Gautama lay down that if in conversation, sitting lying down or on the road, the Sudra assumed a position equal to that to the Brahmin, he should be flogged.[72] And if a Chandala touched an Arya woman he must pay the fine of hundred Panas.[73]

The above discussion indicates the strictness of the Dharmashastras and Ancient Law texts regarding the practice of Untouchability. The societal practices were not far from the rules of Dharmashastrans which can be seen from the following study.

---

65. Us' ana Samhita. IX, 61.
66. Us' ana Samhita. IX, 76.
67. Us' ana Samhita. IX, 72.
68. Us' ana Samhita. IX, 19.
69. Udaharane Jihvacchedah, adavne sarir bhedoh. XII 4-6.
70. Manu, VIII 279.
71. Manu, VIII 281.
72. Vaci pathi sayyayamasana iti samibhavato dandated anam. Apastamba. Dharmasutra. II 10, 27,11, Gautama Dharmasutra. XII, 7.
73. Arti samhita, III, 18.

(C) Idea of Karma and Re-birth[74] as a Factor

According to Hindu doctrine of Karma and Rebirth, the birth of an individual in a certain caste is the direct result of his good and evil deeds through a long succession of births and rebirths. If the good deeds out-balance the evil deeds, one is rewarded with a higher ritual status being born into higher castes after his death. On the other hand, if evil deed out balances the good deeds, one is punished by being born in a lower caste.

It is enjoined in the Hindu scriptures that a man should do his duty which his caste determines for him; and those who do so will be rewarded by rebirth in a higher caste in future birth.

The idea of karma and rebirths has been an important factor to discriminate. It is supposed that the bad deed in the previous birth culminate in the lower birth origin. So it is the very idea which imposed various kinds of disabilities upon them and also to the degradation of Untouchables and Sudras.

(D) Lower Origin of Sudras as a Factor

Lower origin of Sudras has been another factor responsible for the imposition of disabilities upon them. The lower origin of Sudras is emphatically emphasised by Dharma Shastras at Various times. The Nintieth rhythm of the Purushsukta occurring in Rigveda Says:

> "... The Brahmin was his mouth; the Rajana was made his arms; the being called the Vaishya was his thigh and the Sudra sprang from his feet."

Similarly in Santi Parva, **Bhrigu** makes following statement:

> "... This world, having been created by Brahma entirely Brahmanic, became afterwards separated into castes in consequence of works. Those who were found of sensual pleasure, fairly, irascible, prone to violence, who had forsaken their duty and red limbed, fell into the condition of Kshatriyas. . . . Those who were addicted to mischief

74. O' Malley, Indian Caste Customs. 1974, pp. 18-19.

and false hood, who lived by all kinds of works; who were black and fallen from purity, sank into the condition of Sudras."

These passages indicate the lower origin of Sudras and this knowledge had created a feeling of inferiority in the mind of Sudras whereas it created a feeling of superiority in the higher caste Hindus. And such feelings resulted in the practice of Untouchability consequently resulting in the imposition of disability.

(E) Caste and its Association to Occupation as a Factor

Increasing contempt for manual and the association of the idea of impurity to certain occupation during post-vedic period was also an important factor. As certain groups of people were associated with the occupations which were held in contempt such as scavenging, leather work, removing dead cattles from the village and so on, they were considered Untouchable with whom contact was defiling. The contempt for manual work was severe enough that if a Brahmin took to manual occupations, he fell from his status. Baudhyana states that the Brahmin who tend cattle, live by trade, work as artisans, actors, servants or users should be treated like Sudras.[75] Gautama goes a step further and states that if an Arya adopts the occupation of a Non-Arya (i.e. Sudra) he is reduced to the position of Sudra.[76]

Thus, it is evident that the association of the so called Untouchables groups to the manual works and to the work that were considered impure, was a very important factor responsible for the practice of Untouchability. But the unfortunate fact is that even today certain occupations are considered impure and manual work is held in contempt. And tragedy is that in villages even today, overwhelming majority of Sudras are engaged in manual works. particularly in occupations that are held to be onerous. They work mainly as agricultural labourers, but many sections of them are associated

75. Baudhyana, Dharmshastra, II. 4, 7, 15.
76. Aryanaryayorvyatiķsepe Harmaneh samayam, X 67.

with a variety of specialised occupations such as scavenging, leather work, etc.[77]

(F) Certain Undesirable Habits as a Factor

Certain undesirable habits on the part of Sudras also played as a factor. Gautama provides that the Sudra servant should use the shoes, umbrellas, garments and mats which are thrown away by the people of higher castes.[78] There are also evidences about the Sudra servants eating the remanants of food of their masters. Similarly, they persisted in eating beef which was considered the most heinous crime by the caste-Hindus. As regard this, historians are of the view, that upper castes also followed the eating of beef during the Vedic period. But during the period of Dharmashastras, the eating of beef was totally condemned. But these groups persisted in the eating of beef and thus they were condemned.[79]

Finally, the religious practices of Untouchables were markedly different from those of upper castes. They had different deities for worship which are considered to be lower deities than the deities of the higher castes. And similarly cultural and ritual elements occupied a minor position in their religious system.

(G) Low Economic Position of the Sudras as a Factor

As has been discussed earlier, those Aryans and non-Aryans who were dispossessed of their properties such as cattles, etc. and impoverished as a result of external and internal conflicts, were reduced to the position of Sudras. As a result of their low economic position they had to serve as a labouring class and some of them had to choose occupations that were considered impure. As they were economically dependent upon higher caste and some of them were following the occupations that were considered impure, various disabilities were imposed upon them. It is clear that their low economic position played a significant role in the practice of Untouchability. It is clear from the following statement also. "If a Sudra grew wealthy, he could

77. Andre Beteille, Castes: Old and New, Bombay, 1969, p. 90.
78. Jirnanyupamacchatravasah kuraani, X58.
79. B.R. Ambedkar, The Untouchables, 1948, Chapter X.

engage not only another Sudra as his servant but another Kshatriya, Brahmin or Vaishya".[80] This statement implies that sound economic condition could change the social status.

And even today, at the village level, a large proportion of Sudras are working as agricultural labourers for landlords and tenants belonging to higher castes.[81] And the economic dependence upon higher castes has also resulted in their exploitation and down-trodden condition.

(H) Psychological Factors

According to *Alder*, a vinnese psychologist, one of the strong motive in human being is the "will to power". According to this theory every individual, tends to control others whom he considers inferior to himself. On the other hand, every individual who considers himself inferior to other individuals, tends to submit himself under the control of those whom he considers his superior.[82]

As has been seen, there were various reasons on the basis of which, the people belonging to higher Varnas might have considered themselves superior to lower castes. On the other hand, there were many factors which motivated the people belonging to lower castes to conclude that they were inferior to people belonging to higher Varnas. Once this feeling of superiority developed in the higher castes they began to control the behaviour of lower castes, as the will to power theory indicates. On the other hand because of their inferiority feelings, the lower castes people submitted themselves to the control and power of the higher castes. And in this way various disabilities were imposed upon the lower caste people.

(i) Support by Society as a Factor

Generally speaking, it is the society where we exist so if we do not have the backing and support of society for anything it would be difficult to pursue such a thing so, it may be noted that society played a pivotal role in segregation of higher and

---

80. R.S. Sharma, Sudras in Ancient India, 1958, p. 102.
81. Andre Beteille, Castes : old and new, 1969, p. 92.
82. It is important to note that Alder was of the view that the superiority complex originates as a result of inferiority feelings.

lower castes and for the miserable condition of lower caste. In the context of down-trodden condition of untouchable, the expression "society" has been used to mean Hindu society. Untouchability was not only practiced by caste Hindus but Untouchables themselves practiced Untouchability against those whom they considered lower in position than themselves. Thus "Society" has been used in a relative term referring to the groups of people who considered themselves superior to Untouchables. Thus, a washerman is included in the term society in relation to the Chandala but in relation to higher caste, they are considered Untouchable.

The society during British period enforced the practice of Untouchability by providing sanctions in the form of excommunication and social boycott which proved to be very effective in enforcing disabilities against lower caste people. The efficacy of these sanctions were increased because of the indifferent attitude of the courts which usually did not interfere in such cases. When a Gawada Saraswat Brahmin attended a Brahma samaj dinner at which Pariaha were present, he was outcasted by the head of the math. The court held that the head of the math was not guilty of criminal defamation by excommunicating him.[83] The Untouchables themselves used to excommunicate those who deviated from the desired behaviour. For instance, Gharagapur Julahas excommunicated the members of their own castes for associating with Jaswara Chamars.[84] Similarly in *Khamani* v. *Emperor*[85] caste Panchayat would have been privileged if it excommunicated Mangali Prashad for associating with Untouchables and shaking hands with them.. But as it was found that caste Panchayat did not consider the matter nor a formal decision was reached by it; it was defamatory for individuals to impute that a bhurji had become a sweeper simply by joining a procession in which sweepers were included.

Another sanction which was provided by society for the enforcement of disabilities against the lower castes was secondary boycott.

83. Sri Sudhratendra Thirtha Swami V. Prabhu, AIR 1923.
84. Desai, V., Emperor 33, *Criminal Law Journal*, p. 472 (Allahabad) 1931.
85. AIR, 1926, Allahabad, p. 306.

It meant depriving the offenders of the services of the village servants and withdrawal of economic relations such as earning money, buying food, borrowing money, having occupation, etc.[86] Not only this, it extended to areas where untouchables possessed enforceable legal rights such as, the right of foot path. And as receiving such services was requisite for retaining good social standing in society, people were much susceptible to such tools of enforcement. The effectiveness of such a tool increased more because of lack of any legal remedies against such secondary boycotts due to British policy of not enforcing the traditional service relations.[87] Regarding the effectiveness of this tool, State committee concluded:

> "We do not know any weapon more effective than social boycott which could have invented for the suppression of the depressed classes. The method of open violence pales away before it for it as most far-reaching deadening effects. It is the most dangerous because it passes as a lawful method consistent with the theory of freedom of contract".[88]

Thus, it enflows from the above discussion that there were numerous miseries and suffering faced by the lower castes people and certain factors were behind their down-trodden and degraded condition. The discriminatory justice was also in place to further oppress the lower castes. Because of these facts we still have a segregated society with have and have nots.

86. For detailed discussion see Hutton, Caste in India : Its Nature, Function And Origin, pp. 205-06.
87. The court refused to enforce traditional service relations as early as 1854. In Phagoona Nayee V. Monya Matha 1854, S.D.A. 465 (Bengal) the court held that there was no right to enforce customary services of the barbars even where the receiving of such services was requisite for retaining good standing in one's caste, similarly, the service castes exclusive right to serve was also held to be unenforceable in Coopa Mooto, V., Bàupen II SUA 77 (Madras) 1844.
88. Report of the Depressed classes and Aboriginal tribes Committee, Bombay Presidency, Bombay (Starte Committee) March 1930, p. 58.

5

Pre-Constitutional Measures for Upliftment of Scheduled Castes and Scheduled Tribes

In the previous chapter the discussion was about the causes for degradation of Scheduled Castes and Scheduled Tribes. As we all know that change is the very nature of society, so due to this phenomenon, certain changes took place in the then existing society too. The then leaders and prevailing circumstances of the world and community too, were the reasons behind this change. It was endeavoured to ameliorate the down-trodden condition of masses, especially of weaker section of society (i.e. Scheduled Castes and Scheduled Tribes). Different measures were adopted to uplift their inhumane condition. Broadly these measures can be dealt under following heads:

(i) Social Attempts towards upliftment of Scheduled Castes and Scheduled Tribes.

(ii) Legislative Attempts towards upliftment of Scheduled Castes and Scheduled Tribes.

(I) SOCIAL ATTEMPTS TOWARDS UPLIFTMENT OF SCHEDULED CASTES AND SCHEDULED TRIBES

Under this head the role and contribution of the leaders or social reformers for the betterment of the condition of Scheduled Castes and Scheduled Tribes is discussed. This sort of upliftment came through social reformers. Apart from the social reformers, the depressed class itself helped themselves to improve and uplift their condition. So, for the academic clarity the discussion can be made in two sub-heads:

A. Attempts made by social reformers.
B. Attempts made by depressed class itself.

(A) Attempts made by Social Reformers

It was more or less the later half of the Eighteenth century which witnessed the rise of social reformers. A well planned campaign started against the down-trodden condition of the weaker section of the society in the beginning of 20th century. The social reformers in different period of history have raised their voices and tried to tackle their problems in their own ways.

Reformers in early period of history believed in changing the attitude of people to bring about certain reliable changes in the behaviour of society towards Untouchables and Adivasis. The best way was for them to change the attitude of society by way of preaching. The religious reformers adopted this means to tackle the problem. Buddhism, Jainism and Sikhism preached against down-trodden condition of Untouchables and Adivasis.

In ancient period Lord Buddha, moved by the plight of Untouchables, preached compassion for all. He tried to eliminate the influence of superstition and blind prejudice from religion. Jainism also used the same approach to eradicate Untouchability by preaching the notion of equality among men and making Ahimsa, necessary for daily conduct of men. Guru Nanak, a Prominent preacher of Sikh religion, also preached against Untouchability.[1] Guru Govind Singh, the tenth Guru of Sikhs, called the low caste people as the son of Guru.

Swami Vivekanand,[2] Ravindra Nath Tagore,[3] Kabir,[4] Sankaracharya,[5] Ramanujacharya,[6] Raman Maharishi[7] also tried to tackle this problem by preaching the notion of equality and fraternity among people.

Reformers, belonging to religion other than Hinduism adopted conversion as a means to eradicate the practice of Untouchability. Christian missionaries were first to adopt this means to make Untouchables free from the effect of such evil by guaranteeing them quality in their religion.[8]

Schwartz, who was one of the leading missionaries in the South India converted 18,000 lower caste people in the early 1805. The missionaries not only converted individual but whole groups.[9] The converts got changed their lifestyles to a great extent. Not only this, but they were allowed to read, English and got opportunity to join administrative and professional jobs.

Guarantee of equality, access to English education and ability to join administrative and professional jobs attracted the Sudras and other low castes people towards Christian religion. The Arya Samaj was formed by Swami Dayanand Saraswati with a view to prevent conversion to Christianity and to retain

1. Castes are folly, names are Folly;
   All creatures have one shelter, that of God
   Under the Guru's instruction, regard all men as equal
   Since, Gods light is contained in the heart of each.
2. Stand against Untouchability and other rigidities connected with the caste.
3. Why do they shun your touch, my friend, and all call you unclean. Whom cleanliness follows at every step, making the earth and air sweet.
4. Selfless service to humanity without any reservation of caste and creed is what matters.
5. Real Dharma is neither the Varna nor the Varnashram.
6. A chandal can be purer than myself.
7. Everyman is divine, his habit may be evil.
8. Kenneth, W. Jones, Communalism in the Punjab; The Arya Samaj Constitution, Vol. 28, 1968, pp. 39-54.
9. Lala Lajpat Rai, The Arya Samaj.

converts to Hinduism with the same rights and facility as was available in Christianity. The Arya Samaj launched the "Shuddhi" Movement in 1891 under the leadership of Lala Munshi Ram aimed at to reconvert the Christian and Mulism into Arya Samaj through shuddhi who were mostly form lower castes.

The Arya samaj guaranteed equality even in Hindu religion. It also gave the lower castes and the depressed classes, the right to wear the sacred thread, the symbol of high caste status. It gathered momentum in Punjab, Kashmir, Uttar Pradesh and Bihar and in many other places where the lower castes and depressed class people came into the fold of Arya Samaj. Lala Lajpat Rai made a big dent in orthodox Hinduism by admitting a number of Untouchables and Sudras into the Arya Samaj. Though he belonged to the upper caste, yet he ate food prepared by Untouchables and Sudras.

Another important means adopted to combat the evil practice of Untouchability was by raising social standard of Untouchables by adopting various welfare measures such as education etc. This means was adopted usually by various social reform agencies. The Brahma Samaj adopted this means to deal with this evil under the leadership of Keshub Chandra Sen. In Bombay, the Prarthana Samaj worked actively for the depressed classes under the leadership of M.G. Ranade, R. Bhandarkar, N.G. Chandravarkar. It started night schools for low caste in Bombay especially for workers.

Similarly, Mahatma Joyti Ba Phule founded Satya Sodhak Samaj[10] in Maharastra, which conducted a movement for radical social and religious reforms.[11] As early as 1851, Mahatma Phule had started a school for the children of depressed classes.[12] The pioineering work of Mahatma Phule was followed by social reform movement led by Shiv Ram Jamba Vamble. He started a Magazine to propagate his views and made petitions to British Government to improve their lot.[13] Similarly, V.R. Sindh started the Depressed classed mission

10. The Samaj worked for the welfare of all including the depressed classes.
11. G.S. Ghurye, Caste and Race in India, pp. 165-66, 171-72.
12. A.C. Paranjpe, Caste, Prejudice and the Individual, 1970, p. 127.
13. *Ibid.*, p. 31.

society in 1906, which undertook educational activities as their main programme for improving the lot of Untouchables.[14] Under the name of Veda Samaj, a society was started in Madras which was later changed to Brahma samaj of South India. R. Venkataraman of the Madras Brahma samaj focussed his attention on the need for welfare measures for the depressed classes in the South India. K. Ranga Rao started a free school for the depressed classes at Mangalore which was taken over by the Depressed classes mission of Madras established in 1909.[15] The servants of India society founded by Gopal Krishna Gokhle in 1905 declared elevation of the Depressed classes as one of its aims. Along with above mentioned social reform agencies, individual reformers have also adopted the welfare measures as a means to free the Untouchables from the evil practice of Untouchability. Sahu Chhatrapati of Kolhapur passed a Mahar Vatan Abolition Act in his State in 1918.[16] The Mahars thereby became outright owners of their land and were freed from doing a hundred odd jobs for the village in return for a small piece of land they were allowed to cultivate. He recruited Untouchables as clerks in the State service and admitted a few educated Untouchables at Bar. In 1919 he legally prohibited the segregation of Untouchable children in schools.[17]

Social reformers like Dr. B.R. Ambedkar, Shri. Narayan Guru, V.D. Savarkar and Mahatma Gandhi took this problem very seriously and tried to deal with it by adopting various measures.

Dr. B.R. Ambedkar, a great leader of Mahar community in Maharashtra, stayed in America for three years and took his doctorate in Economics from Columbia University, returned to India in 1917. Soon after returning to India, He choose removal of Untouchability and improving the lot of Untouchables as his main goals. He took many steps to accomplish his goal of freeing the Untouchables from the evil practice of Untouchability.

---

14. C.H. Heimsath, Indian Nationalism and Hindu Reform (1964), p. 296.
15. *Ibid.*, p. 253.
16. A.C. Paranjpe, Caste, Prejudice and the individual, 1970, p. 31.
17. *loc. cit.*

He felt that by changing the dirty habits of Untouchables he may change the attitude of the higher caste people, and will grow a self respect in them also. He urged the Untouchables to stop the dragging of dead cattles out of the village. He wanted them to give up eating beef, alcoholic drinks and begging. He asked them to become literates and send their children to schools. He wanted them to dress well and have self-respect for themselves.[18] In 1927, he organised a Satyagrah to establish the right of Untouchables to draw water from a public reservoir.[19] In 1929 and also in 1930 he organised a Satyagrah for entering the Parvati Temple at Poona and Kala Ram Temple in Nasik. But at all these places, there was a violent opposition from the orthodox Hindus. As a result, he could not succeed.

Ambedkar found that his effort to improve the lots of Untouchables and to make them free from the practice of Untouchability, was not bringing in satisfactory result, so he began to think of conversion. As early as 1934, he had announced that he would relinquish Hindusim and embrace some other faith. As a result of growing resentment because of his failure to improve the lots of Untouchables he thought they could not improve unless they gave up Hinduism and embrace some other religion. Thus on 14th October 1956 a few days before his death, he along with his thousands of followers accepted Buddhism at an impressive ceremony in open at Nagpur.[20] But even conversion could not bring any significant change in the position of Untouchables.

Another significant reformer who made the removal of Untouchability as his main aim was Sri Narayana Guru whose field of activity was restriced to Kerala. Unlike Dr. Ambedkar Sri Narayana Guru never encouraged Untouchables to enter into Hindu Temple forcibly. He knew the country and its Government which was not yet prepared for such a radical change in traditional attitude towards exterior castes. The Guru

18. B. Kuppuswamy, Social change in India, 1972, p. 140.
19. A.C. Paranjpe, Caste prejudice and the individual, 1970, p. 32.
20. Donald Eugene Smith, India: As a Secular State, 1963, p. 167. "The ceremony was conducted by Mahathevar Chandramani, the oldest Buddhist Monk in India. The convers took the three-fold Buddhist Vow : "I take refuge in the Buddha, I take refuge in the Dhamma (Law), and I take refuge in the Sangha (Buddhist order).

had therefore started to build and consecrate[21] temples of sanskritic deities with sanskritic rituals for the use of lravas.[22]

In addition to building temples for the lravas, Narayana Guru also established S.N.D.P. Yogam in 1902 with his gospel, "One Caste, One Religion, One God."[23] He started a number of schools and colleges throughout the Kerala. He simplified rituals regarding worship, marriage and funerals. He also established an order of Sanyasis to help the community regarding its religious and spiritual matters. He travelled widely and helped the lower caste people to clean up their houses and streets and to develop clean habits.[24]

Another successful reformer was Shri V.D. Savarkar, who took various measures for removal of Untouchability during 1924 to 1937 in Ratnagiri. Like Narayana Guru who consecrated many temples in Kerala for lravas, V.D. Saverkar also built a Patitpawan temple; which was open for all Hindus including, Untouchables.[25]

Gandhiji, the most humanitarian reformer of 20th century, took Untouchability seriously and adopted various measures, some traditional and some non-traditional, to ostracise this evil from Indian Society. He realised that nomenclature of Untouchables who were referred to as "Adi dravidas", "Antyajas", "Ati-Sudras", "Avarnas", "Bhangis", "Pariahs", "Panchamas", "Chamars", etc. had wrong effect upon the mind of Untouchables themselves. Not only this, such names stimulated the feelings of disgust amongst Hindus towards them. Thus, he gave currency to the word "Harijan" for them, which means people dear to Hari (God), coined by Narasimha Mehta, a Saint poet of Gujarat.[26]

21. Aiyappan, Social Revolution in a Kerala Village, 1965, p. 135.
22. lravas were the Untouchable community of Kerala. Ezhavas and lravas are used interchangeably as both these expressions are used for the Untouchable community of Kerala. Nairs are higher caste community in Kerala.
23. B. Kuppuswamy, *op. cit.*, p. 139.
24. *Ibid.*, p. 139.
25. *Ibid.*
26. Ratna G. Revankar, The Indian Constitution : A Study in the Backward Classes, 1971, p. 115.

With a view to open the forbidden road for Untouchables, leading to a temple, a Satyagrah was launched by Kerala Congress under the leadership of Mahatma Gandhi, in Vyokam, a village in the State of Travancore. Gandhiji explaining the significance of the Satyagrah said:

> "The Vyokam satyagrahis are fighting a battle of no less significance than that of Swaraj. They are fighting against an age old wrong practice. It is supported by orthodoxy, superstition, custom and authority. This is only one among the many battles that must be fought in the holy war against irreligion masquarding as religion, ignorance appearing in the guise of learning. If their battle is to be bloodless, they must be patient under the severest trials."[27]

The Government and people of Travancore State were strongly against this Satyagrah. The Government of Travancore put up barricades and prohibited Untouchables from entering the streets near the temple.[28] Although, later on the Government of Travancore, in response to Gandhiji's[29] appeal removed the barricades. However, due to resentment of Hindus, the Satyagrah was suspended. Although the Vyokam Satyagrah did not succeed, it made the problem of Untouchability, a problem of National importance which is clear from the following statement of Aiyappam:

> "The Vyokam satyagrah, though it has failed to produce any effect on the Travancore Government or on the upper caste in Kerala, made Untouchability a problem of national importance."[30]

On the failure of Vyokam Satyagrah Gandhiji realised the complexity of the problem. He knew that in order to eradicate

27. M.K. Gandhi, Removal of Untouchability, 1954, p. 115.
28. B. Kuppuswamy, *op. cit.*, p. 142.
29. Gandhiji wrote in *Young India* "...........opening of roads is not the final but the first step in the ladder of reform, temples, public wells, and public schools must be open to Untouchables equally with caste Hindus—quoted in B. Kuppuswamy, p. 142.
30. Quoted in B. Kuppuswamy, *op. cit.* p. 142.

the practice of Untouchability, the mind of the masses must be changed. Thus, he started a weekly "Harijan".[31] Weeks after weeks, it published news of temple, wells and schools being thrown open to Untouchability in various parts of country. Through this weekly, Gandhiji aroused conscience of the whole nation against the practice of Untouchability and tried to educate Hindu opinion on the question of Untouchables. He was successful in bringing about great changes in the very psychology and attitude of the vast masses of caste Hindus towards their brethren, then so-called Untouchables. But, unfortunately, this weekly could not reach to the illiterate masses in the villages who needed it most.

In order to intensify his efforts for the improvement of Untouchables, he started the All India Anti-Untouchability league which was later renamed, as Harijan Sewak Sangh on 30th September, 1932. A large public meeting of Hindu leaders from all over India was held at Bombay under the Presidentship of Pandit Madan Mohan Malviya. It was resolved there to set-up an all India organisations, with its headquarter at Delhi, and branches in different provincial centres, for the purpose of carrying on propaganda against the observance of Untouchability with Shri G.D. Birla as President and Shri A.V. Thakkar as General Secretary. In this way the All India Harijan Sevak Sangh was formed with the object of "eradication by truthful and non-violent means of Untouchability in Hindu society with all its incidental events and disabilities suffered by the so-called Untouchables and to secure for them absolute equality of status with the rest of Hindus".[32]

Sangh workers lanuched a compaign throughout the country for throwing open the wells, hotels, temples, schools and other public places to Harijans. Dr. Ambedkar and some of his colleagues were also the members of Harijan Sewak Sangh but later, they dissociated themselves from the Sangh because of differences of opinion.

A year after the formation of All India Harijan Sewak Sangh, Gandhiji with his colleagues and workers undertook a

31. Mahant Mahabir Das, A National Penitence : Removal of Untouchability, 1976, p. 10.
32. Swami Sundaranand, Hinduism and Untouchability, Chapter III, p. 110.

country-wide and historic journey called "Harijan Yatra" with a view to arousing the conscience of the people against Untouchability.[33] The Harijan yatra commenced on 7th of November,1933 and came to an end in Banaras at the end of July 1934. This tour was a great success.

In addition to the above measures, Gandhiji organised various meetings and gave speeches all over India keeping the removal of Untouchability in mind. He tried to educate the people also by writing in "Young India". He worked as a model for caste Hindu. He believed that people do what they see others doing and not that what they are taught to do and thus, he himself set an example. He cleaned his own latrine and called upon all Hindus to follow him so that stigma could be removed from the Harijans who had to perform the degrading task. He adopted Harijan girl as his daughter and lived in Harijan quarter during his tours. In Delhi, the Bhangi colony used to be his head quarter whenever he visited the capital.[34] The above discussion shows that social reformers adopted various measures to eradicate this evil.

(B) Attempts made by Depressed Classes itself

The Untouchables were aware of the fact that the disabilities imposed upon them were the direct result of their low social and ritual status. The Untouchable groups in various parts of India had made attempts to raise their own social and ritual status in order to become free from various disabilities imposed upon them on the ground of Untouchability. They attempted to do so by the process of sanskritization (i.e. change in ritual procedures and up to some extent in culture), which had been first observed and described by Srinivas as:

> "A process by which a low Hindu caste or tribal or other group changes its customs, rituals ideology and way of life in the direction of a high and frequently twice born caste. Generally such changes are followed by a claim to a higher

33. Swami Sundaranand, *op. cit.*, p. 121.
34. *loc. cit.*

position in the caste hierarchy than that traditionally conceded to the claimant caste by local community."[35]

The Untouchables tried to raise social status by sanskritizing their eating habits, their occupations and their names whereas they tried to raise their ritual status by emulating the religious practices of higher castes and also by changing their marriage practices. They gave up eating of beef and dead animals. At least two generations ago Jaiswara Chamars in the vicinity of Madhopur began to out law the eating of beef, in order to gain the respect of the higher castes.[36]

Priviously Chamars were considered degraded because of their eating carrion beef. Often they had been accused of poisoning cattle in order to obtain the meat, but later they maintain that beef eating is banned and those who continue to do so will be outcasted immediately. The bhangis of Jodhpur declared that they would not remove the nightsoils of dhobis and dholis.[37] Similarly, the Chamars of Madhopur refused to carry manure to the Thakur's fields inspite of the strong resistance on the part of Thakurs. The Chamar women refused any longer to make dung cakes for the Thakur's household.[38] Thus, by giving up the occupations what they considered degrading for themselves, have tried to raise their social status.

The depressed classes also started sanskritizing their names. The bhangis of Jodhpur no longer keep Muslim names but have replaced them by names of Hindu Gods, such as Ramchandra, Ganesh Ram, etc. They also made conscious effort to suppress their traditional Gotra for further sanskritization, and emulated the specific Gotra forms of higher castes such as Verma, Pandit, Solanki, etc.[39]

Some Sudras or Untouchables have made more extreme efforts to elevate their social status and thus became free from various disabilities imposed upon them. The Noniyas of

35. M.N. Srinivas, Religion and society among the Coorgs of South India, 1965, p. 30.
36. Bernard Cohn, The changing status of Depressed Castes, 1955, pp. 72-73.
37. Shyamlal, Caste and Political Mobilization : The Bhangis, 1981, p. 33.
38. Bernard Cohn, *op. cit*, p. 73.
39. Shyamlal, *Ibid.*, p. 34.

Madhopur district went so for as to put the sacred thread and called themselves by the title of "Chauhan Rajputs". Although, their action was met with violence by the lords of the village, but later on the resistance downed and they began to wear the sacred thread. Similarly, Chamars in Jaunpur and Azamgarh districts have started wearing sacred threads, calling themselves "Harijan Thakurs".[40] The bhangis of Jodhpur have also attempted to raise their social religious status by wearing sacred threads.[41]

Various attempts by Untouchables to raise their social status were not individual in character or effect nor were they legislated by large formal gatherings. Rather, a leader or a group of leaders in the caste in one village may feel the need for changing a traditional behaviour, and the change is talked over in the village. Then active propagandising followed from the initiating village or villages. Ultimately, it was decided that those who did not confirm to the new pattern of behaviour will be out-casted.

Consistent with efforts to raise their social status, the Untouchables had made conscious efforts to raise their ritual status by suppressing their distinctive traditional religion, by sanskritizing their rituals still further and by emulating the specific religious forms of higher castes. Thus the sacrifice of a pig which formerly began in the Chamar's wedding ceremony in Madhopur, had now been given up and was replaced by cutting of nutmeg.[42] The practice of giving dowry had been introduced, although the boy's father was still has to give a token payment to the girl's father. Chamar wedding had been lengthened from one day to three days, so as to resemble Brahmins weddings. A Brahmin priest was called to conduct every ceremony of the wedding except the final rite.[43] A new emphasis on pilgrimages had helped the Untouchables to sanskritize their rituals even more fully.[44]

40. Bernard Cohn, *op. cit.*, p. 73.
41. Shyamlal, *op. cit.*, p. 34.
42. Beranard Cohn, *op. cit.*, p. 75.
43. *Ibid.*
44. *Ibid.*, p. 75.

Although, the illustrations in the above discussion showing the attempt of the depressed classes to become free from various disabilities by sanskritizing their social and ritual status has been taken only from some main sources the depressed classes in various parts of India are attempting to free themselves from these disabilities in the same manner. The basis of such attempt is that if the Untouchable groups themselves resemble to higher castes, in social and ritual standards, the practice of Untouchability will slowly and steadily cease towards them. No doubt, such a reasoning is realistic and some changes in the behaviour of higher castes towards lower caste have been observed as is clear from the study made in Madhopur[45] and Jodhpur.[46] But such changes in behaviour of higher castes towards lower castes occur only when they succeed in sankritizing their style of life. However, in past such attempts were strongly resisted by upper castes. In such a circumstances sanskritizing their lifestyle was not an easy matter for Untouchable groups. In some cases the Untouchable groups were prevented from sanskritizing their style of life by variety of sanctions.[47] One and most effective of the sanctions was economic boycott. As most of the Untouchables were economically dependent upon upper caste, they can not dare to offend them (upper castes) by pressing too for their legal claims to equality. Those who dare to behave as the equal of their master on ceremonies or social occasions might find themselves deprived of their sources of livelihood.

Apart from economic sanction, there were a threat of physical violence also.[48] Such threat of physical violence was there to protect them. And it had been common for

---

45. *Ibid.*, pp. 53-76.
46. Shyamlal, *op. cit.*
47. Andre Beteille, Caste : Old and New, 1969, pp. 120-22.
48. When the lower castes came for remedy before the court of law, the courts refused such victims any remedy. What to say of Unotouchables, even a backward class community were prevented from raising their social or ritual status. In Sheo Shankar *v.* Emperor, AIR 1940 Oudh, p. 348, when Brahmins tore the sacred thread from the neck of an ahir who lad lately taken wearing it, the court held that since he was a Sudra, the wearing of a thread was not "part of his religion *vis-à-vis* to a higher rank. Therefore, no offence was committed as the injury was not his religious susceptibilities.

Untouchables to be beaten by caste-Hindus when they attempted to claim equal social or religious status.

When Untouchable groups failed to raise their social and ritual status because of various sanctions, a deep resentment was their amongst them against the upper castes.[49] As a result, they leaned towards other religions such as Buddhism, Islam, Sikkism, Christianity, where the equality was guaranteed. And they became converts. In Maharashtra over 2,000,000 Harijans became converts to Buddhism. Many Harijans become convert to Islam. But even the conversion to other religion did not give them equality of status in the eyes of higher castes, although such conversions gave the feeling of self-respect[50] to the converts who refused to accept the degraded position assigned to them in the Hindu society.

(II) LEGISLATIVE DEVELOPMENT TOWARDS UPLIFTMENT OF SCHEDULED CASTES AND SCHEDULED TRIBES

During the British period laws with regard to abolition of Untouchability by private persons did not attracted Government sanction as it is today. During that period discriminatory practices with regard to religion were recognised and enforced. Courts-granted injuctions to restrain member of a particular castes from entering into temples. For a member of a particular caste to knowingly pollute a temple by his presence and touch was a criminal offence.[51]

In 1850 the Government of India enacted Caste Disabilities Removal Act, which declared any law or usage which inflicted on any person forfeiture of right of property or in any way affected his right of inheritance due to caste to cease to be enforceable by law.[52]

Queen Victoria's proclamation in the year following India's mutiny in 1857, made it abundantly clear that no particular religion, faith or observance would be treated differently on

49. Andre Beteille, *op. cit.*, pp. 125-26.
50. *Ibid*, p. 126.
51. Atman, V., King Emperor, AIR 1924 (Nagpur) (1), p. 121.
52. Smith, Donald Eugene, India As a Secular State, p. 70.

account of the caste. The proclamation read "Firmly relying ourselves on the truth of Christianity and acknowledging with gratitude the solace of religion we disclaim alike the right and desire to impose our conviction or any of our subjects we declare it to be our royal will and pleasure that none be in any way favoured none molested or disqualified by reason of their religion, faith or observance but all shall alike enjoy the equal and impartial protection of law."[53] Despite the official proclaimation the treatment with Harijans was not uniform throughout India. Until 1911 the State of Jaipur maintained separate Courts of law for Untouchables was required to wear crown's feathers on their turbans. Many of the hereditry Indian princes enforced Untouchability in their territories and in some States the Untouchables were not permitted to enter the same school with upper caste children.[54]

> "In the early of the 20th century the debates on communal safeguard centred primarily around the method of selecting Indian representative to the legislative bodies which were gradually being developed."[55]

Dr. Ambedkar brought the oppressed and inhumane condition of Untouchable in focus for the first time at the Round Table Conference. At the conference, he spoke about the loathsome condition of the Untouchable in India and said "Hundred fifty years of British rule did not alter even a little the position of Untouchables. They were prevented from drawing water from the wells, from entering into temples, etc. by the caste Hindus. The Government itself prevented their recruitment in the Police and Military service on the ground that they were Untouchables." He demanded the aboilition of Untouchability and establishment of equal citizenship. Ambedkar tried to solve the problem of Untouchablility through different angle by trying to make Untouchables politically strong. Thus he demanded separate electorates for Untouchables at the Second Round Table Conference, held at

53. *Ibid.*, p. 71.
54. Smith, Donald Eugene, *op. cit.*, p. 299.
55. *Ibid.*, p. 71.

London in 1931. But it was seriously opposed by Mahatma Gandhi who claimed to represent all Hindus including the Untouchables. Speaking at the minorities committee Gandhi jee declared, "We do not want the Untouchables to be classified as a separate class. Sikhs may remain such in perpetuity, so may Muslims and Christians. Will the Untouchables remain Untouchables in perpetuity? I would rather feel that Hinduism died than that Untouchability lived."[56] As a result of this disagreement between Dr. Ambedkar and Gandhijee, no consensus was reached in the conference. Subsequently on 14th August 1932, the then Birtish Prime Minister, Ramsay Mc Donald announced communal award which granted separate electorates for the Untouchables.[57] Gandhijee thought that this would distrupt the Hindu community into fractions; viz touchables and untouchables.[58] As a protest against separate electorates, Gandhijee started a hunger strike while in Yervada Jail at Poona.[59] This serious step by Gandhijee created a tense atmosphere in the entire nation.[60] Dr. Ambedkar was called for help to control the situation. Dr. Ambedkar was asked to forsake[61] the separate electorate for the Untouchables which was granted by the Communal Award at his insistence. Ultimately Dr. Ambedkar compromised and accepted joint electorates where 148 seats were reserved for Untouchables as against 71 given by Award. The agreement signed by Dr. Ambedkar and his colleagues and the Hindu leaders, is known

56. B. Kuppuswamy, *op. cit.*, p. 145.
57. Tara Chand, History of Freedom Movement in India, Vol. IV, 1972, p. 181.
58. Swami Sundaranand, Hinduism and Untouchability, p. 11.
59. Tara Chand, *op. cit.*, p. 183.
60. Tagore at Shanti Niketan felt as if "a Shadow is darkening today over India like a shadow Caste on by an eclipsed sun. He further exclaimed, the people of a whole country is suffering from a poignant pain of anxiety, the universality of which carries in it a great dignity of consolation. Mahatmaji was through his life of dedication on has made India his own has commenced his vow of extreme self-sacrifice." quoted in Tara Chand, *op. cit.*, p. 186.
61. A.V. Thakkar, who worked with Dr. Ambedkar in Starte Committee also asked him to forsake the award. See Dhananjay Keer. Dr. Ambedkar's life and Mission, p. 206.

as Poona Pact.[62] As a result of this Pact, Ambedkar failed to make the Untouchables politically as strong as he desired to make them.

As has been seen above that initially the law gave sanction to the customs which prohibited entry of Harijans in Temples. Against this the first major movement started in the princely State of Travancore, when a member of the Assembly made a representation to the Maharaja's Government urging that steps to be taken to bring about such reforms.[63] But the Government refused to interfere on the ground that such action would be a violation of religious neutrality. Following this attempt, several other unsuccessful attempts were made in the following decade in Travancore, Bombay and Madras Legislature; and also in the Legislative Assembly of Delhi.

The Madras Legislative Council, on Nov. 1, 1932, unanimously resolved that the Government should recognise the public sentiment and bring forward a legislation to enable trustees to throw open temples to all Hindus.[64] On December 1, 1932, Subbayar, a former Chief Minister of Madras, moved a bill outlining the procedure to enable the trustees to ascertain the will of the people regarding temple entry.[65] In the same period, in Legislative Assembly of Delhi, Ranga lyer moved a bill on the lines of the Nov. 1932 resolution of the Madras Legislative Council.[66] For moving such bills either in Central or in Provincial Legislature, the assent of Governer-General was necessary. But the Governer-General refused to give assent to the bills on the ground that they affected many devotees who lived outside Madras State but came to these temples.[67] Thus the bill moved in Madras Legislative Council failed.

But the Governer-General gave assent to the Bill introduced by Ranga lyer in the Legislative Assembly of Delhi in 1933.[68] This Bill did not provide for positive interference with

62. Dhananjay Keer, *op. cit.*, p. 214.
63. Donald, E. Smith, *op. cit.*, p. 239.
64. B. Kuppuswamy, *op. cit.*, p. 148.
65. *Ibid.*
66. *loc. cit.*
67. *loc. cit.*
68. *loc. cit.*

social and religious institutions, but nearly tried to remove the official recognition of Untouchability by courts and executives but the bill was bitterly opposed by the orthobox Hindus, and the bill was withdrawn.[69]

A major breakthrough, as far as temple entry was concerned, came with the 1936, proclamation[70] of the Maharaja of Travancore on November 11, which reads as follows:

> "Profoundly convinced of the truth and validity of our religion, believing that it is based on divine guidance and all comprehending toleration, knowing that in its practice it has throughout the centuries adopted itself to the needs of changing times solicitious that none of the our Hindu subjects should, by reason of birth or caste, or community, be denied the consolation and solace of Hindu faith, we have decided and hereby declare, ordain and command that, subject to such rules and conditions as may be laid down or imposed by us for preserving their proper atmosphere and maintaining their ritual and observances, there should henceforth be no restriction placed on any Hindu by birth or religion on entering or worshiping at temple controlled by us and our Government."[71]

The background of Maharaja's proclamation was a situation in which members of the Untouchable class were becoming increasingly re-strive and had come to the verge of abandoning Hinduism in favour of a religion in which they would be treated as equals.

Following temple entry proclamation of Travancore several legislative attempts to attain the same objective were made in the Province of Madras[72] and other provinces.

In 1938, the Madras Legislature passed the Malabar Temple Entry Act which threw open the temple in Malabar. In July 1939, at the insistence of the workers of the Harijan Sewak Sangh and Congress leaders, the temple at Madurai was opened to the Harijans. This event was followed by opening of the temples in

69. Donald Eugene Smith, *op. cit.*, p. 239.
70. A. Aiyyapan, *op. cit.*, p. 137.
71. L. Elayaperumal Committee Report, pp. 3-4.
72. Donald, E. Smith, *op. cit.*, p. 241.

other districts of Madras. In the same year, a Temple Entry Authorisation and Indemnity Act, 1939 was passed by the Madras Legislature authorising the trustees to throw the temples open to the excluded classes. If, in their opinion, "worshippers of such temples are generally not opposed." The Bombay Legislature also passed Madras Temple Entry Indemnity Ordinance (I of 1939) for this purpose which was similar to Madras Act and also contained penal provision, making it an offence to obstruct Harijans from worshipping in an open temple. Similar Bills were also in process in the central provinces, Berar and in the United provinces.

Other social disabilities came for the first time before the British rulers when, the Government of Bombay had to consider the case of Mahar boy who was refused admission to Government school at Dharwar. In 1858, it was announced that "all schools maintained at the sole, cost of Government shall be open to all classes and of its subjects without distinction.[73] But the above measure taken by the Government was not effective at all as was clear from the press note of 1915 in which it was pointed out that the depressed class boys in village schools were often not allowed to enter into the school room but were accommodated outside the room on the varandah.[74]

In 1917, the Indian National Congress decided to include "Social reform" regarding depressed classes as a programme of its action and adopted the following resolution:

> "The congress urges upon the people of India the necessity, justice and righteousness of removing all disabilities imposed by custom upon the depressed classes, the disabilities being of a most variations and oppressive character, subjecting those classes to a considerable hardship and inconveniences.[75]

In 1920, Gandhiji wrote "Untouchability cannot be given secondary place in the programme. Without the removal of Untouchability Swaraj is a meaningless term."[76] Thus from 1920

73. Elayaperumal Committee Report, p. 3.
74. *Ibid.*, p. 3.
75. Quoted in S. Natrajan, A century of social reform in India, p. 144.
76. Quoted in B. Kuppuswamy, *op. cit.*, p. 142.

onwards, the Indian National Congress under the leadership of Mahatma Gandhi became committed to the removal of these social disabilities of depressed classes. In its session in Ahmedabad in December, 1921, the Congress resolved to start a voluntary organisation throughout the country and signed a pledge to remove the evil of Untouchabilty.[77]

With the passage of time, such resolutions and pledges confirming the rights of Untouchables to equal use of Government facilities, schools, wells and tanks, etc. were multiplied. In 1923, the Bombay Legislative Council passed a resolution that Untouchables be allowed to use all public watering places, wells, school and dispensaries, etc. It also declared that no grant would be paid to any aided educational institutions which refused admission to the children belonging to the depressed classes.[78]

In 1925, a Bill was introduced by Madras Legislative Council throwing open all public roads, streets or pathways, giving access to any public office, well, tank or place of public resort, to all classes of people irrespective of caste and creed.[79]

In 1938, the Madras Legislature passed the first comprehensive Penal Act[80] to remove the social disabilities. The Act made it an offence to discriminate against Untouchables not only with regard to public supported facilities but also to any other "secular institutions" to which general public is admitted. The violation of the provisions of the Act was made a cognizable offence, with a small fine for the first offence, and a larger fines and upto six month imprisonment for subsequent offences.[81] The Act also barred judicial enforcement of any customary right or disabilities based on membership in such a group.[82]

---

77. *Ibid.*, p. 142, The pledge read, "As a Hindu, We believe in the justice and necessity of removing the evil of Untouchability and shall on all possible occasions seeks personal contact with the endeavour to render service to the submerged classes."
78. Elayperumal Committee Report, p. 3.
79. Elayperumal Committee Report pp. 3-4.
80. Madras Removal of Social Disabilities Act, 1938 (XXI of 1938).
81. *Ibid.*, Section-6.
82. *Ibid.*, Section-2.

(A) Under the Provisions of Government of India Act, 1935

Under Sec. 298 (1) of the Government of India Act, 1935, it was provided that :

"No subject of his Majesty domiciled in India shall on grounds of religion, place of birth or descent, colour or any of them be ineligible for office under the crown in India or prohibited on any of such grounds from acquiring, holding and disposing of property or carrying on any business, occupation, trade or profession in British India.

(1) Nothing in this section shall affect the operation of any law which[83] :

(a) Prohibits either absolutely or subject to exceptions, disposition of agricultural land situated in any particular area and owned by a person belonging to some class recognised by the law as being a class of persons engaged in or connected with agricultural tribe in favour of or for the benefit of any person not belonging to that class.

(b) Recognises the existence of some rights, privileges or disability attaching to the members of a community by virtue of some personal law or custom having the force of law.

(2) Nothing in this section be construed as derogating from the special responsibility of Governor-General or of a Governer for the safeguarding of legitimate interest of minorities."

Another section 275 of the Government of India Act, 1935 which corresponds the Article 16 of the Constitution of India was as follows:

"A person shall not be disqualified by sex for being appointed to any civil service or civil post under the crown

83. Sec. 298 (2).

in India other than such a service or post or may be specified by any general or special order made.

(a) By the Governor General in the case of services and posts in connection with affairs of the federation;
(b) By the Governer of a Province in the case of services and posts in connection with the affairs of the province; and
(c) By the Secretary of the States in connection with appointment made by him.

Provided that any such agreement with respect to join services and posts as is mentioned in chapter II of this part this Act may provide for the powers conferred by this section on the Governor General and the Governer of a province being exercised with respect to services or posts to which the agreement applies by the Governor or a special Governor."

At a later stage the problems of Scheduled Castes and Scheduled Tribes were deleberated by Constituent Assembly and elaborate provisions have been made in favour of Scheduled Castes and Scheduled Tribes:

(B) Constitutent Assembly Debates

It is the most obvious fact that our Constitution is the sacred and refined outcome of the Constituent Assembly Debates. The Constituent Assembly had elaborately deliberated on incorporating certain specific provisions regarding upliftment of Scheduled Castes and Scheduled Tribes. The Constituent Assembly was very much concerned about the protection of minorities and weaker section of population, specially Scheduled Castes and Scheduled Tribes. India had a composite population, having a number of groups based on religion, language, caste or backwardness such as the Scheduled Castes and Scheduled Tribes, AngloIndian, Muslims, Sikhs, Parsis, Indian Christians etc.

The Principal minority group which were involved in the Constitutional debate on safeguard were the Muslims, Scheduled Castes and Scheduled Tribes, Sikhs, Indian Christians and the Parsis etc.

According to 1941 census the percentage of communal minority was as under.[84]

Muslims	24.5%
Scheduled Castes	12.5%
Sikhs	1.5%
Indian Christian	.81%
Anglo Indian	.04%
Parsees	.04%

There had been a long standing controversy as to whether Scheduled Castes would be considered as a separate minority or as a depressed segment of the total Hindu Community. Though this disagreement did not alter the fact. Finally the Scheduled Castes were treated as a distinct entity and certain safeguards specifically applicable to them were ultimately adopted.

The problem of the demand for safeguards for communal minorities were finally resolved by the Constituent Assembly until it had virtually completed the drafting of the entire Constitution in November 1949. Under the terms of the Cabinet Mission statement, the Advisory Committee was to be the principle instrument for securing just consideration of minorities problem. This Advisory Committee chaired by Sardar Vallabh Bhai Patel, was a Mini Assembly with adequate representation of all communities and sections of the people.

This committee deliberated various matters in two sub committee namely:

(i) The Fundamental Rights sub-committee
(ii) The Minorities Sub-committee

The Minorities sub-committee consisted, as on May 1949 of Shri H.C. Mukherjee (Chairman) and 25 members, including Maulana Abul Kalam Azad, C. Rajgopalachari, B.R. Ambedkar, K.M. Mushi, Jogendra Singh, S.P. Mukherjee and Homi Mody. In June 1947 three more members lsmail Chundrigar, Mohammed Sadaulla, Chaudhary Khali Guzzaman were included. This Minorities Sub-Committee considered the rights sub-committee

84. Spann, R.P. Constitutionalism In Asia, p. 56.

recommendations; and suggested certain changes in its report to the parent advisory committee.

The minorities rights and protections were put under two heads:

(i) Fundamental right to equal religious freedom, and denominational rights for all religious groups, and right of the individual members of such religious groups, cultural rights of the minority committee.
(ii) Representation in the legislatures and executive services.

However, when the report came before the Assembly it contained following recommendations:

(i) Separate electorate and weightage should be rejected. The Assembly should adopt joint electorate with seats reserved for minorities on a minority basis.
(ii) The demand that seats be reserved for the minorities in cabinet should be rejected.
(iii) The demand for reservation of posts for minorities in public services on a population basis should be accepted.
(iv) Special officers should be appointed to safeguard the interest of the minorities and report on infringements of their rights.

The Constituent Assembly deliberated over above recommendations and finally made provisions in Constitution according to the recommendations. These provisions are scattered in our Constitution and are very much helpful for the upliftment and amelioration of the status of Scheduled Castes and Scheduled Tribes.

6

Safeguards Under Constitution of India

> "Legislation can not by itself normally solve deep-rooted social problems. One has to approach them in other ways too, but legislation is necessary and essential so that it may give that punch and have that educative factor as well as legal sanctions behind it which help public opinion to be given a certain shape".
>
> —*Pt. Jawahar Lal Nehru*

The framers of the Indian Constitution were conscious about the prevailing miserable and appealing living condition of the Scheduled Castes and the Scheduled Tribes who have remained far behind and segregated from national and social life and have continued to be socially oppressed and economically exploited for centuries due to various types of disabilities. In free India any discrimination and exploitation by any section of society against other sections could not be justified either morally or legally. The framers realised that the colonialism of the higher castes be ended through the Constitution of India.

The framers of the Indian Constitution took care to safeguard the interests of the Scheduled Castes and Scheduled Tribes to give them a sense of security, to protect them against any discrimination and to help them to get integrated in the mainstream of national life. With this in view, a number of provisions have been incroporated in the Indian Constitution for safeguarding specifically the social, economic, educational and political interests of the Scheduled Castes and the Scheduled Tribes. The policy of the Constitution is to do away with caste and to strive to create a casteless society. There is, thus, no safeguard to any one specifically based on caste except to the Scheduled Castes and the Scheduled Tribes to some extent.

A wide range of safeguards for the Scheduled Caste and the Scheduled Tribes are covered by the provisions relating to the fundamental rights. Article 14, 15, 16, 17, 23, 24 and 25(2)(b) seek to protect them from hostile and discriminatory State action. Besides the Fundamental rights, Directive principles of state policy obligate the State to ensure the welfare of certain sections of the people. Article 46 requires the State to take special care in promoting education and economic interests of the weaker section of the people and in particular of the Scheduled Castes and the Scheduled Tribes.

There are certain specific provisions relating to upliftment of the Scheduled Castes and the Scheduled Tribes viz. Articles 330, 332, 334, 338, 341 and 342, etc. These provisions are there to help them to get integrated in the main stream of national life. The provisions relating to Scheduled Castes and Scheduled Tribes can be divided under the head of following safeguards :

(i) Social Safeguards.
(ii) Educational and Economic Safeguards.
(iii) Service Safeguards.
(iv) Political Safeguards.
(v) Administrative Safeguards.

(I) SOCIAL SAFEGUARDS

The Indian society since time immemorial has been such a society, where people of various caste, creed, race and language resides and there are vast disparities found in the Hindu religion. Our Hindu society itself recognises this type of social system that in a very same religion some are known as so-called higher caste and other are lower caste. The higher caste people had always humiliated the lower castes and these lower castes were subjected to numerous atrocities. These atrocities had resulted into the conversion of the Scheduled Castes and the Scheduled Tribes in other religion. This conversion was so severe that the social reformers of Hindu society thought that it could end up in the disappearence of multiple Hindu society.

To uplift the people of so called lower origin, our Constitution framers have safeguarded the interest of the Scheduled Castes and the Scheduled Tribes. They have endeavoured, at every level, to eradicate the prevailing malpractices of Hindu society. Keeping all these views in mind the framers of our Constitution have incorporated the following provisions through different articles which have been dealt with under relevant heads. These articles can be collectively said as social safeguards for the Scheduled Castes and the Scheduled Tribes.

(A)	**Article 14**	: Equality before law.
(B)	**Article 15**	: Prohibition of discrimination on ground of religion, race, caste, sex or place of birth.
(C)	**Article 17**	: Abolition of Untouchability.
(D)	**Article 23**	: Prohibition of traffic in human beings and forced labour.
(E)	**Article 24**	: Prohibition of employment of children in factories etc.
(F)	**Article 25(2)(b)**	: Provision relating to Temple Entry.

(A) Article 14 : Equality before Law

Part III of the Constitution deals with a series of fundamental rights guaranteed to the citizens and non-citizens, which provides for social safeguards. The first and the foremost of these is "Equality before law." Article 14 States :

"The State shall not deny to any person equality before the

law or the equal protection of the laws within the territory of India."

This doctrine of natural equality first found its expression in the Declaration of Rights of Man, 1789, proclaimed by the National Assembly of France. It stated : "Men are born and always continue free and equal in respect of their rights." The same ideal was echoed in the American Declaration of Independence, which proclaimed. "We hold these truths to be self-evident, that all men are created equal. . .". It got a further backing in the Declaration of Human Rights wherein Article 7 states: "All are equal before the law and are entitled without any discrimination to equal protection of the law. All are entitled to equal protection against any discrimination in violation of this declaration and against any incitement of such discrimination."[1] Equality guaranteed in Article 14 of the Constitution is an extension of the principle ensured in the Preamble of Indian Constitution. The phrase "equality before the law" means that the State should not differentiate between the citizens either in the promulgation or application of law. In short, it means justice in its all aspects. It is the negation of differential treatment, impartiality at the alter of justice. The principle of equality before the law has been beautifully explained by *Ivor Jennings* : "Equality before the law means that among equal the law should be equal and should be equally administered that like should be treated alike."[2] Similarly, "equal protection of the laws" means that equal treatment should be meted out in like circumstances irrespective of any considerations whatever. The law of the land should be the same to highest and the lowest. Article 14 guarantees the principle of equality in general terms. This is further exemplified and particularised in Article 15. It has been rightly held that Article 14 is the genus of the guarantee of equality of which Article 15 is the species.[3] So, equality is further guaranteed by Article 15.

1. Ratna, G. Revankar, The Indian Constitution—A Case Study of Backward Classes. (1971), pp. 43-44.
2. Ivor Jennings, Law of the Constitution, p. 49.
3. See *Supra* 1.

(B) Article 15 : Prohibition of Discrimination on Grounds of Religion, Race, Caste, Sex or Place of Birth

(1) The State shall not discriminate against any citizen on grounds only of religion, race, caste, sex, place of birth, or any of them.

(2) No citizen shall, or grounds only of religion, race, caste, sex, place of birth or any of them be subject to any disability, liability, restriction or condition with regard to—

   (a) access to shops, public restaurants, hotels and places of public entertainment; or

   (b) the use of wells, tanks, bathing ghats, roads and places of public resort maintained wholly or partly out of State funds or dedicated to the use of the general public.

Article 15(1) expresses a particular application of the general principle of equality embodied in Article 14. Where the law comes within the prohibitory line of Article 15(1), it cannot be validated by recourse of Article 14. The combined effect of Articles 14 and 15 is not that the State can not pass unequal laws, but if it does pass unequal laws, the inequality must be based on some reasonable ground, and that, due to Article 15(1) religion, race, caste, sex or place of birth alone is not, and can not be, a reasonable ground for discrimination.

So, Article 15(1) prohibits the State to discriminate on the ground of religion, race, caste, sex or place of birth. It can be inferred (though indirectly) from the Article 15(1) that State would not make any legislation which further degrade or oppress the condition of Scheduled Castes or Scheduled Tribes.

Article 15(2) is wider in the sense that it prevents the imposition of disabilities with respects to religion, race, sex, place or birth, etc. In addition to prevent such restriction on the ground of caste, it forcefully recognizes the rights of Scheduled Castes and Scheduled Tribes to have access to shop, public restaurants, hotels and places of public entertainment, and to use the wells, tanks, bathing ghat, roads and places of public resort maintained wholly or partly out of State funds or dedicated to the use of general public.

Article 15(2) does have many important implications. As a result of this Article, the State can not make law which either permits private individuals or Government agencies to discriminate against such people with respect to such facilities, and, if the State does so, the court may strike down such laws as violative of Article 15(2).[4] On the other hand, if the State implements the prohibition by bringing a legislation penalizing such discrimination by private individuals, the Court may uphold such legislation under this Article.[5] Apart from this, if any person claims the right to exclude such persons from such places on the ground of customary rights, the Court may declare such custom as unreasonable in view of Article 15(2).[6]

It can be observed that the main objective of Article 15(2) is to abolish malpractices found in society, to forge a new society free from disparity. Article 15(2) has been specifically furthered by Article 17.

(C) Article 17 : Abolition of Untouchability

Untouchability is a unique Hindu social institution which emerged in the remote past. The so-called Untouchables have been suffering the stigma of Untouchability followed by servitude, illiteracy and grinding poverty. Due to its serious adverse effect on the Indian society in general and on Untouchables in particular, it has been vehemently opposed by many sensible persons including saints, social reformers and political leaders in the past.

Mahatma Gandhi who realised the danger of 'Untouchability' has rightly said that—

> "Untouchability is a curse that is eating into the vital of Hinduism, and I often feel that unless we take due precaution and remove this from our midst, Hinduism itself is in danger of destruction."[7]

Dr. B.R. Ambedkar also in his preface to his book "The

4. D.D. Basu, Commentary on the Constitution of India, p. 295.
5. *Ibid.*, p. 295.
6. Armugha V. Narayana, AIR 1958 Madras 282.
7. Hingorani, Anand, "My Philosophy of life by M.K. Gandhi, p. 159.

Untouchables"[8] cites instances of the practice of Untouchability and observed:

> "Untouchability is not a short or temporary feature. It is a permanent one. To put it straight, it can be said that the struggle between Hindus and the Untouchables is a permanent phenomenon and it is eternal, because the high caste people believe that the religion which has placed you at the lowest level of the society is itself eternal. No change according to time and circumstances is possible."

Eventually the founding fathers of the Indian Constitution, visualized a society based on Justice, liberty, equality and fraternity. To achieve this object Constitution-makers wanted to integrate the long neglected people of India into Indian society so as to make them feel that they were also son of Indian soil, breathing the same air as others and to assimilate them in common stream of national life. Keeping this aim in their mind Constitution-makers framed the Constitution.

During the course of the discussion on the floor of the Constituent Assembly, *Sardar Vallabh Bhai Patel,* stated that, removal of Untochability is the main idea, if abolition of Untouchability is provided as a fundamental right, as an offence, necessary adjustment will be made in the law that be passed by the legislature.[9]

So, with a view to achieve the integration of long neglected people of India into Indian society the Constitution of India has abolished Untouchability through Article 17.

Article 17 states that:—

> "Untouchability" is abolished and its practice in any form is forbidden. The enforcement of any disability arising out of Untouchability shall be an offence punishable in accordance with law."

"Untouchability" has been abolished but the Constitution, nowhere defines the expression Untouchability. But in order to

---

8. Ambedkar, B.R., The Untouchables, p. 1.
9. C.A.D., Vol. 3, pp. 434, 435.

examine the implication of present article it becomes necessary to see how the expression is used. It may be reviewed in broader and in narrower sense.

Untouchability in its broadest sense might include all instances in which one person treats another as ritually unclean and as a source of pollution. In this sense even a temporary state of pollution and avoidance of persons who are temporarily polluted, may be considered the practice of untouchability. If the expression Untouchability is expressed in this sense then avoiding people, such as women at child-birth, menstruating women, mourners, persons with contagious disease, etc. may be considered the practice of Untouchability. People who have become Untouchable because of being ex-communicated from the membership of a group, might also be considered Untouchable and the practice of avoiding such people might be considered the practice of Untouchability, if the expression "Untouchability" is interpreted in this broadest sense.

In some what narrower sense the expression would include all instances in which a person was stigmatised as unclean or polluting or inferior because of its origin or membership in a particular group[10] i.e., where he is subjected to invidious treatment because of difference in religion or membership of a group which is considered lower. In this sense avoiding the food touched by a Muslim or a Christian by a caste-Hindu might be considered the practice of Untouchability. Preventing people belonging to different religion into Hindu temple and *vice-versa* might be considered the practice of Untouchability.

But the High Court of Mysore has refused to interpret the expression so broadly; in *Devarajiah* v. *Padmanna*[11] where the

10. A definition suggested, but not adopted by the Joint Committee on The Untouchability (offences) Amendment and Miscellaneous Provisions Bill, 1972 tried of cover such interpretation. The definition was as follow : "Untouchability" means and includes subjecting a member of Scheduled Castes or others to any discrimination, disability, suffering, restriction, liability or any condition on the ground of pollution and isolation, caste, race, religion or any of them of such person or of his parents of family".

11. AIR, 1958 Mysore 84—The Court Stated that a literal construction of the term would include persons who are treated as untouchables either temporarily or otherwise for various reasons, such as their suffering from epidemic or contagious disease or on account of

orthodox Jains issued pamphlet contending that the non-Jains had no right to enter the Jain temple and offer worship therein or to take food with Jains. Mysore High Court said that the conduct of Jains towards non-Jains was neither the practice of Untouchability. The court said that the expression "Untouchability" has been put within inverted commas which clearly indicates that the subject matter of Article 17 is not Untouchability in its literal or grammatical sense but the practice of its as it had developed historically in this country.[12] The court further observed that Untouchability with which the Article 17 is concerned is that which "refers to those regarded as Untouchables in the course of historical development.[13] The same view was expressed by the Cuttuck High Court in *Kendra Sethi* v. *Metra Sahu*[14] where, the High Court said, "We understand the word to import a sort of social disability that certain classes of people suffer by reason of birth in particular castes."

---

social observance such as are associated with birth of death or due to social boycott resulting from caste or other disputes.

12. *Ibid.*, p. 85.
13. *Ibid.*, p. 85.
14. (1963) 29 Cuttuck L.T. 364.
15. The Untouchability Offence Bill, 1954, attempted to define the expression untouchable in the following manner—

"Untouchable" means a member of Scheduled castes as defined in Clause 24 of Article 366 of the Constitution, and includes any other person who by custom or usage is regarded as an "Untouchable" by any community or section thereof.

Explanation I-A : Member of Scheduled Caste shall not cease to be such member if he resides in any locality other than the locality specified in relation to him in any public notification issued or any law made by Parliament under Article 341 of the Constitution.

Explanation II-A : Member of Scheduled Caste who has been converted from the Hindu religion to any other religion shall, notwithstanding such conversion, be declared to be an "Untouchable" for the purpose of his Act.

The Joint Select Committee considered whether the expression "untouchable" used in the Bill should be retained or substituted by any other appropriate word or words and came to conclusion that the deletion of the expression "Untouchable" would not stand in the way of attaining the object of the Bill.

Thus the courts restrict the expression to the imposition of various kinds of disabilities upon those who are considered Untouchable.[15] In this sense the expression does not include invidious treatment due to difference in religion or difference in caste, except in so far as the caste was traditionally considered "Untouchable". Preventing an Untouchable from entry into temple or providing no service to Untouchable, will certainly be considered the practice of Untouchability, in this sense, it is important to note that although the Court has restricted the definition to a particular group of persons that is considered as Untouchable, it has broadened the expression so as to include any kind of invidious treatment[16] against a person who belongs to Untouchable group. Thus, the expression would cover separation, segregation and isolation of such persons from the higher caste Hindus. It also includes the practice of keeping the Untouchables away for misplaced fear of pollution requiring keeping themselves away from the places of public resort and also from temples. It includes economic isolation, social segregation, and disqualification for admission into educational institutions, learned profession, trade and industry. It refer to imposition of disabilities, liabilities, etc. because of a person's birth in a low caste. The expression, Untouchability, thus, refer to wide range of activities that put the persons belonging to untouchable group in an unfavourable position.

The result of abolition of untouchability by Art. 17 is, to free the Untouchables from various kinds of disabilities, indignities, discriminations and liabilities associated with the age-old practice of Untouchability. The freedom of untouchables from such disabilities and indignities automatically give them same rights which the untouchables, hitherto, failed to enjoy. Such rights which accrue to the person as a result of abolition of Untouchability are called civil right[17] by the Protection of Civil Rights Act, 1955. As "Untouchability abolition" clause is a part

16. If the State favours an untouchable for his being so, it cannot be said that the state practices untouchability. In *Paradai Gounder* v. *State of Madras*, AIR 1973 Mad. 458, it was held that acquisition of land for constructing harijan colony did not violate Article 17. The court remarked that what is prohibited under Article 17 is singling out the harijan community for hostile treatment as a socially backward.
17. Protection of Civil Right Act, 1955, Section 2(a).

of Part III of the Constitution, the Untouchables have the right to go to Supreme Court under Article 32 of the Constitution,[18] if their Civil Rights, i.e. the rights accruing them as a result of abolition of "Untouchability", is infringed. It would not be out of place to note here that rights under Article 17 are available not only against the State but also against the private individuals.[19]

The makers of the Constitution recognised that only by abolishing untouchability, the untouchables can not be free from various disabilities from which they suffer nor can they enjoy the rights which accrues to them as a result of abolition of "Untouchability". Consequently, they provided for various measures in the Constitution, to be taken by Government, for implementing this policy. They recognised the complexity of the problem of Untouchability and provided for multi-pronged attack to fight this evil. The Constitution-makers did so by authorising the Parliament to make it offence to enforce disabilities against Untouchables,[20] by recognising certain rights to be granted by State[21] and by asking provisions for improving the status of Untouchables.[22]

The Constitution differentiates between the practice of Untouchability in any form and enforcement of disability arising out of Untouchability.[23] The practice of Untouchability is forbidden whereas the enforcement of disability arising out of

18. Article 32(1) states. "The right to move the Supreme Court by appropriate proceedings for the enforcement of the rights conferred by this is guaranteed."
19. Durga Das Basu, Commentary on the Constitution of India, p. 361.
20. Article 17 ". . . . The enforcement of any disability arising out of 'Untouchability' shall be an offence punishable in accordance with law". And Article 35. . . Parliament shall have, and the Legislatures of State shall not have power to make laws.

    (i) ....

    (ii) For prescribing punishment for those acts which are declared to be offences under this part."
21. Articles 15(2), 25(2)(b).
22. Articles 15(4), 16(4), 330 and 332.
23. See Article 17, which uses the expression—"practice" of Untouchability in any form and "Enforcement of Disabilities arising out of Untouchability". R.V. Kelkar pointed out such a difference in R.V. Kelkar, The Untouchability Offence Act, 1955, pp. 127-44.

"Untouchability" has been made an offence punishable in accordance with law. By forbidding the practice of Untouchability in any form, the Constitution prevents the state from practicing Untouchability. It prevents the State from making any law that may recognise the practice of Untouchability. At the same time it forbids the Court to recoginse the practice of Untouchability. At the same time it forbids the Courts to recognise any claim based on the practice of Untouchability. By so doing the Constitution directs the states neither to legislate in favour of Untouchables nor to recognise any claim of private individuals based on the practice of Untouchability. In addition to forbidding the practice of Untouchability, the Constitution makes it an offence to enforce the disability arising out of Untouchability. Article 17 combined with Article 35 authorises the Parliament to make laws which provides punishment to those who enforces disabilities arising out of "Untouchability".

So, in 1955, Parliament, in exercise of the power conferred under Article 35 enacted the Untouchability (Offence) Act, 1955 in pursuance of the Constitutional proclamation under Article 17. After observing the working of the Untouchability (Offence) Act, 1955 the Parliament had appointed a Sub-committee under the leadership of *Shri Elayaperumal,* in the year 1964, to study the problem of Untouchability with reference to the enforcement of Untouchability (Offence) Act, 1955 and sought suitable recommendations. After a series of deliberations the committee submitted its recommendations to the Parliament in the year 1969.

In pursuance of several debates in Parliament while reviewing the Elayaperumal Report, the legislature again sought to amend the Untouchability offence (Amendment and miscellaneous provisions) Act of 1972. The amended act contemplated stringent punishment in contrast of the earlier act. It also provided for minimum punishment, cumulative punishment and withdrew of the facility of fine and the alternative imprisonment, etc. Further, the Act also provided for higher punishments for second and subsequent offences.

Again, a joint committee of the Parliament (1972) undertook an extensive study of the working of the

Untouchability (Offences) Act, 1955 and made its recommendations in the year 1974. Some of its recommendations were:

(1) The abolition of *"Untouchability"* should be taken to have conferred upon the Untouchables certain legally enforceable immunities and privileges of citizenship the "civil rights".
Therefore, the law intended and designed to punish the practice of "Untouchability" should be described as civil right enforcement legislation. Accordingly, the committee felt that the short title of the principal Act—the Untouchability (Offences) Act, 1955 should be changed to the "Protection of Civil Rights Act".

(2) Any disability on ground of "Untouchability" should include any discrimination on that ground.

(3) Any place of public worship established and maintained by a religious denomination should be open to all persons belonging to the same religion.

(4) Prevention of temple entry on the ground of untouchability of a person should be punishable, even if the person concerned does not belong to the same denomination as the person prevented.

(5) No one should be prevented on the ground of untouchability from bathing not only in, or using water of the sacred tanks, wells, springs or water courses, but also of the rivers, lakes or ghats attached to them.

(6) Any disability enforcement on ground of untouchability with regard to the taking part in, taking out any religious or social procession should be made punishable.

(7) Any insult done or attempts to do it to a person on ground of untouchability should be punishable.

(8) A person who justifies or preaches practices of "untouchability" on historical, philosophical or religious grounds should be deemed to encourage or excite practice of untouchability.

(9) A public servant showing any negligence in investigation of the Untouchability Offences Act offences should be punished as an abettor.

(10) Any community local or other practicing "Untouchability" should be liable to a collective fine.
(11) Legal aid should be made available to the victims of the Untouchability Offences Act crimes.
(12) Official machinery including committees at various levels should be planned for overseeing the implementation of "Untouchability" removal measures, and conducting periodic survey of the Untouchability Offences Act enforcement.
(13) Special officers and special courts for the trial of the Untouchability Offences should be constituted.
(14) The reports concerning various measures taken by the various governments should be placed on the Table of the Houses of Parliaments.

In pursuance of these recommendations, the Untouchability Offences Act (1955) was replaced by the *Protection of Civil Rights Act (1976).*[24]

But there were too many loopholes and loose ends in the provisions of these two Acts and because of the ineffective preventive and overall administrative role in mitigating atrocity on the weaker sections, the desired result could not be achieved. Consequently a more effective legislation *Scheduled Castes and Scheduled Tribes (Prevention of Atrocities) Act, 1989* was brought into force from 30 Jan., 1990 in order to check and deter crimes against Scheduled Castes and Scheduled Tribes by persons belonging to higher communities. These enactments have extended the positive discrimination in favour of Scheduled Castes and Scheduled Tribes to the field of criminal law in as much as they prescribe penalties that are more stringent then the corresponding offences under Indian Penal Code and other laws. Special courts have been established in major states for speedy trial of cases registered exclusively under these acts.

The term 'atrocity' with relation to Scheduled Castes and Scheduled Tribes had not been clearly defined before this Act. An attempt was made to define it in the Scheduled Castes and Scheduled Tribes (Prevention of Atrocities) Act, 1989. In

24. Kshirsagar, R.K., Untouchability in India (implementation of the law and abolition), p. 132.

common parlance, "the term atrocity denotes an act which is extremely heinous". In the first report of the commission of Scheduled Castes and Scheduled Tribes, the term included offences like murder, rape, arson and violence resulting in grievous hurt. In conceptualising atrocity, the factor of caste was of utmost consideration. The meaning of the term has undergone a sea-change because of the explanation provided by the Ministry of Home Affairs in 1980-81. According to this explanation, any offence, cognizable or non-cognizable under the Indian penal code, in which the victim is a member of the Scheduled Castes or Scheduled Tribes, is an act of atrocity irrespective of motive.

Various atrocities committed on Scheduled Castes and Scheduled Tribes can be classified under different heads, namely, physical, mental and emotional torture, assault on person and property, dishonour and human indignity atrocities born of social, religious and cultural differences. So it is necessary to know that what type of atrocities being committed on the Scheduled Castes and Scheduled Tribes. There are various types of atrocities[25] being committed on the Scheduled Castes and Scheduled Tribes.

1. *Physical:* Beating and manhandling causing hurt, grievous hurt, permanent disabilities, removal of limbs eyes, ears, nose, hands, legs, etc. Causing nuisance, Sexual exploitation, molestation and rape, Denying on customary right of passage, Murders and mass killings.
2. *Mental & Emotional*: Giving derogatory names to the caste/tribe, passing sarcastic remarks on self and members of family, insult, intimidation and assault.
3. *Property:* Burning of houses and grave arson cases, Looting colonies, theft and dacoities, Grabbing land and encroachment, grabbing cattle, theft, robbery and dacoity, Encroachment on houses, Agricultural land and lifting of cattle, ejection from rightful possession not allowing to enjoy easementary rights, Extorting money on some count or another, Cheating Dishonest claim, Destruction of property.

25. Central Bureau of Investigation Bulletin, 2006 p. 84.

4. *Dishonour:* Shaving of the head, Blackening of the face and forced to Donkey ride, Forcing to take-off clothes, Made to eat or drink obnoxious substance, Remarks derogatory to human dignity, Parading naked, making sleep naked and have sex with near relations like daughters, etc., Polluting and fouling water.
5. *Social, Religious & Cultural*: Barring access to temples and other religious places, not allowing mounting a horse on the occasion of marriage, not allowing the use of band, not allowing the use of wells and other water resources, social boycott, Untouchability, blocking of the marriage procession.
6. *Economic* : Begar, bonded labour, loaning, loaning on a heavy rate of interest, after mortgage, pledge to the poor, free labour, compelling forced labour, barter, work without adequate payment.
7. *Political:* Intimidation and coercion for votes, harassment on being elected, preventing for voting.
8. *Legal*: Implicating in false cases, Fabrication of documents and evidence.
9. *Police:* There are complaints that police indulge in all sorts of atrocities, using third-degree methods, taking bribes and exercising undue influence.

The legislation named Scheduled Castes and Scheduled Tribes (Prevention of Atrocities) Act, 1989[26] has been passed to combat the menaces of atrocity on the weaker sections, i.e., Scheduled Castes and Scheduled Tribes and their overall amelioration for their assimilation into the mainstream of social consciousness and national development, without which there can be no real social progress and harmony.

(D) Article 23(1): Prohibition of Traffic in Human Beings and Forced Labour

Article 23(1) of the Constitution of India provides for the prohibition of trafficking in human beings and forced labour. Before the enactment of the Constitution there were many areas of the country where the weaker section of society, i.e.,

26. Sec. 3 of this Act provides punishment for the offence of atrocity.

Untouchables and Adivasis were being exploited in several ways by higher castes and richer class. For example, in parts of Rajasthan which was in Pre-Independence days a cluster of Princely States, there existed a practice under which labourers who worked for a particular landlord could not leave him to seek employment elsewhere without his permission. Very often this restriction was so severe and the labourer's dependence on the 'master' was so absolute that he was just a slave in reality. The local laws had supported such practices. Pre-independence history is replete with such examples. These types of social evils were rampant in other parts of our country. To abolish such a deep-rooted evil, our framers of the Constitution have incorporated Article 23 as a fundamental rights in our Constitution.

Article 23(1) runs as follows:

> "Traffic in human beings and begar and other similar forms of forced labour are prohibited and any contravention of this provision shall be an offence punishable in accordance with law".

Although Article 23(1) does not specifically mention Scheduled Castes and Scheduled Tribes but it is evident from the past that usually those who were exploited and oppressed belonged to weaker section of society. Because of this fact this Article has a special significance with regards to Scheduled Castes and Scheduled Tribes.

Article 23(1) simply prohibits:

- Traffic in human beings,
- Begar, and
- Other similar forms of forced labour.

The expression "Traffic in human beings" commonly known as 'Slavery' implies the buying and selling of human beings as if they were chattels, and such a practice is now abolished by the Constitution.

"Begar" means involuntary work without payment. To ask a man to work without remuneration constitutes Begar. It is a

Fundamental Right of a person, citizen or non-citizen, not to be compelled to work without wages. Article 23(1) is not restricted to begar alone but includes "other similar form of forced labour". It means to compel a person to work against his will. Begar commonly connotes forced labour for which no wages are paid, or, if some payment is made, it is grossly inadequate. It means making a person work against his will and without paying any remuneration.[27] To ask a person to work and then not to pay his wages saviours of begar but a voluntary agreement to do extra work for payment is not begar or forced labour.

In *Peoples Union for Democratic Rights* v. *Union of India*,[28] the Supreme Court considered the scope and ambit of Article 23 in details. The court held that the scope of Article 23 is wide and unlimited and strike at "traffic in human beings, begar and other forms of forced labour" whenever they are found. It is not merely "begar" which is prohibited by Article 23 but also all other forms of forced labour. "Begar is a form of forced labour under which a person is compelled to work without receiving any remuneration. This Article strikes at forced labour in whatever form it may manifest itself, because it is violative of human dignity and contrary to basic human values. The practice of forced labour is condemned in almost every international instrument dealing with Human Rights. Every form of forced labour "begar" or other forms is prohibited by Article 23 and it makes no difference whether the person who is forced to give his labour or service to another is paid remuneration or not. Even if remuneration is paid, labour or services supplied by a person would be hit by this Article, if it is forced labour, e.g. labour supplied not willingly but as a result of force or compulsion. This Article strikes at every form of forced labour even if it has its origin in a contract voluntarily entered into by the person obligated to provide labour or service. If a person has contracted with another to perform service and there is a consideration for such service in the shape of liquidation of debt or even remuneration he cannot be forced by compulsion of law, or otherwise to continue to perform such

27. S. Vasudevan *v.* S.D. Mittal, AIR 1962 Bombay, pp. 53-67.
28. AIR 1982 SC, p. 1963.

service as it would be forced labour within the meaning of Article 23. No one shall be forced to provide labour or service against his will even though it is under a contract of service. The word "force" was interpreted by the Court very widely. *Bhagwati, J.* said, "the word 'force' must therefore be construed to include not only physical or legal force but also force arising from the compulsion of economic circumstances which leaves no choice or alternatives to a person in want and compels him to provide labour or service even though the remuneration received for it is less than the minimum wage." Thus a person who provides labour or service to another for remuneration which is less than minimum wage amounts to forced labour under Article 23. In the instant case, it was held that the deduction of Re.1 per worker per day by the jamadars from the wages payable to workers employed by contractor for Asiad projects in Delhi as a result of which the workers did not get the minimum wage of Rs. 9.25 per day was violative of Article 23 of the Constitution. The Court directed the Government to take necessary steps for punishing the violation of fundamental rights of citizens guaranteed by Article 23 by private individuals.

In *Sanjit Roy* v. *State of Rajasthan,*[29] it has been held that the payment of wages lower than the minimum wages to the person employed on Famine Relief Work is violative of Article 23. Whenever any labour or service is taken by the State from any person who is affected by drought and scarcity condition the State cannot pay him less wages than the minimum wage on the ground that it is given them to help to meet famine situation. The State cannot take advantage of their helplessness.

In *Deena* v. *Union of India,*[30] it was held that labour taken from prisoners without paying proper remuneration was "forced labour" and violative of Article 23 of the Constitution. The prisoners are entitled to payment of reasonable wages for the work taken form them and the Court is under duty to enforce their claim.

In *Dubar Goala* v. *Union of India,*[31] the petitioners, who were licensed porters at Howrah Railway Station, voluntarily entered

29. AIR 1983 SC, p. 328.
30. AIR 1983 SC, p. 1155.
31. AIR 1952 Cal. p. 496.

into an agreement to do two hours extra work for the railway administration. They challenged the validity of this agreement and asked the Court to restrain the railway administration from compelling the porters to perform begar or forced labour. The Calcutta High Court held that "the petitioners could not be said to be doing begar or forced labour within the meaning of Article 23." The very idea that the petitioners had voluntarily agreed to do extra work by entering into a contract to the effect repels the idea of their work being a forced labour. There was no element of force or illegality in the system of license or in realising the fees for such licenses. The Railway authorities had the power to regulate the use of station. The petitioners were paid some remuneration for their two hours labour. Further, they get the benefit of a reduced licence fee, and in addition they were allowed the privilege of free use of the railway premises for earning their livelihood. In the circumstances the extra work done by them was not forced labour within the meaning of Article 23(1).

In *Kahason Thangkhul* v. *Simtri Shaili,*[32] a custom required that each householder of the village should offer one day's free labour to the headman of the village. It was held that the custom was violative of Article 23(1) of the Constitution which prohibits begar and other form of forced labour.

The various State laws make it an offence to compel a person to work against his will or without payment of wages to do any work. In an interesting case of *State* v. *Banwari,*[33] the respondents challenged the validity of the U.P. removal of Social Disabilities Act. The appellants who were barbers and dhobis had refused to shave and wash clothes of *Harijans.* They were therefore convicted under section 6 of the above Act. It was held that the Act did not contravene Article 23 of the Constitution. The Court said that when a person is prohibited from refusing to render service merely on the ground that the person asking for it belongs to a Scheduled Caste he is not thereby subjected to forced labour. Likewise, the payment of Wages Act, 1926, which provides that every employer is responsible for payment of wages to his employees, had been held to valid.

32. AIR 1961 Manipur, p. 1.
33. AIR 1951 All, p. 615.

A serious socio-economic problem in India had been that of Bonded labour. Bonded labour is widely prevalent in many regions in India. The main feature of the system is that the debtor pledges his person or that of a member of his family for a loan and is released only on the repayment of the debt. The practice seems to be fairly old. It existed on a wide scale during Moughal period. Bonded labour system was widely prevalent where the lower and depressed class was most numerous. In Andhra Pradesh, Orissa, Madhya Pradesh, Gujarat, Bombay and Kerala where the aboriginal population is found the system is wide spread. In other regions also the Scheduled Castes and Scheduled Tribes are the victims of Bonded labour system.[34]

Article 23 has abolished the system of Bonded labour. Bonded labour has been made unconstitutional under Article 23 as it is a form of forced labour. But unfortunately no serious efforts were made to give effect to this article. It was only in 1976 that Parliament enacted *The Bonded Labour System (Abolition) Act, 1976* providing for the abolition of bonded labour system with a view to prevent the economic and physical exploitation of weaker section of people, i.e., Scheduled Castes and Scheduled Tribes. Under Article 35 of the Constitution for the purpose of punishing acts which results in bonded labour. The Preamble of the Act states that it is to provide for the abolition of bonded labour system with a view to prevent the economic and physical exploitation of the weaker section of the people and for the matters connected therewith or incidental thereto.[35] This Act strikes at the system of bonded labour. In spite of the Constitutional and legal provisions abolishing bonded labour, the implementation of the law has been very tardy at the administrative level. There were many difficult problems involved in eradication of such labours e.g... Problem of identification of bonded labours, problem of rehabilitation (after release from the bondage), etc. The slow implementation of the law has given rise to several judicial pronouncement by way of Public Interest litigations.

In *Bandhua Mukti Morcha* v. *Union of India*[36] the Supreme Court held that when an action is initiated in the Court through

34. Sivaramayya, B., Inequalities and the Law, p. 148.
35. Bonded Labour System (Abolition) Act, 1976, p. 1.
36. AIR 1984 SC 802.

Public Interest litigation alleging the existence of bonded labour the Government should welcome it as it gives the Government an 'opportunity to examine whether bonded labour system exists and as well as to take appropriate steps to eradicate that system. This is the Constitutional obligation of the Government under Article 23 which prohibits "Forced labour" in any form.

In *Neerja Chaudhary* v. *State of M.P.*[37] the question before the Court was that how to Court identify bonded labour. The court has said :

> "Whenever it is found that any workman is forced to provide labour for no remuneration or nominal remuneration, the presumption would be that he is a bonded labour under the employer or the State Government is in a position to prove otherwise by rebutting such presumption."

However, The Article 23(1) of the Constitution is a general provision with regard to abolition of Trafficking, Begar and Forced labour, etc. and enabling the state to make appropriate laws in this regard the real beneficiaries of this Article is the weaker section of the society and particularly the Scheduled Castes and Scheduled Tribes.

(E) Article 24 : Prohibition of Employment of Children in Factories, etc.

> "No child below the age of fourteen years shall be employed to work in any factory or mine or engaged in any other hazardous employment."

Though, according to the bare language of Article 24 it cannot be inferred that the Article is any how related with Scheduled Castes and Scheduled Tribes. But dealing with the Article 24 in deep, would show that it is generally for all and particularly for the welfare of children of Scheduled Castes and Scheduled Tribes.

37. SCC 1984, Vol. 3, 243.

In respect of child labour, India is an outlier in the modern world. As *Mysron Weiner* has argued, "Modern states regard education as a legal duty", and "compulsory primary education is the policy instrument by which the state effectively removed children from the work force."[38] In India, child labour persists on a significant scale. Child labour is neither illegal nor is schooling compulsory.Attitudes to child labour among policy makers in India believe the modern progressive view of childhood being a period of learning through school, and not a period of employment.

Child labour usually refers to children up to the age of 14, following the ILO Convention. The International Labour Office (ILO) resolution on age of employment, concerning Minimum Age for Admission to Employment (Convention No. 138), recommends that no person below 15 years be considered suitable for employment (on the grounds that a child should compulsorily complete a certain number of years of school). The United Nations Convention on the Rights of the Child (1989), however, refers to children as persons below the age of 18.

If we consider the age group 5-14, and the definition of worker as in the Census of India, then, in 2001, there were 12.6 million child workers in the country. We have more child workers than the entire population of Belgium. More than 50 percent of child workers (6.7 million children) are concentrated in the five States of Uttar Pradesh, Andhra Pradesh, Rajasthan, Bihar and Madhya Pradesh.

Child labour is predominantly a rural phenomenon. Rural areas account for 85 percent of child workers and the incidence of child labour is higher in rural areas than in urban areas. Almost 80 percent of estimated child workers are employed in the agricultural sector. Nevertheless, there are some urban pockets with a high incidence and visible concentration of child labour in specific industries such as gem polishing in Jaipur, slate making in Markapur, and silk weaving in Varanasi.

Although the incidence of child labour has declined over the years, clearly it remains a big problem. Furthermore, there are a large number of children who are not attending school either, and can be viewed as potential child workers.[39]

38. As quoted in *The Hindu* 10 October, 2006.
39. Madhura Swaminathan, *The Hindu*, 10 Oct. 2006.

Infact, child labour is a socio-economic problem. It is generally considered that illiteracy, ignorance, low wages, unemployment, low standard of living and social life all are root cause of child labour. It is a fact that the Scheduled Castes and Scheduled Tribes are oppressed class and more or less these classes suffer from the above mentioned condition which result in their children forced in labour, unwillingly. These children are required to seek employment either to supplement the income of their families or to have a gainful occupation in the absence of availability of school going facilities at various places. Their poverty forces them to send their children to seek employment.

In Indian social system, majority of workers are from socially and economically backward classes, viz. Scheduled Castes and Scheduled Tribes in our society there have been discrimination based on the caste. Because of this fact the children of this marginalised section have very limited opportunity. Their lower strata of social hierarchy put an encumbrance in their upliftment. The other contributing factors include the uneven distribution of wealth. Poor families have also lost faith in the present day education system which is not cognizant of the structural pattern existing in the Indian society. The children working as child labour are generally drop-outs, who usually leave school even without obtaining primary education, therefore, they do not find formal education renumeratives. So it is better for them to become a bread earner and in some cases gain experience towards becoming a skilled labour.

Indian Constitution framers were aware of the fact that children are the future of the country and a ruined present can not give a prosperous tomorrow."[40]

Pt. Jawahar Lal Nehru had once said :

> "Children, I think, all over India have the first claim on us, because they represent the India of tomorrow."[41]

In fact, the framers of our Constitution were quite aware of the intensity of the problem of child labour. So they

40. R.P. Rai, Child labour—A myth or reality in *The Sphere of Human Rights. Law Review*, 2000-01, p. 157.
41. Jawaharlal Nehru's speeches, 1949-53

incorporated a fundamental right prohibiting child labour in form of Article 24.

Although efforts were on to abolish the child labour before the enactment of Constitution also. The very first Act in this regard was the Children (Pledging of labour) Act, 1933. This was followed by the Employment of Children Act, 1938 and after the enactment of Indian Constitution, to further and strengthen the spirit of Article 24, the legislature has passed many Acts, viz. Indian Factories Act, Mines Act, 1952, The Merchant Shipping Act, 1958, The Motor Transport Workers' Act, 1951, The Bidi and Cigar Workers' Act, 1966 and the Child Labour (Prohibition and Regulation) Act, 1986.

The Child Labour (Prohibition & Regulation) Act, 1986 was the culmination of efforts and ideas from the deliberation and recommandations of various committees on child labour. The current legislation in India does not ban all forms of child labour. The Child Labour (Prohibition and Regulation) Act, 1986, is concerned only with "the engagement of children in certain employment" and accordingly lists specific occupations (Part A) and processes (Part B) in which the employment of children in banned or is to be regulated. The occupations specified in the Act include work in the railways, ports and the sale of fireworks, and the processes specified include bidi-making, carpet weaving, and the manufacture of soaps, matches, and cement.

On August 1, 2006, the Ministry of Labour added the following occupations to the list of hazardous occupations: domestic servants, workers in dhabas, restaurants, hotels, motels, teashops, resorts, spas or other recreational centres. The notification will become effective on October 10, 2006, that is, today. This is a welcome step but far from adequate.

Implicit in the above legislation is the view that certain types of employment are hazardous and only child labour in those employments is to be prohibited or regulated. The ILO Convention (No. 182) on the Worst Forms of Child Labour, 1999, also attempts to make a distinction between hazardous and non-hazardous employment. The convention seeks the immediate elimination of certain types of child labour including slavery (sale of children, debt bondage, etc.) prostitution, drug trafficking, and other hazardous activity (or "work which is likely to harm the health, safety or morals or children").

There is no doubt that bonded labour and other extremely exploitative forms of child labour should be ended at once, and require priority attention. Nevertheless, there are problems with defining hazardous activity; ultimately, all forms of labour are hazardous to the well-being of children.[42]

The Courts too, have strictly interpreted the provisions of different child labour prohibition Acts and given benefit to children so that this social evil could be rooted out.

In People's Union for Democratic Rights v. *Union of India,"*[43] in was contended that the Employment of Children Act, 1938 was not applicable in case of employment of children in the construction work of Asiad projects in Delhi since construction industry was not a process specified in the schedule of the Employment of Children Act. The Employment of Children Act, 1938 only prohibits employment of children below 14 years of age in the railways and other means of transport. But, the Court rejected this contention and held that the construction work in hazardous employment and therefore under Article 24 no child below the age of 14 years can be employed in the construction work even if construction industry is not specified in the Schedule of the Employment of Children Act, 1938, expressing concern about the "Sad and deplorable ommission". *Bhagwati, J.* advised the State Government to take immediate steps for inclusion of construction work in the schedule to the act, and to ensure that the Constitution mandate of Article 24 is not violated in any part of the Country.

In *Labour Working on Salal Hydro Project* v. *Jammu and Kashmir,*[44] the Court has reiterated the principle that the construction work is a hazardous employment and children below 14 years cannot be employed in this work.

In a landmark judgment in *M.C. Mehta* v. *State of Tamilnadu*[45] the Supreme Court has held that children below the age of 14 years cannot be employed in any hazardous industry,

42. Madhura Swaminathan, *The Hindu*, 10 Oct. 2006.
43. AIR 1982 SC, p. 1473.
44. AIR 1984 SC, p. 177.
45. SCC 1996 SC, p. 796.

mines or other works and has laid down exhaustive guidelines how the state authorities should protect economic, social and humanitarian rights of millions of children, working illegally in public and private sections. The matter was bought before the Court by a public spirited lawyer *Mr. M.C. Mehta* by way of public interest litigation (PIL) under Article 32 of the Constitution. He told the Court about the plight of the children engaged in Sivakasi Cracker Factories. Though the Constitution provides in Article 24 that the children should not be subjected to exploitation and the law prohibits employment of child labour, yet there are 17 million children working in the organised sector as estimated by the Planning Commission. According to estimate from various non-government sources, the actual number of working children range from 44 million to 100 million. Despite the Constitutional provisions and various legislative enactments passed by many States which prohibit employment of child labour. The child labour is a big problem and has remained unsolved, even after fifty-nine years of Independence.

The Court directed setting up of Child Labour Rehabilitation Welfare Fund and asked the offending employer to pay for each child a compensation of Rs. 20,000 to be deposited in the Fund and suggested a number of measures to rehabilitate them in the phased manner.

The Court made it clear that the liability of the employer would not cease even if he would desire to disengage the child presently employed and asked the government to ensure that an adult members of the child's family get a job in a factory or any where in lieu of the child.

In those cases where it would not be possible the appropriate Government would, as its contribution, deposit Rs. 5,000 in the fund for each child employed in a factory or mine or in any other hazardous employment.

The authority concerned has thus two options either it should ensure alternative employment for the adult whose name would be suggested by the child concerned or it should deposit a sum of Rs. 25,000 in the fund.

The Court made it clear that in case of getting employment for an adult, the parent or guardian shall have to withdraw the child from the job. Even if no employment would be provided, the parent shall have to see that his child is spared from the requirement of the job as a alternative source of income. Interest income from deposit of Rs. 25,000 would become available to the child's family till he continues his studies upto the age of 14 years.

To start with, the Court said, work could be taken up regarding hazardous employments and then to be followed by comparatively less hazardous and so on. The Court issued following directions to implement above directions:

(1) A survey about the child labour within 6 months.
(2) 'The Court identified nine industries first where the work could be taken up namely—the match industry in Sivakasi, Tamilnadu, the Diamond Polishing Industry in Surat, Gujarat, the precious stone Polishing Industry in Jaipur, Rajasthan; the Glass Industry in Ferozabad, the Brass-ware Industry in Moradabad, the hand-made Carpet Industry in Mirzapur, Bhadohi and Lock-making Industry in Aligarh, all in Uttar Pradesh; the Slate Industry in Markapur, Andhra Pradesh; and the Slate Industry in Mandsaur; Madhya Pradesh of priority action.
(3) The employments given could be in the industry where the child is employed, a public sector undertaking, and could be manual in nature in as much as the child in question must be engaged in doing manual work. The undertaking chosen for employment shall be one which is nearest to the place of residence of the family.
(4) In those cases where no alternative employment is available, to the adult member of child's family, the parents would be paid income from interest of Rs. 25,000 and the employment given or payment made would cease if the child is not sent for education by parents.
(5) On discontinuance of the employment his education could be ensured until they complete the age of 14 years and shall be free as required by Art. 45 of the

Constitution. It would be the duty of the Inspectors to see that this call of the Constitution is carried out.

(6) For the collection of Funds, a district could be the unit of collection so that executive head of the district keeps a watchful eye on the work of the Inspectors. In view of the magnitude of the task a separate cell in the labour department of the concerned Government would be created to monitor this work. Overall monitoring by the Ministry of Labour, Government of India would be beneficial and worthwhile.

(7) The Secretary of the Ministry of Labour of the Union of India would apprise the Court within one year about the compliance of the direction of the Court in this regard.

(8) In so far as the non-hazardous jobs are concerned, the Inspector shall have to see that the working hours of the child are not more than 4 to 6 hours a day and it receives education at least for two hours each day. The cost of education shall be borne by the employer.

(F) Article 25(2)(b) : Provisions relating to Temple Entry

The Constitution also recognises the right of all classes and section of Hindus to enter into the Hindus religious institutions of a public character, by authorising the State to throw open such institutions to all classes and sections of Hindus by the virtue of Article 25(2)(b).

Article 25(2) states that :

> Nothing in this Article shall affect the operation of any existing law or prevent the state from making any law.
>
> (a) ....
>
> (b) Providing for social welfare and reform or the throwing open of Hindu religious institutions of a public character to all classes and sections of Hindus.

Although, the temple entry movement was first started in the Princely State of Travancore when a member of assembly made a representation to the Maharaja's Government urging that steps to be taken to bring about such reform. But the Government refused to interfere on the ground that such action would be a violation of religious neutrality. Following this attempt, several other unsuccessful attempts were made in the following decade in Travancore, Bombay, Madras and also in the Legislative Assembly of Delhi.

A major breakthrough, as far as temple entry is concerned, came with the 1936 proclamation of the Maharaja of Travancore. The Maharaja issued a proclamation on Nov. 11, 1936.[46]

The proclamation was acclaimed by many prominent leaders as courageous and far reaching reform.[47]

Following temple entry proclaimation of Travancore, Several other legislative attempts to attain the same objectives were made.[48] The Constitution-makers were aware of the fact that a right which guarantees temple entry to Scheduled Castes and Scheduled Tribes must be inserted in the chapter of fundamental rights.

Public temple is a "place of public worship", and is defined as a place of public religious worship, or which is dedicated generally to, or used generally by persons profession any religion, or belonging to any religious denomination or any section thereof for performance of any religious service, or for

---

46. Profoundly convinced of the truth and validity of our religion, believing that it is based on divine guidance and on all comprehending toleration knowing that in its practice it was throughout the centuries adopted itself to the needs of changing time, solicitous than none of our Hindu subjects should by reason of birth or caste or community, be denied the consolation and solace of Hindu faith, we have decided and hereby declare ordain and command that, subject to such rules and conditions as may be laid down or imposed by us for preserving their proper atmosphere and maintaining their ritual and non-ritual and observances, there should henceforth be no restriction placed on any Hindu by birth or religion on entering or worshipping at temples controlled by us and our Government.
47. Donald, E. Smith, India as a secular state 1963 p. 240.
48. (a) Malabar Temple Entry Act (XX of 1938).
    (b) Madras temple Entry indemnity ordinance (I of 1939).
    (c) Bombay Hindu Temple Worship (Removal of Disabilities) Act, (XI of 1938).

offering prayers therein; and includes all lands and subsidiary shrines appurtenant or attached to such places." Article 25(2)(b) articulates ahead of public morality and a social reform measure when it requires a Hindu temple to be opened to the Hindus for unfettered public religious worship; and further provides that it should be thrown open to all classes and sections of co-religionist Hindus. The temple entry by the Scheduled Caste men on equal and non-discriminatory basis along with other persons professing the same religion or belonging to the same religious denomination is a head of social reform, and a law providing for this is deemed not to affect religous freedom of the caste Hindus, In term Clause (2)(b) of Article 25 confers no right of temple entry; but enables the state of provide for this as a social reform and welfare measure. Indeed no conferment of separate temple entry right is necessary as any opposition to temple entry by the Scheduled Caste men must be an enforcement of a disability arising out of Untouchability. Under article 17 "Untouchability" having been abolished, this is clearly an offence punishable in accordance with law. The prevention, resistance or opposition to temple entry too arising out of "Untouchability" is made an offence punishable in accordance with section 3 of the Untouchability Offence Act. Whosoever prevents any person from temple must be guilty not only of practicing Untouchability but also be instrumental to deny him freedom to prefer or practice religion equally along with persons professing the same religion or belonging to the same religions denomination as him. Nothing can justify any opposition by a caste Hindu to temple entry of the *harijans*. Even an argument founded on his own religious freedom worship in exclusion cannot be accepted. He cannot avail of his freedom of worship by denying similar freedom to his co-religionists including the untouchables who might profess the same religion and thus be his co-religionists. The freedom of a higher caste Hindu should be presumed to touch its farthest point at which the similar freedom of Untouchables begins. It is declared that right of religious freedom can not affect the operation of a social reform law, or for that matter, a temple entry law,[49] *Mahatma Gandhi* said,[50]

49. Venkataramana Devaru *v.* State of Mysore, AIR 1950 S.C. 255.
50. M.K. Gandhi, Removal of Untouchability, p. 130 (1951).

"Temple entry is one spritual act that would constitute the message of freedom to the Untouchables and assure them that they are not out castes before God."

The Constitutional direction intended to provide the legal articulations of the spiritual sentiments expressed by Mahatma Gandhi. The Part III of the Constitution of India remove the impediment of caste from the path to entry into temples. It confers legally enforceable right to temple entry upon the Scheduled Castes and Scheduled Tribes at par with other caste Hindus. Scheduled Castes and Scheduled Tribes are entitled equally to enter into a temple. Article 25(2)(b) protects the rights to enter into a temple for purpose of worship. This, however is not an unlimited right. Thus, for instance, no Hindu can claim, as part of the right protected by Article 25(2)(b), that a temple must be kept open for worship at all hours of the days and night, or that he should personally perform those religions services in a temple which the Acharyas or Pujaris alone are entitled to perform. The Courts have recognised the need to place some limitations on the right conferred by 25(2)(b).[51] A denominational temple is not required to change its essential denominational character. The case would be otherwise, if the Untouchables alone are required to stay out, or are prevented from entering into any part of the temple only on the ground of "Untouchability". In Varaha Devaswan temple case the accused person, al Saraswath Brahmins, joined in preventing certain harijans and also a man who was a theeya, a Scheduled Caste from entering into the nalambalam the inner portion for offering prayers of the "Shree-kovil". They were prosecuted under Sec. 3 of the Untouchability Offences Act, 1955. Thus, any act of entry prevention is an offence only if the temple is a place of public worship, and is open to other persons professing the same religion as the person prevented, or belongs to the same religions denomination as the latter.

The above discussed Articles clearly establish the fact that our Constitution-makers were totally aware of malpractices and unjust behaviour made to Scheduled Castes and Scheduled Tribes. So they, at the time of making the Constitution, kept all

51. P.S. Charya *v.* State of Madras, AIR 1956 Mad., p. 541.

the aspect of disparity, injustice and segregation in mind and made the provisions accordingly. They incorporated Articles 14, 15, 17, 23, 24 and 25(2)(b) in Part III, i.e. Fundamental Right of Constitution of India. All these Articles have helped to a great extent to eradicate the malpractices at micro and macro-level. So that these castes have started to feel self-respect and are coming back to the mainstream of national life.

(II) EUCATIONAL AND ECONOMIC SAFEGUARDS

The Constitution-makers recognised that punishing those who enforced various disabilities against Scheduled Castes and Scheduled Tribes and authorising the state to grant various rights to Scheduled Castes and Scheduled Tribes were not enough to eradicate the deep rooted and long established idea and practice to Untouchability from our country; unless the Scheduled Castes and Scheduled Tribes are made educationally and economically strong. Because the importance of education in the transformation of Scheduled Castes and Scheduled Tribes in a welfare state is well known. Eradication of illiteracy by teaching the Scheduled Castes and Scheduled Tribes constitutes the keynote of the problem of educational backwardness. Education is the birth right of every citizen. But a mere literacy drive can not serve the purpose. Education is not mere literacy; it should aim at the development of individual personality of the Scheduled Castes and Scheduled Tribes. It is only through education, the Scheduled Castes and Scheduled Tribes could be made to realise their rights and privileges and the role they have to play in the national life of the country. The future of these castes depends on their progress in the field of education. Education is the only means to place them along a clear-cut path to realise their aspiration of life. Apart from their other causes social, educational and economic conditions play a great part in the assesment of the poverty of the mass. Economic conditions have constituted the keynote of backwardness in India. Social evil and economic backwardness are so interrelated that they can not be treated in isolation. Because of this interrelation, economic amelioration of Scheduled Castes and Scheduled Tribes deserves special mention in any plan for the welfare of Scheduled Castes and Scheduled Tribes.

The Constitution-makers recognised the timidity of Scheduled Castes and Scheduled Tribes resulting from their low social status, lack of education and economic dependence upon higher castes. To make Scheduled Castes and Scheduled Tribes free from such timidy and inferiority, the Constitution-makers have also made various provisions under the Constitution, directed towards raising their educational and economic standard. To raise their educational and economic status and consequently to improve their self-image, so that they may assert their rights, the Constitution provides safeguards through different Articles. These Articles are as under:

(A) Article 15(4)	:	Special provision for the advancement of Scheduled Castes and Scheduled Tribes.
(B) Article 15(5)	:	Provision for Reservation of Scheduled Castes and Scheduled Tribes in private educational institutions
(C) Article 46	:	Promotion of Educational and Economic interest of Scheduled Castes and Scheduled Tribes.
(D) Article 275(1)	:	Grants from the Union to certain States.

(A) Article 15(4) : Special Provision for the Advancement of Scheduled Castes and Scheduled Tribes

Article 15(4) has special provision for socially and educationally backward classes including Scheduled Castes and Scheduled Tribes. This Article was not there in original Constitution (i.e. the Constitution which came into effect on 26th Jan. 1950). During the last fifteen months of the working of the Constitution certain difficulties have been brought to light by judicial decisions and pronouncements especially in regard to fundamental right. Soon after the enforcement of the Constitution a case reached the Supreme Court from the State of Madras regarding Article 15 of the Constitution. The case was *State of Madras* v. *Champakam Daroirajan*.[52] The facts of the case

52. AIR 1951, S.C., p. 226.

were as under. By virtue of certain orders issued prior of the coming into force of the Constitution, popularly known as "Communal G.O." the seats in Medical and Engineering colleges in the State of Madras were reserved and even after the advent of the Constitution, the G.O. was being acted upon which was challenged by Smt. Champakam as violative of the Fundamental rights guaranteed to her by Article 15(1) and Article 29(2) of the Constitution of India. The full bench of Madras High Court declared the said G.O. as void and unenforceable with the advent of the Constitution. The State of Madras took the matter before the Supreme Court and the special bench of seven judges of Supreme Court heard the matter and came to the unanimous conclusion that the allocation of seats in the manner aforesaid is violative of Articles 15(1) and 29(2). Soon after the said decision was rendered, the Parliament intervened and in exercise of its constituent power passed Constitution (first Amendment) Act, 1951 inserting clause (4) in Article 15 which reads :

> "Nothing in this Article or in clause (2) of Article 29 shall prevent the State from making any special provision for the advancement of any socially and educationally backward classes of citizens or for the Scheduled Castes and Scheduled Tribes".

It is pertinent to note that the Parliament which enacted the first amendment to the Constitution was in fact more or less the very same Constituent Assembly which had framed the Constitution. So, it may be inferred that the original Constituent Assembly too agreed for insertion of Article 15(4) which conspicuously and directly relates to Scheduled Castes and Scheduled Tribes. *Dr. Ambedkar* submitted that there is no Hindu who has not a caste and consequently, if reservation is made in favour of Scheduled Castes, Scheduled Tribes and Backward classes which are nothing else but a collection of certain castes, those who are excluded are persons who belong to certain castes. Therefore, in the circumstances of this country, it is impossible to avoid reservation without excluding some people who have got a caste.

Article 15(4) empowers the State that if the State thinks fit it can make some specific provisions for socially and educationally depressed classes (i.e. Scheduled Castes and Scheduled Tribes). If the State enacts any specific provisions for socially and educationally oppressed class; it is valid by the virtue of Article 15(4) and no one can challenge that provisions because of being discriminatory.

This question arose in the case of *Dr. Ram Krishna* v. *Union of India*,[53] in which the constitutionality of Sec. 3 of Scheduled Castes and Scheduled Tribes (Prevention of Atrocities) Act, 1989 was challanged. The Supreme Court held that the special act is protected under Article 15(4) of the Constitution, which provides for special provisions to be made for the benefit of the members of the Scheduled Castes and Scheduled Tribes. The court reasoned that Article 15(4) embodies the doctrine of "protective discrimination" and the word 'advancement' in clause 4 of Article 15 is not subject to any qualification or restriction. By no principle of interpretation it could be said that from the context it should be construed in restricted sense, as amounting to social and educational advancement.

The expression 'Special provision for the advancement' is an expression of very wide import and bring within its sweep each and every kind of advancement. This is because the Scheduled Castes and Scheduled Tribes occupy a special position in our Constitution. They have endured great ill-treatment as Untouchables for centuries, apart from their backwardness. It is in the fitness of things that every endeavour are to be made to correct this long standing and historical discrimination.

A special provision does not only mean to provide for education, agricultural programmes, schemes for training to pursue trade or business free education, free hostel facilities, advancement of loan and special procedure of recovery of loan, etc. It would also include an affirmative action by the state to make them stand on their own feet, to bring them into the mainstream of the national life, to live with dignity, self-respect and with their head held high. This is only possible if they are permitted to live in the society without fear or suppression from

53. AIR 1994, M.P., p. 143.

the upper caste or the top echelons of the society belonging to another caste, creed or religion.

The court concluded that Section 3 of the said Act enumerates offences against the Scheduled Castes and Scheduled Tribes by members of the Upper castes, by persons who are not members of Scheduled Castes and Scheduled Tribes. The provisions for offences enumerated in Section 3 of the Act is actually meant for the purpose of achieving the aforesaid object. The legislature has jurisdiction and authority to make such Act and the Act is protected under Article 15(4) of the Constitution and according to the scheme of the objectives of Constitution.

In furtherence of the power given to state by virtue of Article 15(4) the state can reserve seats for Scheduled Castes and Scheduled Tribes in different professional colleges. The States have made provisions regarding reservation of seats. At this point a question arises that what should be the limit for that special provision of reservation of seats.

In the case of *M.R. Balajee* v. *State of Mysore*[54] the Court dealt with this question for the first time. In this case the State Government by order reserved 68 percent of seats in the Engineering and Medical colleges and other Technical institutions for the educationally and socially backward classes and for the Scheduled Castes and Scheduled Tribes, and the rest of the 32 percent of the seats were left open for the merit pool. While striking down such reservation the court observed that it would be extremely unreasonable to assume that in enacting Article 15(4), the Parliament intended to provide that where the advancement of the backward classes or the Scheduled Castes and Scheduled Tribes was concerned, the Fundamental Right of the citizen constituting the rest of the society were to be completely and absolutely ignored. The court held that reservation shall be less than 50 percent.

In *Pradeep Jain* v. *Union of India*[55] the question of reservation of seats in Medical Colleges for the MBBS and Postgraduate medical course on the basis of domicile or residential qualification and institutional preference came up for

54. AIR 1963, S.C., p. 649.
55. AIR 1984, S.C., p. 1420.

consideration. The Court held that effort must always be made to select the best and meritorious students for medical and technical education by providing equal opportunity to all citizens. Further, it was held that the reservation should in no event exceed the outer limit of 70 percent. This decision was followed by *Nidamarti Mahesh Kumari* v. *State of Maharastra & Others*.[56] where region wise reservation of seats in Medical College for admission to MBBS Courses came up for consideration. The court made extensive reference to Pradeep Jain's case. The Court held that the reservation based on residential requirement or institutional preference should not exceed the outer limit of 70 percent of the total number of the open seats after taking into consideration other kind of reservation validly made and the remaining 30 percent of the seats should be made available for admission to students on all India basis irrespective of the State or the University from where they come.

Taking into consideration the principles of the above decisions it was held in *Deepak Sibal* v. *Punjab University*[57] that reservation shall not exceed 50 percent of the general seats after deducting the number of seats reserved for Scheduled Castes, Scheduled Tribes and other backward classes.

Here one more question regarding Article 15(4) arises that if any Scheduled Castes and Scheduled Tribes student comes in the merit of general student then whether he would get admission under reserved catagory or general catagory. This question was dealt with in *Ashish Meity* v. *State of West Bengal*,[58] and the opinion given by the Supreme Court was that any Scheduled Castes candidate when selected in open competition on the basis of their merits, they will not be counted nor any adjustment can be claimed against the quota reserved for the Scheduled Castes.

Further, it can be observed that for the benefit of Scheduled Castes and Scheduled Tribes the State Government can make provisions for the relaxation of marks in admission to professional institutions. In the case of *State of Madhya Pradesh* v.

56. AIR 1986, S.C., p. 1362.
57. AIR 1989, S.C., p. 913.
58. AIR 1995, Cal., p. 38.

Nivedita Jain[59] it has been held that relaxing the condition relating to the minimum qualifying marks for entry into medical college in the state respect to the Scheduled Castes and Scheduled Tribes candidates did not violate either Article 14 or Article 15 of the Constitution, since the relaxation could not be said to be unreasonable. It was pointed out that in the absence of any law to the contrary it is open to the state Government to relax the rule prescribing the minimum qualifying marks to ensure that the interest of these category of student was protected and they receive such state protection to the extent as is necessary for their upliftment.

In *Prakash Kiran* v. *State*[60] the Government reserved 125 seats for the Scheduled Castes and Scheduled Tribes candidates and in the selection test the number of the candidates was not available and the Government reduced the qualifying marks for the reserved quota from 40% to 35%. It was held that such reduction is not arbitrary and under the ambit of power given to State by Article 15(4) of Constitution of India.

Where some concession has been given to the Scheduled Castes and Scheduled Tribes in respect of marks to be obtained in the entrance test for admission to post graduate courses in medicine, it was held that such concession in marks is not violative of any provision. In the case of *Dr. Anupama Gupta* v. *Secretary Medical Health, Lucknow*.[61] The cut off merit for General candidate was 50% and the merit was reduced to 40% for the candidates who belongs to Scheduled Castes and Scheduled Tribes category. This reduction was held valid by Supreme Court.

Further, in the case of *Ajit Kumar Singh* v. *State of Bihar*,[62] where State of Bihar had provided minimum qualifying marks of 50% for general category and 40% for the reserved category but when the required number of students under the reserved categories were not available the qualifying marks was further reduced from 40% to 30%; it was held that reduction in eligibility criteria marginally is not improper. The court

59. AIR 1981 S.C., p. 2015.
60. AIR 1989 Pat., p. 238.
61. AIR 1992 All., p. 3.
62. AIR 1994 S.C., p. 2515.

observed that the state has been given the power under Article 15(4) of Constitution of India to strengthen that segment of society which is socially and educationally backward and specially the Scheduled Castes and Scheduled Tribes.

As it is clear that the legislature has the power to make laws subject to the provision of the Constitution under Article 162 of the Constitution of India. The executive power of the state extends to the matters with respect to which the legislature of the state has the power to make laws. If there is no legislation covering the field and the selection of the candidates for admission to medical college is proposed to be made then the State Government will undoubtedly be competent to pass executive order in this regard.

After repeal of the West Bengal Medical and Dental College (Regulation of Admission) Act, 1973; there being no legislation covering the field of admission to the medical colleges in the State, the order passed by the Government that 22% of the total seats would be reserved for Scheduled Castes students and 6% seats would be reserved for Scheduled Tribes in different teaching institutions where MBBS and BDS course are being prosecuted, are not liable to be struck down as the order finds support from Article 15(4) of the Constitution. The executive power of the State extends to make rules and adopts suitable policy to promote the cause and welfare of under privileged section of the community at large. Thus, the reservation of seats in the educational institutions in matter of admission by executive order is not unconstitutional.[63]

The member of Scheduled Castes and Scheduled Tribes have occupied a special position in our Constitution. They had to endure great ill-treatment for centuries and the reserved discrimination. Clause (4) of Article 15 is justified not only because of their backwardness but also on the ground that such discrimination is meant to right historic wrong.[64]

Clause (4) of Article 15 is a special provision in derogation of the Fundamental Right of the citizens provided under Article 15(1) of the Constitution, and clause (4) was inserted in Article 15 by I[st] Constitutional Amendment Act, 1951 to nullify the

63. Ashish Merity *v.* State of West Bengal, AIR 195 Cal., p. 38.
64. Ms. Mohini Jain *v.* State of Karanataka, AIR 1992 S.C., p. 1858.

effect of the decision of the Supreme Court of India. In *State of Madras* v. *Champakam Dorairajam,*[65] Article 15(4) authorised the State to make any special provision for the advancement of the backward classes of citizen, the object being to make special provision to carry out the Directive Principles enshrined under Article 46 of the Constitution. In terms of the provisions envisaged under clause (4) of Article 15 the State can adopt a policy in harmonious liaison with the Directive principles of the Constitution of India as enshrined in Article 46 of the Constitution and the State is competent to pass executive order to make such reservation. The State has discretion to fix the quota of seats by way of reservation for the Scheduled Castes and Scheduled Tribes candidate by an executive order also.

(B) Article 15(5) : Reservation of Seats for Scheduled Castes and Scheduled Tribes in Private Educational Institutions

The new clause 5 provides that :

"Nothing in this Article 15 or in sub-clause (g) of clause (1) of Article 19 shall prevent the State from making any special provisions, by law, for the advancement of any socially and educationally backward classes of citizens or for the Scheduled Castes or Scheduled Tribes in so far as such special provisions relate to their admission to educational institutions, including private educational institutions whether aided or unaided by the State, other than the minority educational institutions referred to in clause (1) of Article 30."

Article 15(5) has been added to our Constitution by 93rd Constitutional Amendment Act, 2005, by this amendment the legislature has nullified the effect of decisions given by our Hon'ble Supreme Court in cases namely *T.M. Pai Foundation* v. *State of Karnataka,*[66] *Islamic Academy* v. *State of Karnataka*[67] and *P.A. Inamdar* v. *State of Maharashtra.*[68] In T.M. Pai Foundation

65. AIR 1951 S.C., p. 226.
66. AIR 2003 S.C., p. 335.
67. AIR 2003 S.C., p. 3724.
68. AIR 2005 S.C., p. 3226.

and P.A. Inamdar case it has been held that the State can not make reservation of seats in admissions in privately run educational institutions. There the admissions can be done on the basis of common admission test conducted by the State or private institutions and on the basis of merit. In Islamic Academy case the Court held that the State can fix quota for admissions to these educational Institutions but it can not fix fee and also admissions can be done on the basis of common admission test and on the basis of merit. In P.A. Inamdar, however, the Court has overruled the Islamic Academy ruling to the effect that the "State could fix the quota for admissions to private professional educational institutions." This amendment enables the State to make provision for reservation for the above categories of classes in admission to private educational institutions. The Amendment, however, keeps the minority educational institutions out of its purview.

The clause emphatically declares the intention of the legislature to further and strengthen the cause of Social Justice, by way of educational upliftment of marginal section of society. The reservation provided under this clause shall provide for a quality education to the students of socially and educationally backward class and Scheduled Castes and Scheduled Tribes, because it is always presumed that the educational standard of private professional institution happens to be good. This clause is a step taken in good spirit and in right direction.

(C) Article 46 : Promotion of Educational and Economic Interest of Scheduled Castes and Scheduled Tribes

The next Article which provides for educational and economic safeguards to weaker section in general and Scheduled Castes and Scheduled Tribes in particular is mentioned under Article 46 of the Constitution. This Article is placed under the head of Directive Principle of State Policy which is incorporated under Part IV of the Indian Constitution.

Protection of the interests of the Scheduled Castes and Scheduled Tribes and the weaker sections of the society are first charge on the State which have to be adjusted with the interests of the community at large.[69] India's system of preferential

69. M.R. Balaji *v.* State of Mysore, AIR 1963 S.C., p. 663.

treatment for historically disadvantaged sections of the populations is unprecedented in scope and extent.[70] India has great social and cultural diversity. Often we take great pride in the country's cultural diversity while the cultural diversity on the one hand adds to the splendour of India, on the other hand adds to our shame and sorrow. The social and economic disparties are indeed despairingly vast. The Scheduled Castes, Scheduled Tribes and the other socially and educationally backward classes (i.e., the weaker sections of the people) have long journey to go. They need aid, facility, launching and propulsion. Their needs are their demands. The demands are matter of right and not of philanthropy. They ask for parity not for charity. The days of Dronacharya and Eklavya are over. They claim their Constitutional right to equality of status and of opportunity *vis-à-vis* socio-economic justice. Several bridges have to be erected, so that they may cross the Rubicon. Professional education and employment under the State are thought to be two such brigdes.[71] among the countries in the world, whether they are developed or developing; India can claim to have had more experience than any other country, with the system of public policy which sought to safeguard the interest of weaker sections through preferential treatment.[72]

So the Constitution of India provides for *inter-alia*, Justice—social, economic and political, and equality of opportunity and status to all its citizens including the weaker sections of the society who constitute the bulk of the population. These solemn pledges have been translated into some specific provisions of the Constitution; Part III of the Constitution guarantees certain Fundamental Rights to the individual which are in general negative in character but envisages some positive rights also. For example, the right to equality in its various facets require affirmative actions on the part of State for the benefit of the socially and educationally backward classes which includes Scheduled Castes and Scheduled Tribes primarily is a

70. Marc Galanter, Competing Equalities : Law and the Backwardness in India, 1984, p. 1.
71. K. C. Vasanth Kumar *v.* State of Karnataka, AIR 1985 S.C., p. 1495.
72. B.A.V. Sharma, Reservation Policy in India, 1982, p. 1.

representation of egalitarian concept.[73] The same concept has been expressed with greater vigour and clarity in the Directive Principles of State Policy in Part IV of the Constitution of India. The directives require the State, *inter alia,* to promote the welfare of the people by securing and protecting a social order in which justice—social, economic and political should confirm in all the institutions of national life.[74] If further enjoins the State that it should in particular, strive to minimise the inequalities in income, and endeavour to eliminate inequalities in status, facilities and opportunities, not only amongst individuals but also amongst groups of people residing in different areas or engaged in different vocation.[75] Article 46 specifically provides:

> "The State shall promote with special care the educational and economic interests of the weaker sections of the people, and in particular, of the Scheduled Castes and Scheduled Tribes, and shall protect them from Social injustice and all forms of exploitation."

The term "weaker section" though finds place in Article 46, yet it has not been defined any where in the Constitution. An attempt was made in the Constituent Assembly to define it but was given up. Members of the Scheduled Castes and Scheduled Tribes have ordinarily been accepted as belonging to the weaker sections.[76]

The obvious purpose of Article 46 is to promote the welfare of those who are socially handicapped in the peculiar Indian context.[77] The expression "educational and economic interests was deliberately used to emphasize that the educational and economic interests and their advancement go hand in hand. Without education the economic assistance may not be really fruitful or effective and that lack of education was

73. Articles 14, 15(1), 15(2), 15(4), 16(4) and 335.
74. Article 38(1).
75. Article 38(2): The clause is inserted by the Constitution (44th Amendment) Act, 1978.
76. Shanti Star Builders *v.* Narayan K. Totame, 1990, SCC(1), p. 520.
77. S.K. Agrawal, Content of Directive Principles in the Indian Constituton.

primarily responsible for the perpetuation of social and economic injustices against them.[78] The phrase "Shall protect them from social injustice and all forms of exploitation" is both comprehensive and pertinent.

Thus the Directive Principles embody a commitment which was imposed by the Constitution-makers on the State to bring about socio-economic regeneration of the teeming millions who steeped in poverty, ignorance and social backwardness. They incorporate a pledge to the coming generations of what the State would strive to usher in.[79]

Article 46 constitutes only a Directive Principle unenforceable by the judiciary and the Directive Principles are nothing more than mere directions for the States to undertake particular lines of action for the benefit of weaker sections of society.[80] They serve as nothing more than a pointer to the humanitarian ideal of the Constitution. This fact was stressed by *Dr. Ambedker* when he interpreted.

"Directive Principles are nothing but obligations imposed by the Constitution upon the various Governments in the country, if the Government failed to carry them out, no one could ask for specific performance."[81]

Further, the State could only discharge them through legislation. It implies that the State, in regard to these matters, has the implied power to make a law.

In *Sukhvindra Kaur* v. *State of Himachal Pradesh*[82] the question before the Himachal Pradesh High Court was to determine the reasonability of reservation of seats in Himachal Pradesh medical college. The Court while making reference to Article 46 observed: "The Government has got the right to make reservation for the betterment and amelioration of weaker and economically backward sections of the community and to

78. State of Kerala *v.* Jacob Mathew, AIR 1964 Ker., p. 313.
79. Keshwanand Bharti *v.* State of Kerala, AIR 1973 SC, p. 1461.
80. Article 37. "The provisions contained in this part shall not be enforceable by any court, but the principles therein laid down are nevertheless fundamental in the governance of the country and it shall be the duty of the State to apply these principles in making laws."
81. During Ist Constitutional Amendment, 1951.
82. AIR 1974 H.P., p. 465.

implement the Directive Principle of State Policy as contained in Article 46 of the Constitution."

In *State of Kerala* v. *N.M. Thomas,*[83] Rule 13-AA of the Kerala state subordinate services rules, 1958, which exempted any member of Scheduled Caste or Scheduled Tribe who is already in service for a specified period, from passing the test for promotion, was in question. Upholding the validity of the rule, the Supreme Court held that it was permissible to give preferential treatment to Scheduled Castes or Scheduled Tribes under Article 16(1) outside Article 16(4). While making reference to Article 46 the court observed that giving preference to an unrepresented backward community in matters of public employment is perfectly valid and would not contravene Articles 14, 16(1) and 16(2). The court pointed out that the Article 16(4) removed every doubt in this respect in the words of Ray, C.J. :

> "The classification of employees belonging to Scheduled Castes or Scheduled Tribes for allowing them an extended period of two years for passing the test for promotion is just and reasonable classification having a rational nexus to the object of providing equal opportunity for all citizens in matter relating to employment or appointment to public office."[84]

It is submitted that the decision of the court in Thomos case reflects the new judicial trend towards the legitimation of the governmental initiatives to level up the social, educational and economic status of the disadvantaged and the oppressed section of the society. This ruling would give a free hand to the State to exhaust all possible ways to raise the social standard of the backward groups who because of their lack of resources, attainments and background can not successfully compete with more advanced sections of the population.

In *Madhaw Singh* v. *State of Bihar,*[85] section 12 of the Bihar Money Lender's Act, 1975 was questioned. The section imposed

83. AIR 1976 S.C., p. 490.
84. State of Kerala *v.* N.M. Thomas, AIR 1976 S.C., p. 490.
85. AIR 1985 Pat., p. 72.

certain restrictions on the rights of money lenders in regard to usufructuary mortgages and their redemption. Upholding the provisions reasonable and in public interest the Patna High Court observed, "Agricultural debtor being weaker section of the society, section 12 must be considered to be in furtherance of the Directive Principle contained in Article 46, namely, protecting them from social injustice and all forms of exploitation".

This shows that the action of the State which remains within the scope of a particular directive would always be upheld by the court in the public interest. But if such an action goes beyond the scope of the relevant directive the same is likely to be struck down, as arbitrary.

In *re Krishnadas Mondal*,[86] which is an interesting case on the point, the question related to the payment of grants to students belonging to Scheduled Castes and Scheduled Tribes who resided in the hostels. The grant in question was restricted to students whose parents income was below Rs. 3600 per annum. This was challenged as contravening the provision of Article 46 of the Constitution and also as an unreasonable restriction. Referring the fundamental character of the Directive Principles contained in Article 37, the court found that the state which implemented Article 46 was reasonable and in public Interest.

These cases make it ample clear that the judiciary has been quite sensitive to the interests of the weaker sections of the society.

(D) Article 275(1) : Grants from the Union to Certain States

Article 275 deals with grants given to States for implementation of welfare schemes to better the conditions of Scheduled Tribes. It provides:

(1) Such sums as Parliament may by law provide shall be charged on the consolidated fund of India in each year as grants-in-aid of the revenues of such States as Parliament may determine to be in need of assistance,

86. AIR 1985 S.C., p. 430.

> and different sums may be fixed for different States : Provided that there shall be paid out of the consolidated fund of India as grants-in-aid of the revenues of a State such capital and recurring sums as may be necessary to enable that State to meet the costs of such schemes of development as may be under taken by the State with the approval of the Government of India for the purpose of promoting the welfare of the Scheduled Tribes in that State or raising the level of administration of the Scheduled areas therein to that of the administration of the rest of the areas of that State.

The grants made under this Article are of a discriminatory nature, but, since they are made for purpose of launching welfare schemes for the benefits of Scheduled Tribes and Scheduled Areas and aim at the correction of inter-state financial disparities, they can not be considered unconstitutional but these special provisions should be treated as supplementary benefits to amplify the general welfare schemes of the States, for the advancement of Scheduled Tribes and the development of Scheduled Areas.

In view of the change in emphasis in the conditions governing the grants made under Article 275, particularly during the third plan, which laid special emphasis on population, the Scheduled Areas Commission has suggested the criteria for allocating grants as follows:

(a) Population;
(b) Level of development reached by the State in welfare activity for the Scheduled Tribes and in raising the level of administration in the Scheduled Areas at the beginning of each plan period; and
(c) Financial position of the State along with its willingness to contribute its quota.[87]

Besides, the commission made a special reference to the problem of the border States. In view of frequent foreign

87. Report of the Scheduled Areas and Scheduled Tribes Commission, 1961-62, p. 78.

aggressions, the border states experience a severe dislocation of their economy. Hence, these border States should be given greater assistance to counter balance the effects of dislocation. After a detailed study of the problem of grant-in-aid, considering the views of the State Governments, the commission commented on Article 275 as follow :

> The Article, thus, does not contain sufficient safeguards for the proper expenditure of the funds given to the States, as provided in the Constitutions of the United States, United Kingdom, Canada, etc. beyond allocating funds to the States, the Union Government has no adequate machinery for ensuring that the funds given have been properly spent and for the purposes intended. I recommend that the Department to be set-up at the centre in the Ministry of Home Affairs should contain an accounts cell exclusively for the purpose of maintaining accounts of the funds disbursed to the State Governments, Union territories and non-official organisations.[88]

The above discussed Articles (i.e., 15(4), 15(5), 46 and 275(1)) make one thing clear that our Constitution-makers not only wanted to eradicate the social evils but they were willing for all round upliftment of Scheduled Castes and Scheduled Tribes. Keeping this objective in mind our Constitution-makers provided for Article 15(4) in Part III of Constitution of India which is the basic structure of the Constitution.[89] Besides this in Part IV of Constitution which relates to Directive Principles of State Policy it is supposed that the State would try to uplift the educational and economic condition of Scheduled Castes and Scheduled Tribes through legislation. Under Article 275(1) there is a provision for issuing grant by Union to those States who have the population of Scheduled Tribes or which has been declared as Scheduled Areas.

These are provisions which try to equate the Scheduled Castes and Scheduled Tribes with rest of society, so that this

---

88. Report of the Scheduled Areas and Scheduled Tribes Commission, 1961-62, pp. 81-82.
89. Keshwanand Bharti *v.* State of Kerala, AIR 1973 SC 1461.

segment of society could be brought back in the main stream of national life.

(III) SERVICE SAFEGUARDS

It is an obvious fact that the Constitution authorises preferences for the Scheduled Castes and Scheduled Tribes. It is only because of perpetration of social and economic injustices by so-called higher caste on the lower castes that the Constitution thought it necessary "to accord favoured treatement to the lower caste who were at the bottom of the scale of social values and who were afflicted by social and economic disabilities".[90]

The Constitutional policy of compensatory discrimination was based upon the notion that certain groups in India were inherently unequal and were victims of social discrimination and thus required satisfaction and compensation. They believed that the meaning of equality based upon individual achievement was too hypocritical in a caste-ridden society where group identification had historically been used for the purposes of discrimination and separation.[91] To them, there was nothing; paradoxical in the idea that individual claims of equality might sometimes clash with an otherwise desirable social goal, including a policy of making the community equal as a whole.[92] They believed that equality was furthered by favouring both competence and need-based claims.[93] Even if quotas involved social castes, imposed unfair burdens on those excluded or affected standard or meritocracy, the benefits accruing to the society would in the long-run outweigh the costs, raise self-respect and self-development of the victims of social discrimination who lacked in resources, opportunities, background and incentive to achieve success on the terms of formal equality. Undue insistence on uniform standard would have perpetuated inequality.

90. C.M. Arumugam *v.* S. Rajgopal, AIR 1976 SC 939.
91. J.N. Hutton, Caste in India.
92. M.R. Balaji *v.* State of Mysore, AIR 1963 SC 649.
93. State of Kerala *v.* N.M. Thomas, AIR 1976 SC, pp. 490, 515, 535.

Some impairment of efficiency and standards was seen as inherent in the very idea of providing service safeguards to providing Scheduled Castes and Scheduled Tribes. The policy of providing service safeguards to Scheduled Castes and Scheduled Tribes were, however, required to strike a balance between competing claims of equalities. Since the members of the Scheduled Castes and Scheduled Tribes were too weak or crippled to take initiative, it was the State which had to make remedial measures to correct the society's inbuilt discrimination against certain groups trapped in the cycle of deprivation due to structural reasons with worst possible life chances.

Dr. Ambedkar argued before the Constituent Assembly that in our country there are castes but the castes are anti-national. In the first place because they bring out separation in social life. They are anti-national because they generate jealousy and antipathy between the Caste and Class. He suggested that the difficulty must be overcome if we wish to become a nation in reality for fraternity can be a fact only when there is a nation. Without fraternity, equality and liberty will be no deeper than the coats of paint.[94] While explaining the scope and significance of reservation Dr. Ambedkar observed: "The seats to be reserved, if the reservation is to be consistent with Article 16 of the Constitution must be confined to minority seats" and he suggested that reservation of 30% seats would be adequate and consistent.

Keeping all these aspects in mind our Constitution-makers have provided for following safeguards for Scheduled Castes and Scheduled Tribes.

- **(A) Article 16(4)** : Reservation of Posts in Public Employnments.
- **(B) Article 335** : Claims of Scheduled Castes and Scheduled Tribes to services and post.

(A) Article 16(4) : Reservation of Post in Public Employments

This aspect is to be dealt with under Article 16. Artcle 16(1)

94. See C.A.D., Vol. 12, p. 980.

represents one particular aspect of the guarantee of the general principle of equality enshrined in Article 14.[95] It ensure to all citizens' equality of opportunity in matters relating to employment in State services. Unlike Article 14 which is negative in form, Article 16(1) lays emphasis on the affirmative action of the State. According to *J. Mathew* in *State of Kerala* v. *N.M. Thomas* case,[96] "equality of opportunity as dealt with in Article 16(1) means something more than mere formal equality. It means differential treatment of persons who are unequal."

Clause (4) of Article 16 enables the State to make reservation in appointments or posts in favour of any under-represented as well as unrepresented backward classes of citizens Article 16(4) runs as follows:

> "Nothing in this article shall prevent the State from making any provision for the reservation of appointments or posts in favour of any backward class of citizens, which in the opinion of the State, is not adequately represented in the services under the State."

Article 16(4) empowers the State to make special provision for the reservation of appointments of post in favour of any backward class of citizens which in the opinion of the State are not adequately represented in the services under the State. Thus, Article 16(4) applies only if two condition are satisfied.

1. The classes of citizens is backward, and
2. The said class is not adequately represented in the services of the State. Though the second test can not be the sole criterion.[97]

The expression Backward class of citizens has not been defined in the Constitution and this has been the most difficult question before the Hon'ble Supreme Court. In the matter of *General Manager Southern Railway* v. *Rangachari*[98] the Supreme

95. State of Kerala *v.* N.M. Thomas, AIR 1976 SC, p. 490.
96. *Ibid.*, p. 343 (per Methew) J.
97. M.R. Balaji *v.* State of Mysore, AIR 1963 SC, 649.
98. AIR 1962 SC. 649.

Court has observed that the expression "Backward class of citizens" as used in Article 16(4) has a wider conotation. This expression affirmatively includes Scheduled Castes and Scheduled Tribes because these class themselves are most backward class of citizen.

Again in *Indira Sawhney* v. *Union of India*[99] the significance of this expression was considered by the specially constituted bench of 9 judges of the Supreme Court and several shades of opinion were expressed before the court. Here it seems necessary to mention the substance of the argument emerging from the submission made before the Supreme Court.

Shri N.A. Palkhiwala argued that a secular, unified and casteless society is the basic feature of the Constitution and caste is a prohibited ground of distinction under the Constitution and should be erased altogether from the Indian society. He argued that the caste can never be the basis for determining backward classes referred in Article 16(4) of the Constitution. The report of the Mandal Commission has treated the backward classes as synonymous with the backward castes and has proceeded to identify backward classes solely and exclusively on the basis of caste, ignoring all other considerations including poverty. It has indeed invented castes for non-Hindus where none exists and the report has divided the nation into two sections which will spell disaster to the unity and integrity of the nation. It is not permissible to start with castes to determine whether a caste is backward class, argued *Shri K.K. Venugopal* for the petitioner in Mandal Commission case. He relied upon the provision in clause (2) of Art. 38[100] and Art. 46[101] to say that the objective is

---

99. AIR 1993 SC. 477.
100. Article 38: State to secure a social order for the promotion of welfare of the people: (1) The state shall strive to promote the welfare of the people by securing and protecting as effectively as it may a social order in which justice, social, economic and political, shall inform all the institutions of the national life.

     (2) The State shall, in particular, strive to minimize the inequalities in income, and endeavour to eliminate inequalities in status, facilities and opportunities, not only amongst individuals but also amongst groups of people residing in different areas or engaged in different vocations.
101. Article 46: Promotion of educational and economic interests of Scheduled Castes and Scheduled Tribes and other weaker sections.

to minimize inequalities in income not only amongst the individuals but also amongst the group of persons and to help the weaker section of the society. The economic criterion is an important one and must be applied in determining backward classes and also for excluding those sections or identified groups who may be for the sake of convenience be referred to as the 'creamy layer'. Since castes do not exists amongst Muslims, Christians and Sikhs, caste cannot be the basis of identification. He argued that the expression "backward class of citizens in Article 16(4) cannot be construed as backward caste. Backwardness may be social and educational and may also be economic and the authority entrusted with the task must first settle the criteria or the indicators for determining backward classes and then it must apply the said criteria to each and every group in the country.

A secular and socialists society can never countenance identification of backward classes on the basis of caste which would only perpetuate and accentuate caste difference and generate antagonism and antipathy between caste.

The only basis for identification of backward classes should be occupation-*cum*-means which was done in the State of Karnataka at a particular stage which aspect is dealt with and approved by this court in *Chitralekha.* v. *State of Mysore*[102] was the argument advanced by *Shri P.P Rao* appearing for the Supreme Court bar association and also *Smt. Shyamala Pappu.*

Shri Ram Jethamalani appearing for the State of Bihar argued that the provision for reservation is really a programme of historical compensation and poverty is not a necessary criterion of backwardness; it is, in fact, irrelevant. According to him, backward castes in Art. 16(4) meant and means only the members of Sudra caste which is located between the three upper caste (Brahmins, Kshatriyas and Vaishyas) and the outcastes (Panchamas) referred to as Scheduled Castes. Article 16(4) was conceived only for these "middle caste", i.e

---

The State shall promote with special care the educational and economic interest of the weaker sections of the people, and in particular, of the Scheduled Castes and Scheduled Tribes, and shall protect them from social injustice and all forms of exploitation.

102. AIR 1964 SC 1823.

the caste categorised as Sudras in the caste system and for none else. These backward castes have suffered centuries of discrimination and disadvantage, leading to their backwardness, The expression "backward classes" does not refer to any current characteristic of a backward caste save and expect paucity or inadequacies of representation in the apparatus of the Government. The provision for reservation is really a programme of historical compensation and it is neither a measure of economic reform nor a poverty alleviation programme. It is for the Government to determine who are the backward classes and not a matter for the court to decide.

Dr. Rajiv Dhawan, learned counsel appearing for Srinarayana Dharma Paripalana Yogam submitted that Article 16(4) and Article 15(4) occupy different fields and serve different purposes. Article 16(4) enables the State to undertake schemes of positive discrimination. Accordingly, the class of intended beneficiaries under both the clauses are different. The social and educational backwardness which is the basis of identifying backwardness under Article 15(4) is only partly true in the case of 'backward class of citizens' in Article 16(4). The expression "any backward class of citizens" occurring in Article 16(4) must be understood in the light of the purpose of the said clause viz. empowerment of those group and classes which have been kept out of the administration, classes which have suffered historic disabilities arising from discrimination or disadvantage or both and who must now be provided entry into the administrative apparatus. In the light of the fact that the Scheduled Castes and Scheduled Tribes were also intended to be beneficiaries of Article 16(4) there is no reason why caste cannot be an exclusive criteria for determining beneficiaries under Article 16(4).

The Communist Party of India represented by *Sri R.K Garg* as an intervener, submitted that caste + poverty + location + residence should be the basis for identification and not mere caste.

For the State of Madras *Sri Siva Subramanium* supported the entire Mandal Commission Report and according to him backward classes must be identified only on the basis of caste and that no economic criteria should be adopted for the said purpose. He referred to the history of reservation in the State of

Tamilnadu prior to independence and how it has been working there successfully and peacefully over the last several decades. Similarly, *Sri P.S. Poti* appearing for the State of Kerala supported the identification of backward classes solely and exclusively on the basis of caste. He submitted that caste system is scientifically organised in Kerala and therefore, furnishes a perfectly scientific basis for identification of backward classes.

The all India Federation of Backward Classes, Scheduled Castes and Scheduled Tribes and Religious Minorities submitted that caste should be the sole criteria for determining backwardness.

It is important to note the submission made by *Sri K. Parasaran* on behalf of the Union of India. His submission is summerised as follows:

(1) The reservation provided for by clause (4) of Article 16 is not in favour of backward citizens, but in favour of backward class of citizens. What is required to be identified is backward class of citizens and not citizens who can be classified as backward. The homogeneous groups based on religion, race, caste, place of birth, etc., can form a class of citizens and if that class is backward there can be a reservation in favour of that class of citizens.

(2) Caste is a relevant consideration and it can even be the dominant consideration. Indeed, most of the lists prepared by the States are prepared with reference to and on the basis of caste. They have been upheld by the Supreme Court.

(3) Article 16(2) prohibits discrimination only on any or all the grounds mentioned therein. A provision for protective discrimination on any of the said grounds coupled with other relevant grounds would not fall within the prohibition of clause (2). In other word, if the reservation is made in favour of backward class of citizens the bar contained in clause (2) is not attracted even if backward class of citizens are identified with reference to caste. The reason being that the reservation is not made in favour of caste simpliciter but on the ground that they are backward castes

which are not adequately represented in the services of the State.

(4) Whether a class is backward or not and whether it is adequately represented in the service of the State or not are questions of fact and are within the domain of the executive decision. The criteria of backwardness evolved by Mandal Commission is perfectly proper and unobjectionable.

The Supreme Court in Mandal Commission case traversed the entire field relating to the problem starting from Balaji. In *M.R. Balaji* v. *State of Mysore*[103] the Constitution bench while discussing the meaning of the expression, the importance of the caste in the Hindu social structure in the context of social backwardness observed that while dealing with the question as to whether any class of citizen is socially backward or not, it may not be irrelevant to consider the caste of said group of citizens. The court further observed that though the caste of the group citizen may be relevant, its importance should not be exaggerated. If the classification of backward classes of citizens was based solely on the caste of the citizens, it may not always be logical and may perhaps contain the vice of perpetuating the caste themselves. Besides, if the caste of the group of citizens was made the sole basis for determining the social backwardness of the said group, the test would inevitably break down in relation to any section of Indian society which do not recognize caste in the conventional sense known to the Hindu society. The court finally observed that though caste in relation to the Hindus may be a relevant factor for consideration in determining social backwardness of groups or class of citizens, it cannot be made the sole or the dominant test in that behalf.

It is to be noted that Balaji was dealing with Article 15(4) of the Constitution which clause contains the qualifying word "socially and educationally" preceding the expression "Backward classes of citizens".

Accordingly, it was held that the backwardness contemplated by Article 15(4) is both social and educational. Though clause (4) of Art. 16 did not contain any such qualifying

103. AIR 1963 SC 649.

words, yet they came to be read in it and in *Janki Prasad* v. *State of Jammu & Kashmir*,[104] it was observed that it was well-settled that the expression backward classes of citizens in Article 16(4) means the same thing as the expression any socially and educationally backward class of citizens in Article 15(4). Then Constitution bench in *Minor P. Rajendra* v. *State of Madras*[105] held that a caste is a class of citizens and if the caste as a whole is socially and educationally backward reservation can be made in favour of such a caste on the ground that it is a socially and educationally backward class of citizens within the meaning of Article 15(4).

Then in *K.C. Vasant kumar* v. *State of Karanataka*,[106] the five Judges constituting the Constitution bench expressed different opinion and the opinion explained the integral connection between caste, occupation poverty and social backwardness. They recognized that in the Indian context, lower caste are and ought to be treated as backward classes.

The Supreme Court in Mandal Commission case after referring to the above decisions also examined how the words "caste" and "class" were understood in the pre-Constitution India and observed that in pre-independence India, the expression class and caste were used interchangeably and that caste was understood as an enclosed class. The court then referred to the Constituent Assembly Debates with a view to ascertain the intention of the use of the words "backwards class of citizen". The reference was also made in this context to the speech of *Dr. Ambedkar* in the Parliament at the time the First Amendment to the Constitution was being enacted. Dr. Ambedkar as the Minister of Law was piloting the bill and he said the "backward classes are nothing else but a collection of certain castes". The Court then explained why the Constitution could not have used the expression "castes" or "caste" in Article 16(4) and why the word class was the natural choice in the context. The Constitution was meant for the entire country and for all time to come. The system of caste does not exist among non-Hindu. The Constitution is supposed to be a

104. AIR 1973 SC 930.
105. AIR 1968 SC 1012.
106. AIR 1985 SC 1495.

permanent document expected to last for several centuries. It must surely have been envisaged that in future many classes may spring-up answering the test of backwardness, requiring the protection of Article 16(4) of the Constitution. It therefore follows that from the use of the word "class" in Article 16(4), it can not be concluded either that "class" is antithetical to "caste" or that a caste cannot be a class or that a caste as such can never be taken as a backward class of citizens. The Court concluded that caste is nothing but a social class a socially homogeneous class. It is also an occupational grouping, with this difference that its membership is hereditary but involuntary. The court endorsed the observation of Dr. Ambedkar that a caste is an enclosed class and it was mainly these classes the Constituent Assembly had in mind though not exclusively while enacting Article 16(4). Lowly occupation results not only in low social position but also in poverty; it generates poverty 'caste occupation poverty' cycle is thus an ever present reality. All the decisions since Balaji speak of this "caste occupation poverty" nexus. The language and emphasis may vary but the theme remains the same.

In the previous paragraph the meaning of expression Backward classes of citizens has been elaborated. There are certain guidelines which have been laid down by Supreme Court regarding the identification of Backward classes of citizens. The identification of backward classes of citizens vary from State to State, region to region and from rural to urban areas. What should be the basis for identification of backward classes of citizens was considered by the Supreme Court in *Mandal Commission case*[107] and the court answered the issue in broad general terms necessarily dealing with the generalities of the situation and not with the problems or issue of a peripheral nature which are peculiar to a particular State, district or region. While identifying backward class, one can very well begin with caste, which represent explicit identifiable social class grouping, more particularly when Article 16(4) seeks to ameliorate social backwardness and when caste, occupation, poverty and social backwardness are so closely interline in our society and more particularly, when Article 16(4) speaks of class protection and not individual protection.

107. Indira Sawhney *v.* Union of India, AIR 1993 SC 477.

The court, further, reasoned that identification cannot be done with reference to caste alone as besides caste, there may be other communities, groups, classes and denominations which may qualify as backward classes of citizens. For instance, in a particular State Muslim community as a whole may be found socially backward (as in the State of Karnataka and Kerala). Similarly, certain sections and denominations amongst Christians in Kerala who are included among backward communities notified in the former princely State of Travancore as far back as in 1935 may also be surveyed and so on and so forth.

The court, by majority, held that an authority entrusted with the task of identifying backward class may well start with the caste and then apply the criteria of backwardness evolved by it to that caste and determine whether it qualifies as a backward class or not and if it does qualify than what emerges is a backward class. However, the court qualified the term caste used in this context and held that the concept of 'caste' in this behalf is not confined to caste among Hindus. It extends to castes. Whereever they obtained as a fact, irrespective of religious sanction for such practice. Having exhausted the castes or simultaneously with it, the authority may take up for consideration other occupational groups, committee and classes. For example, it may take up Muslim community (after excluding the sections which have already been considered) and find out whether it can be characterised as backward class in that state or region. Similarly, Christians may also be considered. The effort should be made to consider all the available groups, sections and classes of society in whichever order one proceeds. Since caste represents an existing, identifiable, social group spread over an overwhelming majority of the country's population, one may well begin with caste, and then go to other groups, sections or classes.

If a commission or authority begins its process of identification with caste (among Hindus) and occupational groupings among others, it cannot by that reason alone be said to be unconstitutional or illegal. If the real object is to identify backwardness, and if such backwardness is found in a caste, it can be treated as backward; if it is found in other groups, sections or classes, they too can be treated as backward.

Though Article 16(4) does not contain the qualifying words "socially and educationally" preceding the words "backward classes of citizens" but the same meaning can be attached to them. This aspect of the matter was considered in *M.R. Balajee* v. *State of Mysore*[108] whether the backwardness is both social and educational backwardness. Since Balaji it was assumed that the backward class of citizens contemplated in Article 16(4) is the same as the socially and educationally backward classes mentioned in Article 15(4).

The Supreme Court in *Janki Prasad* v. *State of Jammu & Kashmir*[109] speaking for the Constitutional bench observed that Article 15(4) speaks about socially and educationally backward classes of citizens. However, it is now settled that the expression "backward classes of citizens" in Article 16(4) means the same things as the expression "socially and educationally backward classes of citizens" in Article 15(4). In order to qualify for being called a 'backward classes of citizens' one must be member of socially and educationally backward of a class which is material for the purpose of both Articles 15(4) and 16(4).

The Supreme Court in *Mandal Commission case*[110] observed that this proposition of law gained currency without any basis. The Supreme Court observed that said clause (4) of Article 16 does not contain the qualifying words "socially and educationally" as does clause (4) of Article 15. Article 340 does employ the expression 'socially and educationally backward classes' yet that expression does not find place in Article 16(4). The reason was obvious. 'Backward classes of citizens' in Article 16(4) takes in Scheduled caste, Scheduled Tribes and all other backward classes of citizens including Socially and educationally backward classes. Thus, certain classes which may not qualify for Article 15(4) may qualify for Article 16(4) as backward classes of citizens. The court further observed that Article 340 does not expressly refer to services or to reservations in services under the State, though it may be that the commission appointed thereunder may recommend reservation in appointments and posts in the services of the State as one of

108. AIR 1963 SC 649.
109. AIR 1973 SC 930.
110. AIR 1993 SC 477.

the step for removing the difficulties under which Socially and Educationally Backward Classes are labouring and for improving their conditions. Thus, Socially and Educationally Backward Classes referred to in Article 340 is only one of the categories for whom Article 16(4) was enacted; Article 16(4) applies to a much larger class than the one contemplated by Article 340.

The Court concluded that it would not be correct to say that 'backward classes of citizens' in Article 16(4) are the same as the Socially and Educationally backward classes in Article 15(4) In interpreting so it would mean and imply puting a limitation into beneficial provision like Article 16(4). The backwardness contemplated by Article 16(4) is mainly social backwardness and it would not be correct to say that backwardness under Article 16(4) should be both social and educational and Scheduled Caste and Scheduled Tribes are undoubtedly backward for the purpose of Article 16(4).

The backward classes of citizens contemplated by Article 16(4) is not limited to the socially and educationally backward classes referred to in Article 15(4) and Article 340 and the test or requirement of social and educational backwardness cannot be applied to Scheduled Castes and Scheduled Tribes who undoubtedly fall within the expression "backward classes of citizens". The Supreme Court in *Mandal Commission case*[111] further held that it is not necessary for a class to be designated as backward class that it should be situated similarly to the Scheduled Caste and Scheduled Tribe.

In *M.R. Balaji* v. *State of Mysore*[112] the Supreme Court held that the backward classes for whose improvement special provision is contemplated by Article 15(4) are in the matter of backwardness as to the Scheduled Castes and Scheduled Tribes. The correctness of the said decision was questioned in Mandal Commission Case. The Supreme Court in the latter case had drawn reference to observation of *Chinnappa Readdy, J.* in *K.C. Vasant Kumar* v. *State of Karnataka*[113] where the learned judge was pleased to observe that there is no reason to think that Balaji laid

111. AIR 1993 SC 477.
112. AIR 1963 SC 649.
113. AIR 1985 SC 1495.

down the proposition that the socially backward classes were those class of people, whose condition of life were very nearly the same as those of the Scheduled Castes and Scheduled Tribes. There is no point in attempting to determine the social backwardness of other classes by applying the test of nearness to the conditions of existence of the Scheduled Castes. Such a test would practically nullify the provision for reservation for socially and educationally backward classes other than Scheduled Caste and Scheduled Tribes.

The Supreme Court in *Mandal Commission Case*[114] asserted that there is no warrant to import any such *a-priori* notions into the concept of other backward classes. The court found no reason to qualify or restrict the meaning of the expression "backward classes of citizens" by saying that it meant those other backward classes who are situated similarly to the Scheduled Castes and Scheduled Tribes. Artcile 16(4) does not expressly refer to the Scheduled Castes or Scheduled Tribes and so there is no reason why their backwardness should be treated as a standard fot the backwardness for all those claiming its protection.

It is not possible or advisable for the court to lay down any such procedure or method, observed the Supreme Court, but it must be left to the authority appointed to identify and the authority may adopt such method or procedure as it thinks convenient and so long as its survey the entire population no objection can be taken to it. The relevancy of the criteria evolved by *Mandal Commission*[115] has not been questioned by either of the parties before the court and the court found no fault with the criteria evolved by the Mandal Commission.

The Supreme Court while considering the scope of Article 16(4) of the Constitution in the context as to whether the same is exhaustive of the topic of reservations in favour of the backward classes, in *Mandal Commission case*,[116] also referred to the earlier decision of the court in *State of Kerala* v. *N.M. Thomas*.[117] The Supreme Court explored the meaning and the scope of the expression "reservation" and the court expressed

114. AIR 1993 SC 477 (541).
115. AIR 1993 SC 477 (541).
116. AIR 1993 SC 477 (541).
117. AIR 1976 SC 490.

the view that the meaning and scope has to be ascertained having regard to the context in which it occurred. The relevant words "any provision for the reservation of appointments or posts." Whether the said words contemplates only form of provisions namely reservation simpliciter or do they take in other forms of provisions like preference, concession and exemptions. The court held that reservation is the highest form of special provision, while preference, concession and exemption are lesser form. The court held that the Constitutional scheme and context of Article 16(4), the concept of reservation takes within its sweep all supplemental and ancillary provisions as also lesser types of special provisions like exemptions, concessions and relaxations, consistent no doubt with the requirement of maintenance of efficiency of administration.

Several concessions, exemptions and other measures issued by the Railway Administration as noticed in the '*Akhil Bhartiya Soshit Karmachari Sangh* v. *Union of India*'[118] case are instances of supplementary incidental and ancillary provisions made with the view to make the main provision of reservation effective i.e., to ensure that the members of the reserved class fully avail the provision of reservation in their favour.

In *Thomas*[119] there was no provision for reservation in favour of the Scheduled Caste and Scheduled Tribes in the matter of promotion to the category of the Upper Division Clerks (UDC). Certain tests were required to be passed before promotion and the Lower Division Clerks (LDC) belonging to the Scheduled Caste and Scheduled Tribe were not able to pass the required tests with the result that there was stagnation. Rule 13AA was accordingly made empowering the Government to grant exemption to the members of the Scheduled Castes and Scheduled Tribes from passing those tests and the Government exempted the Scheduled Castes and Scheduled Tribes from passing those tests'. This provision of exemption was lesser form of special treatment than reservation. The court reasoned why such a special provisions should not be held to be within the larger concept of reservation. It is in this context that the

118. AIR 1981 SC 298.
119. AIR 1976 SC 490.

words "any provision for reservation of appointment and posts" assume significance. The court held that the word "any" is not merely a surplus but must be given its due meaning. It was argued by the petitioner in *Thomas* before the Kerala High Court that only type of provision that the State can make in favour of the backward classes is reservation of appointments and posts as provided by clause (4) and the said clause does not contemplate or permit granting of any exemptions or concessions to the backward classes and the Kerala High Court accepted the argument. The Supreme Court by majority reversed the view taken by the Kerala High Court holding that such exemption or concession can be extended under clause (1) of Article 16. The Supreme Court while upholding the validity of the notification held that this kind of reservation was warranted by and relatable to clause (4) of Article 16 itself and the court reasoned that clause (4) was exhaustive of the provisions that can be made in favour of the backward classes in matter of employment. But the Supreme Court in the Mandal Commission case while agreeing with the view of its earlier decision rested its finding on different reasoning. The court held that where the State find it necessary for the purpose of giving full effect to the provision of reservation to provide certain exemptions, concessions or preference to the members of the backward classes, it can extend the same under clause (4) itself.

All supplemental and ancillary provisions to ensure full availment of provisions for reservations can be provided as part of the concept of reservation itself. Similarly, in a given situation, the State may think that in case of particular backward classes it is not necessary to provide reservation of appointments or posts and that it would be sufficient if a certain preference or a concession is provided in their favour. This can be done under clause (4) itself.

The court held that clause (4) of Article 16 is exhaustive of the special provisions that can be made in favour of the backward class of citizens. The backward classes having been classified by the Constitution itself as a class deserving special treatment, it shall be presumed that no further classification or special treatment is permissible outside Article 16(4). Then the Supreme court in Mandal commission case considered whether clause (4) is exhaustive of the very concept of reservation or whether reservation can be provided outside clause (4) i.e., Clause (1) of Article 16. The court held that clause (4) is not exhaustive of the concept of reservation; it is exhaustive of reservations in favour of backward classes of citizens alone.

The Supreme Court in *Indira Sawhney* v. *Union of India*[120] case dealt with the matter of permissible extent of reservation. The court observed that limitation can be prescribed by the court on the extent of reservation. The Constitutional bench of the Supreme Court in *M.R. Balaji* v. *State of Mysore*[121] rejected the argument that in the absence of limitation contained in Article 15(4), no limitation can be prescribed. The court observed that a provision under Article 15(4) being a special provision must be within reasonable limits. The court reasoned that when Article 15(4) refers to the special provision for the advancement of certain classes or Scheduled Castes and Scheduled Tribes, it must not be ignored that the provision is a special provision; it is not a provision which is exhaustive in character, so that in looking after the advancement to those classes, the State would be justified in ignoring altogether the advancement of the rest of the society. It is because the interest of the society at large would be served by promoting the advancement of the weaker elements in the society that Article 15(4) authorizes. But the provision which is in the nature of exception completely excludes the rest of the society, that clearly is outside the scope of Article 15(4). It would be extremely unreasonable to assume that in enacting Article 15(4) the Parliament intended to provide that where the advancement of backward classes or the Scheduled Castes and Scheduled Tribes are concerned, the fundamental rights of the citizens constituting the rest of the society were to be completely and absolutely ignored.

A special provision contemplated by Article 15(4) like the reservation for posts and appointments, contemplated by Article 16(4) must be within reasonable limits. The interest of the weaker sections of the society which is a first charge on the State and the Center have to be adjusted with the interests of the community as a whole. The adjustment of these competing claims is undoubtedly a difficult matter, but if under the guise

120. AIR 1993 SC 477 (541).
121. AIR 1963 SC 649.

of making special provision, the State reserves all the seats available in all the colleges, that would be subverting the object of Article 15(4). The court finally ruled that generally and in a broad way a special provision should be less than 50 percent; how much less than 50 percent would depend upon the relevant prevailing circumstances in each case.

Then, in *T. Devadasan* v. *Union of India*[122] this rule of 50% was applied in a case arising under Article 16(4) and on that basis the carry forward rule was struck down.

In *Thomas*[123] the correctness of this 50 percent rule was seriously questioned. It was held that the 50 percent rule as laid down in earlier cases, is a rule of caution and does not exhaust all categories. The court reasoned that Article 16(4) does not fix any limit on the power of the Government to make reservations. Since clause (4) is a part of Article 16 of the Constitution it is manifest that the state cannot be allowed to indulge in excessive reservations so as to defeat the policy contained in Article 16(1) of the Constitution. As to what would be the suitable reservation within the permissible limits would depend upon the facts and circumstances of each case and no hard and fast rule can be laid down, nor can this matter be reduced to mathematical formulae so as to be adhered to in all the cases. The court held that 50 percent rule can not be accepted in all the cases and it is rule of caution and does not exhaust all the categories. The dominant object of Article 16(4) is to make steps to make inadequate representation adequate. The view of *Justice Fazal Ali* was accepted by *Justice Krishna Iyer* and he agreed with the construction of Article 16(4) given by Justice Fazal Ali. However, Chief Justice Ray did not dispute the correctness of the 50 percent rule but at the same time pointed out that this percentage should be applied to the entire service as a whole.

After the decision of Thomas, controversy arose whether the 50 percent rule in Balaji stand overruled by Thomas or does it continue to be valid and in *Vasanta Kumar*[124] two Judges came to precisely opposite conclusions on this question. Justice Chinnappa Reddy held that Thomas had the effect of undoing

122. AIR 1964 SC 279.
123. AIR 1976 SC 490.
124. AIR 1985 SC 1495.

the 50 percent rule in Balaji. Whereas Justice Venkataramiah held that it does not.

The Supreme Court, by majority, in *Mandal Commission*[125] case finally set the dispute at rest. The court held that reservation under Article 16(4) shall not exceed 50% of the appointments or posts, barring certain extraordinary situations. The court reasoned that it is adequate representation and proportional representation what is contemplated in Art. 16(4) of the Constitution. The power conferred under Article 16(4) should be exercised in a fair manner and within reasonable limits. There can be nothing more reasonable than to say that reservation under clause (4) shall not exceed 50% of the appointments or posts, barring certain extra-ordinary situations.

The limitation of reservation was made to 50% by the *Mandal Commission*[126] case. Certain other rule named as carry forward as modified in 1955 for providing unfilled reserved vacancies was struck down in the case of *Devadasan*.[127] The said carry forward rule provided that if a sufficient number of candidates considerd suitable by the recruiting authorities, are not available from the communities for whom reservations are made in a particular year, the unfilled vacancies should be treated as unreserved and filled by the best available candidates. The number of reserved vacancies thus treated as unreserved will be added as an additional quota to the number that would be reserved in the following year in the normal course; and to the extent to which approved candidates are not available in that year against this additional quota corresponding addition should be made to the number of reserved vacancies in the second following year. In *Devadasan*,[128] the UPSC in the year 1960 recommended 16 unreserved posts and 30 for reserved vacancies—a total of 46 and the Government appointed 45 persons out of which 29 belonged to Scheduled Castes and Scheduled Tribes and the said rule and the appointments was challenged being violative of the 50% rule as iniciated in Balaji. It was contended for the petitioner

125. AIR 1993 SC 477 (541).
126. AIR 1993 SC 477 (541).
127. AIR 1964 SC 279.
128. *Ibid.*

that by virtue of the carry forward rules, 65% of the vacancies for the year in question came to be reserved for Scheduled Castes and Scheduled Tribes. The majority speaking through *Mudholkar, J.* upheld the contetion of the petitioner and struck down purporting to apply the principle of Balaji.

But the validity of the decision in Devadasan was challenged before the Supreme Court in *Mandal Commission*[129] case and the court held that the decision of Devadasan so far it struck down the rule is not sustainable as carry forward of vacancies has become impermissible. The court over-ruled the decision in Devadasan. The court held that 50% rule shall apply in the case of carry forward rule as well and a year should be taken as the unit or basis, as the case may be, for applying the rule of 50 percent and not the entire strength. Thus, the result of application of carry forward rule, in that ever manner it is operated, should not result in breach of 50 percent rule, Justice Krishna Iyer in Karmachari Sangh held that the "carry forward" rule shall not result, in any given year, in the selection of appointments of Scheduled Castes and Scheduled Tribes in excess of 50%.

Prior to August 29, 1997, the vacancies reserved for the Scheduled Castes and the Scheduled Tribes, which could not be filled up by direct recruitment on account of non-availability of the candidates belonging to the Scheduled Castes or the Scheduled Tribes were treated as "Backlog Vacancies". These vacancies were treated as distinct group and were excluded from the ceiling of 50% reservation. The Supreme Court of India in its judgment in the *Indra Sawhney* v. *Union of India*[130] held that the number of vacancies to be filled up on the basis of reservations in a year including carried forward reservations should in no case exceed the limit of fifty percent. As total reservations in a year for the Scheduled Castes, the Scheduled Tribes and other Backward classes combined together had already reached forty-nine and a half percent and the total number of vacancies to be filled up in a year could not exceed fifty percent, it became difficult to fill the "Backlog Vacancies" and to hold Special Recruitment Drives. Therefore, to

129. AIR 1993 SC 477 (541).
130. *Ibid.*

implement the judgment of the Supreme Court, an Official Memorandum dated August 29, 1997 was issued by providing that the 50% limit shall apply to current as well as "Backlog Vacancies" and for discontinuation of the Special Recruitment Drive.

Due to the adverse effect of the aforesaid order dated August 29, 1997, various organizations including the Member of Parliament represented to the Central Government for protecting the interest of the Scheduled Castes and the Scheduled Tribes. The Government, after considering various representations, reviewed the position and has decided to make amendment in the Constitution so that the unfilled vancancies of a year, which are reserved for being filled up in that year in accordance with any provision for reservation made under clause (4) or clause (4A) of Article 16 of the Constitution, shall be considered as a separate class of vacancies to be filled up in any succeeding year or years and such class of vacancies shall not be considered together with the vacancies of the year in which they are being filled up for determining the ceiling of fifty percent reservation on total number of vacancies of that year. This amendment in the Constitution would enable the State to restore the position as was prevalent before August 29, 1997.

Amended Article 16(4B) provides that :

> "Nothing in this Article shall prevent the State from considering any unfilled vacancies of a year which are reserved for being filled up in that year in accordance with any provision for reservation made under clause (4A) as a separate class of vacancies to be filled up in any succeeding year or years and such class of vacancies shall not be considered together with the vacancies of the year in which they are being filled up for determining the ceiling of fifty percent reservation on total number of vacancies of that year".

The Scheduled Castes and Scheduled Tribes have been enjoying the facility of reservation in promotion since 1955. In respect of question for providing reservation in promotion, the Supreme Court in its judgement dated November 16, 1992 in the case of *Indra Sawheney* v. *Union of India & Others* expressing the view of the seven judges out of the nine judges constituting the bench that "We see no justification to multiply the risk which could be the consequence of holding that reservation can be provided in matter of promotion. While it is certainly just to say that the handicap should be given to backward classes of citizens at the stage of initial appointment, it would be a serious and unacceptable in road into the rule of equality of opportunity to say that such a handicap should be provided at every stage of promotion throughout his career. That would mean creating a permanent separate category apart from the mainstream.

This ruling of the Supreme Court adversely affected the interests of the Scheduled Castes and Scheduled Tribes. Since the representation of the Scheduled Castes and Scheduled Tribes in service in the States have not reached the required lavel, it is necessary to continue the existing dispensation of providing reservation in promotion in the case of the Scheduled Castes and the Scheduled Tribes. In view of the commitment of the State to protect the interest of the Scheduled Castes and the Scheduled Tribes, the Government have decided to continue the existing policy of reservation in promotion for the Scheduled Castes and the Scheduled Tribes. To carry out this, it is necessary to amend Article 16 of the Constitution by inserting a new clause (4A). It is said article by the way of Seventy-seventh Constitutional Amendment Act, 1995 to provide for reservation in promotion for the Scheduled Castes and the Scheduled Tribes.

Clause (4A) to Article 16 provides that :

> "Nothing in this Article shall prevent the State from making any provision for reservation in matters of promotion to any class or classes of posts in the service under the State in favour of the Scheduled Castes and Scheduled Tribes which in the opinion of State, are not adequately represented in the services under the State."

Consequently, the Parliament has removed the lacunae pointed out by the Supreme Court. The successive two decisions in *Commissioner of Commercial Taxes* v. *G.Sethu Madhava Rao*[131] and in *M. Venkteswaru* v. *State of Madras*[132] the Supreme Court held the right to reservation in promotion stands restored by the Constitution Seventy-Seventh Amendment Act which introduced clause (4A) to Article 16.

One more amendment regarding promotion has been made by Constitution Eighty-Fifth Amendment Act, 2001. This Amendment has been substituted, in clause (4A) of Article 16. Object behind that amendment is that the Government servants belonging to the Scheduled Castes and the Scheduled Tribes had been enjoying the benefit of consequential seniority on their promotion on the basis of rule of reservation. The judgments of the Supreme Court in the case of *Union of India* v. *Virpal Singh Chauhan*,[133] and *Ajit Singh Junuja* v. *State of Punjab*,[134] which led to the issue of the O.M. dated 30 January, 1997 adversely affected the interest of the Government servants belonging the Scheduled Castes and Scheduled Tribes category in the matter of seniority on promotion to the next higher grade. This led to considerable anxiety and representations were also received from various quarters including Members of Parliament to protect the interests of the Government servants belonging to Scheduled Castes and Scheduled Tribes.

The Government reviewed the position in the light of views received from various quarters and in order to protect the interests of the Government servants belonging to the Scheduled Castes and Scheduled Tribes, it was decided to negate the effect of O.M. dated 30 January, 1997 immediately. Mere withdrawal of the O.M. dated 30 January, 1997 could not meet the desired purpose and review or revision of seniority of the Government servants and grant of consequential benefits to such Government servants were also necessary. This required amendment to Article 16(4A) of the Constitution to provide for consequential seniority in the case of promotion by virtue of rule of reservation. It was also necessary to give retrospective effect to the constitutional amendment to Article 16(4A) with

131. AIR 1996 SC 2248.
132. SCC (5) 1996 SC 167.
133. SCC (6) 1995 SC 684.
134. AIR 1996 SC 1189.

effect from the date of coming into force of Article 16(4A) itself, that is, from the 17th day of June, 1995.

By virtue of Eighty-fifth Constitutional Amendment Act, 2001 the Article 16(4A) stands as follows :

> "Nothing in this Article shall prevent the State from making any provision for reservation in matters of promotion with consequential seniority, to any class or classes of posts in the service under the State in favour of the Scheduled Castes and Scheduled Tribes which in the opinion of State, are not adequately represented in the services under the State."

Articles 14 and 16 read with the Preamble gives equality of opportunities in matters relating to employment or appointment to any office under the State. By hierarchical unequal social status and denial of opportunities and facilities due to Untouchability practice against the Scheduled Castes and the Scheduled Tribes requires protective measures to remove the handicaps and disadvantage suffered by the members belonging to the Scheduled Castes and Scheduled Tribes so as to enable them to compete for selection. It was held in *Madhu Kishwar* v. *State of Bihar*[135] that the rule of law should establish a uniform pattern for harmonious existence in a society where every individual should exercise his rights to his best advantage to achieve excellence, subject to protective discrimination. The court observed that the concept of equality, therefore, requires that the law should be adaptable to meet equality. Article 38 mandates to minimize inequality in income and eliminate discrimination in status. Facilities and opportunities not only amongst the individual but also amongst the group of people to secure to them adequate means to improve excellence. Article 46 directs the State to promote with special care the educational and economic interest of the weaker section of the people and in particular of the Scheduled Castes and Scheduled Tribes, and to protect them from social injustice and all forms of exploitations. Equal protection clause, therefore, requires affirmative action for those placed unequally. Equality for unequals is secured by

135. AIR 1996 SC 2178.

treating them unequally. Affirmative action or positive discrimination, therefore, is in-built in equality of opportunity in status enshrined in Articles 14 and 16(1) of the Constitution. Therefore, Scheduled Castes and Scheduled Tribes stands as two separate classes.

Under the Rajasthan State and Subordinate Services (Direct Recruitment by Combind Competitive Examinations) Rule, 1962, relaxation of marks was provided for the Scheduled Castes and Scheduled Tribes candidate by lowering the lowest range of marks fixed for the general candidate but the same benefit was not made available to the candidates belonging to the Other Backward Class (OBC) category. The dissimilar treatment between the two groups was challenged as violative of Arts. 14 and 16 of the Constitution.[136] It was held that the backward classes do not form integrated class with the Scheduled Castes and Scheduled Tribes. The court reasoned that the object of reservation for the Scheduled Castes and Scheduled Tribes is to bring them into the mainstream of the national life. But the objective in respect of the backward classes is to remove their social and educational handicaps. Therefore, they are always treated dissimilar and they do not form the integrated class with the Scheduled Castes and Scheduled Tribes for the purpose of Article 16(4) or Article 15(4) of the Constitution. The rule which expressly provides the benefits to the Scheduled Castes and Scheduled Tribes excluding Other Backward Classes is not void under Articles 14 and 16(4) of the Constitution.

It is expedient to tell that the reservation for Scheduled Castes and Scheduled Tribes can be made by executive order. The Comptroller and Auditor General of India after consultation with the Government of India issued circular providing for reservation in matter of promotion for the Scheduled Castes and Scheduled Tribes candidates and the constitutional validity of the said circular was challenged in *Comptroller and Auditor General* v. *Mohan Lal Mehrotra*[137] on the ground that no executive order can be issued in matter of

136. Chattar Singh *v.* State of Rajasthan, AIR 1997 SC 303.
137. AIR 1991 SC 2289.

reservation and such circulars should be issued by the President of India as required under Article 148(5)[138] of the Constitution. The Supreme Court declined to restrain the Comptroller & Auditor General of India from enforcing the said circular and held that the circular is valid and binding since the Government has approved the circular and the circular was according to the declared policy of reservation. The infirmity that the President has not issued the circular, relates to the form and not the substance. The court finally held that the Government could direct the reservation by executive orders.

But the administrative orders cannot be issued in contravention of the statutory rules. It can be issued to supplement the statutory rules.[139]

The circular issued by the Railway Board introducing reservations for the Scheduled Castes and Scheduled Tribes in the Railway services both for selection and non-selection categories of post and the court upheld the circulars as they were issued in implementation of the policy of the central Government.[140]

The question whether an executive order made in terms of Article 16(4) is effective and enforceable by itself or whether it is necessary that the said 'provision' is enacted into a law made by the appropriate legislature under Article 309 or is incorporated into and issued as a rule by the President or Governor under the provision of Article 309 for it to become enforceable was raised in the *Mandal Commission case*.[141] It was argued by *Mr. Ram Jethmalani* that Article 16(4) is merely declaratory in nature, that it is an enabling provision and it is not a source of power by itself. He argued that unless made into a law by appropriate legislature or issued as a rule in terms of

---

138. Article 148(5) Subject to the provisions of this constitution and of any law made by Parliament, the conditions of service of persons serving in the Indian Audit and Accounts Department and the administrative powers of the C. & A.G. shall be such as may be prescribed by rules made by the President after consultation with the C. & A.G.
139. Santaram Sharma *v.* State of Rajasthan, AIR 1997 SC 1910.
140. Akhil Bharti Soshit Karmachari Sangh *v.* Union of India, AIR 1981 SC 298.
141. Indra Sawhney *v.* Union of India, AIR 1993 SC 477 (538).

the provision to Article 309, the provision so made by the executive does not become enforceable. But the Supreme Court held that a provision under Article 16(4) can be made by the Executive and such a provision is effective at the movement it is made. Until a law is made or rules are issued under Article 309 with respect to the reservation in favour of backward classes. It would always be open to the Executive Government to provide for reservation of appropriate posts or appointments in favour of the backward classes by an executive order. The court held that the Office Memorandum dated 25th September 1991 was executive order issued under Article 73 of the Constitution read with Clause (4) of Article 16 and mere omission of a recital. 'in the name and by the order of the President of India' does not effect the validity and enforceability of the orders.

It is well settled through the decisions of the Supreme Court that the appropriate Government is empowered to prescribe the condition of service of its employee by an executive order in absence of the rules made under the provision of Article 309. Even where the rules under the proviso to Article 309 are made, the Government can issue orders or instructions with respect to the matters upon which the rules are silent. This view has been reiterated in a decision of the Supreme Court in the *Comptroller and Auditor General* v. *Mohan Lal Mehrotra*[142] where it was held that the High Court was not right in stating that there can not be an administrative order directing reservation for Scheduled Castes and Scheduled Tribes as it would alter the statutory rules in force. The rules do not provide for any reservation. In fact the rule is silent about reservation and the Government could direct the reservation by executive orders. The administrative orders cannot be issued in contravention of the statutory rules but it could be issued to supplement the statutory rules.

The Supreme Court in *Akhil Bharatiya Soshit Karmachari Sangh* v. *Union of India*[143] upheld the circular issued by the Railway Board introducing reservation for Scheduled Castes and Scheduled Tribes in Railway services both for a selection

142. AIR 1991 SC 2288.
143. AIR 1981 SC 298.

and non-selection categories of posts which were issued to implement the policy of the Central Government.

Thus, it follows that until a law is made or rules are issued under Article 309 with respect to reservation in favour of backward classes, it will always be open to the Executive to provide for reservation in appointments or posts in favour of backward classes by an Executive order and such a provision is effective the moment it is made.

Under Article 16(4) the lowering of academic standard is also permissible and the government policy of lowering of 5 percent is the tolerable limit by which the standard for the Scheduled Castes candidates has been allowed to come down the minimum qualifying standard for admission to various institution. The candidates belonging to the Scheduled Castes and Scheduled Tribes are eligible for admission to the reserve seat if they attain this minimum standard. Further reduction in the standard is not permissible.[144] It was further held that the mark obtained in the admission test is the determinative factor and the mark obtained in the qualifying examination is irrelevant. Relaxation of the percentage of minimum qualification marks for admission to medical college in case of candidates belonging to the Scheduled Castes and Scheduled Tribes subsequent to the declaration of result of the entrance test could not be said to be unjust and illegal.[145]

It is now settled that the reservation in favour of backward classss of citizens, including the members of Scheduled Castes and Scheduled Tribes as contemplated by Article 16(4) can be made not merely in respect of initial appointment but also in respect of posts to which the promotions are to be made. In *Comptroller and Auditor General* v. *K.S. Jagannathan*[146] the petitioners belonged to Scheduled Caste and were working in the Audit and Account Department of Madras. They appeared for Staff Selection Examination in December 1980. The petitioner contended that instruction in the office memorandum dated 21st January 1977 was not followed by the authority. The Supreme Court found that the object of the said office memorandum was

144. Ravneet Bhatwa *v.* Punjab University, AIR 1990 P&H 329.
145. Awadeesh Nema *v.* State of M.P., AIR 1989 MP 61.
146. AIR 1987 SC 538.

to provide an adequate opportunity of promotion to the members of Scheduled Castes and Scheduled Tribes. The court held that the petitioners are entitled to relaxation of marks of promotion to the higher grade and the relaxed or lower qualifying standard cannot be fixed for all the time but for the number of years and notified so that the candidates appearing for the examination would know what the lower qualifying standard is. The court directed that lower or relaxed qualifying standard has to be fixed every year and before each examination.

By reason of the provisions of Article 16(4) of the Constitution a treatment to the members of the Scheduled Castes and Scheduled Tribes different from that given to others in relation to employment or appointment to any office under State does not violate fundamental rights to equality of opportunity in matter of employment.

It is clear from the above discussion that Constitution of India makes special exception to the concept of equality before law by granting concessions and preferences to Scheduled Castes and Scheduled Tribes. Article 16(4) gives a broad discretion to the State to reserve certain places in public services to the members of the "backward classes of citizens".

It addition, a more specific provision is made in Article 335 for making appointments to the various services from the members of Scheduled Castes and Scheduled Tribes.

(B) Article 335: Claims of Scheduled Castes and Scheduled Tribes to Services and Posts

One more provision relating to the appointment of Scheduled Castes and Scheduled Tribes in various services is Article 335. This Article imposes a Constitutional duty on Union and State to take into consideration the claims of the members of Scheduled Castes and Scheduled Tribes community consistent with the maintenance of efficiency of administration.

The Constitution of India has laid down special responsibility on the Government to protect the claims of the Scheduled Castes and Scheduled Tribes in matter of public employment under Article 335 which reads as under :

"The claims of the members of the Scheduled Castes and

Scheduled Tribes shall be taken into consideration, consistently with the maintenance of efficiency of administration, in the making of appointments to services and posts in connection with the affairs of the Union or of a State."

Ray, C.J. in *State of Kerala* v. *N.M. Thomas*[147] stated that the aim of Article 335 is to consider the claims of the Scheduled Castes and Scheduled Tribes to redress the imbalance in public service and to bring about a parity in all communities in public service.

Article 335 assumes that the Scheduled Castes and Scheduled Tribes have some claims. These claims have to be taken into consideration in appointments to services and posts in connection with the affairs of the Union or of a State. The words 'consistently with the maintenance of efficiency of administration' have generally been read as words of limitation to re-strike the claims of the Scheduled Castes and Scheduled Tribes. Although this Article does not apply to other backward classes, reliance has been placed on these words even to restrict reservations for them. Particularly to deny reservation in promotion.[148]

The words 'consistently with the maintenance of efficiency of administration' are capable of being read differently though they have not been so read by the courts so far. In a mixed and diverse society as in India representation of all sections of society in different walks of life creates an integrated and, therefore, efficient society. Accordingly, representation of the Scheduled Castes and the Scheduled Tribes, which constitute about twenty-five percent of the total population of the country and whose representation in the State administration is negligible, if not totally absent, will lead to efficiency in the administration. Therefore, the Constitution-makers directed that in consistency with the goal of maintenance of efficiency of administration the Scheduled Castes and the Scheduled Tribes must be duly represented in the State administration. It may also be argued that active inclusion of about twenty-five percent

147. AIR 1976 SC 449.
148. Indra Sawhney *v.* Union of India, AIR 1993 SC 477 (538).

of the population into the category from which the administrator have to be selected creates wider choice for the selectors of the administrators. Thus the words 'consistently with the maintentance of efficiency of administration' are not the words of limitation but of guidance that in order to ensure maintenance of efficiency of administration the claims of the Scheduled Castes and Scheduled Tribes must be taken into consideration making of appointments to services and posts in connection with the affairs of the Union and the States.[149] In *State of U.P.* v. *Dina Nath Shukla*[150] the Court also observed : "Thus Article 335 read with Articles 46, 38 and 16 would give the socio-economic empowerment to the Scheduled Castes and Scheduled Tribes and rule of reservation in the matter of appointment to a service or post under the State is part of the constitutional scheme as a positive facility and opportunity available to them.

The Scheduled Castes and the Scheduled Tribes had been enjoying the facility of relaxation of qualifying marks and standards of evaluation in matters of reservation in promotion. The Supreme Court in its judgment in the case of *S. Vinod Kumar* v. *Union of India*[151] held that such relaxations in matters of reservation in promotion were not permissible under Article 16(4) of the Constitution in view of the command contained in Article 335 of the Constitution. The Apex Court also held that the law on the subject of relaxations of qualifying marks and standards of evaluation in matters of reservation in promotion in one laid down by the nine-judge Constitution Bench of the Supreme Court in the case of *Indira Sawhney* v. *Union of India*. Para 831 of Indira Sawhney Judgement[152] also held such relaxations as being not permissible under Article 16(4) in view of the command contained in Article 335 of the Constitution. In order to implement the judgements of Supreme Court, such relaxations had to be withdrawn with effect from July 22, 1997.

---

149. M.P. Singh, Are Articles 15(4) and 16(4) Fundamental Right?
150. AIR 1997 SC 1095-97.
151. Supreme Today, 1996(7) SC 333.
152. Indra Sawhney *v.* Union of India, AIR 1993 SC 477.

In view of the adverse effect of the order dated July 22, 1997 on the interests of Scheduled Castes and Scheduled Tribes, representations had been received by the Government from several quarters including the Members of Parliament. Considering the various representations, the Government has reviewed the position and decided to move for constitutional amendment with a view to restore the relaxations which were withdrawn vide instructions issued by the Department of Personnel and Training on July 22, 1997.

In Article 335 of the Constitution, the following proviso shall be inserted at the end, namely :

> "Provided that nothing in this article shall prevent in making of any provision in favour of the members of the Scheduled Castes and the Scheduled Tribes for relaxation in qualifying marks in any examination or lowering the standards of evaluation, for reservation in matters of promotion to any class or classes or services or posts in connection with the affairs of the Union or of a State."

The above discussed safeguards are made in Constitution for the proper representation of Scheduled Castes and Scheduled Tribes in public employment. By the way of judicial interpretation Scheduled Castes and Scheduled Tribes have been included in the expression "backward class of citizens". There must be a collective effort to strengthen the Scheduled Castes and Scheduled Tribes community educationaly so that they could be adequately represented in public employments.

(IV) POLITICAL SAFEGUARDS

The framers of our Constitution were totally aware of the fact that as long as the depressed section of our society (viz. Scheduled Castes and Scheduled Tribes) would not be politically strengthened, there is no use to provide them with different safeguards. Provisions regarding political safeguards for Scheduled Castes and Scheduled Tribes are meant to equate them with other section of society so that the object of Social justice could be achieved, which is the cornerstone of our Constitution. Though there were efforts to strengthen Scheduled

Castes and Scheduled Tribes politically before the Constitution also, but it became more evident in our Constitution when our Constitution-makers made certain specific provisions regarding political safeguards for Scheduled Castes and Scheduled Tribes. There was a longstanding difference of opinion about these safeguards but ultimately the safeguards were unanimously accepted. The Constitution-makers tried to give proper-representation to Scheduled Castes and Scheduled Tribes in politics. So these provisions have been incorporated in Constitution of India. Even after the enactment of Constitution whenever the question of political representation of Scheduled Castes and Scheduled Tribes arises, the legislature attempts to give proper representation by making amendments in Constitution.

The various Articles which provide for political safeguards to Scheduled Castes and Scheduled Tribes are as follows:

(A) Article 330	:	Reservation of seats for Scheduled Castes and Scheduled Tribes in the House of the People.
(B) Article 332	:	Reservation of seats for Scheduled Castes and Scheduled Tribes in the Legislative Assemblies of the States.
(C) Article 334	:	Reservation of seats and special representation to cease after 'Sixty years'.
(D) Article 243(D)	:	Reservation of seats in every Panchayat.
(E) Article 243 (T)	:	Reservation of seats in every Municipality.
(F) Article 164 (1)	:	Minister-in-charge of Tribal welfare.

(A) Article 330: Reservation of Seats for Scheduled Castes and Scheduled Tribes in the House of the People

(1) Seats shall be reserved in the House of the People for:

(a) the Scheduled Castes;

(b) the Scheduled Tribes except the Scheduled Tribes in the autonomous districts of Assam; and

(c) the Scheduled Tribes in the autonomous districts of Assam.

(2) The number of seats reserved in any State or Union territory for the Scheduled Castes and Scheduled Tribes under clause (1) shall bear, as nearly as may be, the same proportion to the total number of seats allotted to that State or Union territory in the House of the People as the population of the Scheduled Castes in the State or Union territory or of the Scheduled Tribes in the State or Union territory or part of the State or Union territory as the case may be, in respect of which seats are so reserved, bears to the total population of the State or Union territory.

(3) Notwithstanding anything contained in clause (2) the number of seats reserved in the House of the People for the Scheduled Tribes in the autonomous districts of Assam shall bear to the total number of seats allotted to that State a proportion not less than the population of the Scheduled Tribes in the said autonomous districts bears to the total population of the State.

"Explanation"—In this article and in Article 332, the expression "population" means the population as ascertained at the last preceding census of which the relevant figures have been published.

Provided that the reference in this Explanation to the last preceding census of which the relevant figures have been published shall, until the relevant figures for the first census taken after the year 2000 have been published, be construed as a reference to the 1971 census.

It is obvious that the reservation of seats specified in Article 330 is intended to guarantee a minimum number of seats to the Scheduled Castes and Scheduled Tribes. At present, there are 119 seats reserved in the House of the People for Scheduled Castes and Scheduled Tribes. Of these, 79 are reserved for Scheduled Castes and rest for the Scheduled Tribes.[153]

153. M.V. Paylee, India's Constitution, p. 348.

Therefore, if the member of the said castes and the tribes secure additional seats by election to general unreserved seats there would be no repugnancy at all. The claim of eligibility for the reserved seat does not exclude the claim for general seats.

In *V.V. Giri* v. *D.S. Dora,*[154] the Supreme Court held that a Scheduled Tribes candidate can contest an election for both the seats reserved as well as open. At the same time, it also held that a non-Scheduled Tribe candidate residing in a constituency for which there is a reserved seat will be unable to stand for election to that seat. In 1961, Parliament enacted legislation providing for the division of two member constituency and thus a non-Scheduled Caste person will be debarred to contest election to a reserved seat even though residing in that constituency. It further held that Section 54(4) of The Representation of People Act, 1950 is not opposed to Article 330 of the Constitution when it is admitted that Scheduled Tribe candidate could compete for a general seat.

In *Chatturbhuj Vithhldas Fasoni* v. *Moneshwar,*[155] question before the Supreme Court was that what is the effect on the caste if a person of Scheduled Caste adopts another religion? In this case an election tribunal had rejected the nomination papers for a reserved seat submitted by a Mahar who had joined the Mahanubhavya panth, a Hindu sect which repudicated the multiplicity of Gods and the caste system. Reversing the decision of the tribunal the Supreme Court held that the candidate remained a Mahar and was entitled to the seat reserved for Scheduled Castes.

Another question came before the Supreme Court in *Punja Rao* v. *D.P. Meshram*[156] that what is the effect on the caste if a person of Scheduled Caste adopts another religion, namely, Buddhism? It has been held that regardless of the fact that strict compliance to formalities for conversion from a Scheduled Caste to Buddhism were not observed, such a person must be deemed to have been obliterated from the President's order of 1950, in as much as the order contemplates that for treating a person as belonging to a Scheduled Caste, he must be one who

154. AIR 1959 S.C. 1318.
155. AIR 1954 S.C. 236.
156. AIR 1965 S.C. 1127.

professes either Hindu or Sikh religion. And therefore, in accordance with the maxim "*expressio unius est exclusio alterious,*" since these two religions were specially mentioned, the plea that under Article 25 Hindu religion also included Buddhism can't be accepted.

(B) Article 332 : Reservation of Seats for Scheduled Castes and Scheduled Tribes in the Legislative Assemblies of the States

Not only in House of the People but also in the State legislature, the political interest of the Scheduled Castes and Scheduled Tribes are protected by the reservation of seats in both Houses. Here again, the method adopted is the same.

Article 332 provides:

(1) Seats shall be reserved for the Scheduled Castes and the Scheduled Tribes, excepts the Scheduled Tribes in the autonomous districts of Assam, in the Legislative Assembly of every State.

(2) Seats shall be reserved also for the autonomous districts in the Legislative Assembly of the State of Assam.

(3) The number of seats reserved for the Scheduled Castes and Scheduled Tribes in the Legislative Assembly of any State under clause (1) shall bear, as nearly as may be, the same proportion to the total number of seats in the Assembly as the population of the Scheduled Castes in the State or of the Scheduled Tribes in the State or part of the State, as the case may be, in respect of which seats are so reserved, bears to the total population of the State.

(3A) Notwithstanding anything contained in clause (3), until the taking effect, under Article 170, of the re-adjustment, on the basis of the first census after the year 2000, of the number of seats in the Legislative Assemblies of the State of Arunachal Pradesh, Meghalaya, Mizoram and Nagaland, the seats which shall be reserved for the Scheduled Tribes in the Legislative Assembly of any such State shall be:

(a) if all the seats in the Legislative Assembly of such State is existence on the date of coming into force of the Constitution (Fifty-seventh Amendment) Act, 1987 (hereinafter in this clause referred to as the existing Assembly) are held by members of the Scheduled Tribes, all the seats except one;

(b) in any other case, such number of seats as bears to the total number of seats, a proportion not less than the number (as on the said date) of member belonging to the Scheduled Tribes in the existing Assembly bears to the total number of seats in the existing Assembly.

(3B) Notwithstanding anything contained in clause (3), until the re-adjustement, under Article 170, takes effect on the basis of the first census after the year 2000, of the number of seats in the Legislative Assembly of the State of Tripura, the seats which shall be reserved for the Scheduled Tribes in the Legislative Assembly shall be, such number of seats as bears to the total number of seats, a proportion not less than the number, as on the date of coming into force of the Constitution (Seventy-second Amendement) Act, 1992, of members belonging to the Scheduled Tribes in the Legislative Assembly in existence on the said date bears to the total number of seats in that Assembly.

(4) The number of seats reserved for an autonomous district in the Legislative Assembly of the State of Assam shall bear to the total number of seats in that Assembly a proportion not less than the population of the district bears to the total population of the State.

(5) The constituencies for the seats reserved for any autonomous district of Assam shall not comprise any area outside that district.

(6) No person who is not a member of a Scheduled Tribe of any autonomous district of the State of Assam shall be eligible for election to the Legislative Assembly of the State from any constituency of that district.

Article 332 of the Constitution of India provided for reservation of seats for the Scheduled Castes and the Scheduled Tribes in the Legislative Assemblies of the States. Clause (6) of Article 332 stipulated that no person who was not a member of a Scheduled Tribe of any autonomous district of the State of Assam would be eligible for election to the Legislative Assembly of the State from any constituency of that district.

In pursuance of the Memorandum of Settlement signed on the 10th day of February, 2003 between the Government of India, Government of Assam and Bodo Liberation Tigers, and to protect the rights of the non-tribals, the existing representation of the Scheduled Tribes and non-Scheduled Tribes in the Legislative Assembly of the State of Assam from the Bodoland Territorial Council Areas District was proposed to be kept intact. It was therefore proposed to insert a proviso in clause (6) of Article 332 of the Constitution. And the proposed proviso inserted in the Constitution by (Ninetieth Amendment) Act, 2003.

The following proviso is :

> "Provided that for elections to the Legislative Assembly of the State of Assam, the representation of the Scheduled Tribes and non-Scheduled Tribes in the constituencies included in the Bodoland Territorial Areas District, so notified and existing prior to the Constitution of the Bodoland Territorial Areas District, shall be maintained".[157]

In the State Assemblies, out of total of 4047 seats, the Scheduled Castes and Scheduled Tribes have 854 seats, of these 551 are reserved for the Scheduled Castes and the rest 303 seats are reserved for Scheduled Tribes candidates.[158]

If any seat of constituency is reserved for Scheduled Castes and Scheduled Tribes candidate in that case only the member of aforesaid caste or tribe may contest the election from that constituency, which has been notified by the President under Articles 341 and 342.

---

157. President assented this provision on 28th September 2003.
158. M.V. Paylee, *opt. cit.*, p. 348.

In *Bhaiyalal* v. *Harikishan Singh*[159] the appellant was a candidate in the State Legislative Assembly election from a reserved seat had declared that he was a Chamar, which was one of Scheduled Caste in the Constitution (Scheduled Castes) Order, 1951 issued by the President under Article 341. The respondent pleaded that the appellant was a Dohar caste excluded by the order from the category of Chamars. The appellant adduced evidence in support of the plea. The question arose whether an enquiry was permissible? The Supreme Court unanimously answered it in negative. Gajendragadkar, C.J. held that as for categories of Scheduled Castes, the President's Order was conclusive.

Another case which arose under Article 332 was of *Wilson Reade* v. *C.S. Booth*.[160] In this case the election commissioner had rejected nomination papers for a Scheduled Tribe seat of a candidate whose father was a English Man and whose mother was Khasi. The Assam High Court found that even though an Anglo Indian did not prevent him from being a member of the Scheduled Tribe.

It may, however, be noted that elections are to be held on the basis of a single electoral roll, and each voter in the reserved constituency is entitled to vote. There is no separate electorate, e.g. it is not for the Scheduled Castes and Scheduled Tribes only to elect their representatives. Though it may be recalled that *Dr. Ambedkar* had pioneered the idea of separate electorate but ultimately when Gandhiji announced his fast unto death he left his idea. The present day system of election is that though a person belonging to Scheduled Castes or Scheduled Tribes is to be elected to a reserved seat he is to be elected by all the voters in the constituency. This has been done with a view to discourage the sharpening of differentiation between the Scheduled Castes and Scheduled Tribes from other people and to lead to their gradual integration into the main stream of national life as desired by Gandhiji.

159. AIR 1965 S.C. 1557.
160. AIR 1958 Assam 128.

(C) Article 334 : Reservation of Seats and Special Representation to Cease after 'Seventy Years'

Notwithstanding anything in the foregoing provisions of this part, the provisions of this Constitution relating to:

(a) the reservation of seats for the Scheduled Castes or the Scheduled Tribes in the House of the People and in the Legislative Assemblies of the State; and
(b) the representation of the Anglo-Indian community in the House of the People and in the Legislative Assemblies of the States by nomination,

shall cease to have effect on the expiration of a period of 'Seventy Years' from the commencement of this Constitution:

Provided that nothing in this Article shall affect any representation in the House of People or in the Legislative Assembly of a State until the dissolution of the then existing House or Assembly, as the case may be.

Article 334 deals with the reservation of seats to Scheduled Castes and Scheduled Tribes. The reason which weighed with the Constituent Assembly of India in making provision for the reservation of seats for the Scheduled Castes and Scheduled Tribes and representation of the Anglo-Indian community in the House of People and in the State Legislative Assemblies have not ceased to exist. Parliament, therefore, makes the aforesaid reservation and nomination to continue for another ten years. Originally Article 334 provided for the reservation of seats to Scheduled Castes and Scheduled Tribes for a period of ten years only from the date of commencement of the Constitution but by the Constitution (Eighth Amendment) Act, 1959 the words twenty years was substituted for the words ten years. The effects of the amendment was that reservation of seats in the legislatures for the Scheduled Castes and Scheduled Tribes which was originally to cease after ten years was now to cease after twenty years from 26 Jan. 1950. Then again the Constitution (Twenty-Third Amendment) Act, 1969 has given a more liberal interpretation to the reservation by extending it for an another period of ten years. Thus the reservation for the Scheduled Castes and Scheduled Tribes candidates which was originally to cease after ten years from 26 Jan. 1950 was now to cease after thirty years from that date. Again, by the Constitution (Fourty-fifth Amendment) Act, 1980 the term thirty years was substituted by fourty years. Again in the year 1989, Constitution (Sixty-second Amendment) Act, 1989 was passed and through this amendment the reservation of seats was extended to fifty years. At present the word fifty years has been substituted with sixty years by the Constitution (Seventy-nineth Amendment) Act, 1999. Now the reservation of seats for Scheduled Castes or Scheduled Tribes cease after 26 Jan. 2010.

(D) Article 243 (D) : Reservation of Seats in Panchayats

Article 243 (D) was not present in the original Constitution but by virtue of Constitution (Seventy-third Amendment) Act, 1992 (which came into effect on 24 April 1993), there is a provision for reservation of seats for the Scheduled Castes and Scheduled Tribes at Gram Panchayat level.

The object and reason behind the insertion of that Article is the Panchayati Raj Instititions which have been in existence for a long time, it has been observed that these institutions have not been able to acquire the status and dignity of viable and responsive people's bodies due to a number of reasons including absence of regular elections, prolonged supersessions, insufficient representation of weaker sections like Scheduled Castes and Scheduled Tribes.

Article 40 of the Constitution which enshrines one of the Directive Principles of State Policy lays down that : the State shall take steps to organize village panchayats and endow them with such powers and authority as may be necessary to enable them to function as units of self-government. In the light of the experience in the last forty years and in view of the short-coming which have been observed, it is considered that there is an imperative need to enshrine in the Constitution certain basic and essential features of Panchayati Raj Institutions to impart certainty, continuity and strength to them.

Accordingly; it is proposed to add a new part relating to Panchayats in the Constitution to provide for among other things, Gram Sabha in a village or group of villages; Constitution of Panchayats at village and other level or levels; direct elections to all seats in panchayats at the village and intermediate level, if any, and to the office of Chairpersons of

Panchayats at such levels; reservation of seats for the Scheduled Castes and the Scheduled Tribes in proportion to their population for membership of Panchayats and office of Chairpersons in Panchayats at each level.

Article 243 (D) Provides :

1. Seats shall be reserved for:
   (a) the Scheduled Castes; and
   (b) the Scheduled Tribes;
   in every panchayat and the number of seats so reserved shall bear, as nearly as may be, the same proportion to the total number of seats to be filled by direct election in that Panchayat as the population of the Scheduled Castes in that Panchayat area or of the Scheduled Tribes in that Panchayat area bears to the total population of that area and such seats may be allotted by rotation to different constituencies in a Panchayat.
2. Not less than one-third of the total number of seats reserved under clause (1) shall be reserved for women belonging to the Scheduled Castes or, as the case may be, the Scheduled Tribes.
3. Not less than one-third (including the number of seats reserved for women belonging to the Scheduled Castes and the Scheduled Tribes) of the total number of seats to be filled by direct election in every Panchayat shall be reserved for women and such seats may be allotted by rotation to different constituencies in a Panchayat.
4. The offices of the Chairpersons in the Panchayats at the village or any other level shall be reserved for the Scheduled Castes, the Scheduled Tribes and women in such manner as the Legislature of a State may, by law, provide:
   Provided that the number of offices of Chairpersons reserved for the Scheduled Castes and the Scheduled Tribes in the Panchayats at each level in any State shall bear, as nearly as may be, the same proportion to the total number of such offices in the Panchayats at

each level as the population of the Scheduled Castes in the State or of the Scheduled Tribes in the State bears to the total population of the State.

Provided further that not less than one-third of the total number of offices of Chairpersons in the Panchayats at each level shall be reserved for women:

Provided also that the number of offices reserved under this clause shall be allotted by rotation to different Panchayats at each level.

5. The reservation of seats under clauses (1) and (2) and the reservation of offices of Chairpersons (other than the reservation for women) under clause (4) shall cease to have effect on the expiration of the period specified in Article 334.
6. Nothing in this Part shall prevent the Legislature of a State from making any provision for reservation of seats in any Panchayat or offices of Chairpersons in the Panchayats at any level in favour of backward class of citizens.

(E) Article 243 (T) : Reservation of Seats in Municipality

In the same manner by the Constitution (Seventy-fourth Amendment) Act, 1992 Part IX(A) has been added in the Constitution (which came into effect on 20 June, 1993) which provides reservation of seats for Scheduled Castes and Scheduled Tribes in Municipalities. The objects and reasons behind the insertion of this article is, in many states local bodies have become weak and ineffective on account of a variety of reasons, including the failure to hold regular elections, prolonged supersessions and inadequate devolution of powers and functions. As a result, Urban Local Bodies are not able to perform effectively as vibrant democratic units of self-government. Having regard to these inadequacies, it is considered necessary that provisions relating to Urban Local Bodies are incorporated in the Constitution particularly for providing adequate representation for the weaker sections like Scheduled Castes and Scheduled Tribes.

Article 243 (T) provides:

(1) Seats shall be reserved for the Scheduled Castes and Scheduled Tribes in every Municipality and the number of seats so reserved shall bear, as nearly as may be, the same proportion to the total number of seats to be filled by direct election in that Municipality as the population of the Scheduled Castes in the Municipal area of the Scheduled Tribes in the Municipal area bears to the total population of that area and such seats may be allotted by rotation to different constituencies in a Municipality.

(2) Not less than one-third of the total number of seats reserved under clause (1) shall be resrved for women belonging to the Scheduled Castes or, as the case may be, the Scheduled Tribes.

(3) Not less than one-third (including the number of seats reserved for women belonging to the Scheduled Castes and the Scheduled Tribes) of the total number of seats to be filled by direct election in every Municipality shall be reserved for women and such seats may be allotted by rotation to different constituencies in a Municipality.

(4) The offices of Chairpersons in the Municipalities shall be reserved for the Scheduled Castes, the Scheduled Tribes and women in such manner as the Legislature of a State may, by law, provide.

(5) The reservation of seats under clauses (1) and (2) and the reservation of offices of Chairpersons (other than the reservation for women) under clause (4) shall cease to have effect on the expiration of the period specified in Article 334.

(6) Nothing in this Part shall prevent the Legislature of State from making any provision for reservation of seats in any Municipality or offices of Chairpersons in the Municipalities in favour of backward class of citizens.

(F) Article 164 (1) : Minister-in-charge of Tribal Welfare

Although under Article 164(1) it is mentioned that:

"The Chief Minister shall be appointed by the Governor and the other ministers shall be appointed by the Governor on the advice of the Chief Minister, and the ministers shall hold office during the pleasure of the Governor."

But in the Proviso of Article 164 (1), it has been mentioned "Provided that in the State of Bihar, Madhya Pradesh and Orissa there shall be a minister in charge of tribal welfare who may in addition be in charge of the welfare of the Scheduled Castes and backward classes or any other work."

In the year 2000, Bihar and Madhya Pradesh States have been divided in order to create two new states, namely, Jharkhand and Chhattisgarh. Due to division of Bihar, the population of Scheduled Tribes in Bihar have been nearly vanished. Due to this the post of Minister in charge of tribal welfare have been created space for the States Jharkhand and Chhattisgarh and also to abolished this post in Bihar, the Parliament has passed (Ninty-fourth Amendment) Act, 2005, by which Article 164 has been amended.

Amendment of Article 164 : In Article 164 of the Constitution in clause (1) in the proviso for the word 'Bihar' the words "Jharkhand", "Chhattisgarh" shall be substituted.

It is evident from the above, that our Constitution-makers have sincerely endeavoured to strengthen Scheduled Castes and the Scheduled Tribes politically, so that these sections could also come at par with other group of society. They were aware of the fact that it can be done through reservation of seats in Legislature. Through reservation in Legislature, the Scheduled Castes and the Scheduled Tribes could effectively put forward their grievances and get them solved. It can be only Scheduled Castes and the Scheduled Tribes who are aware of the original problems of their caste. So it is expedient to give them proper representation in Legislature by the mode of reserving seats in their favour. Our Parliament has from time to time extended the reservation at various levels. So that Scheduled Castes and the Scheduled Tribes could be ameliorated at every stage of politics, and the voice of Scheduled Castes and the Scheduled Tribes could not get unheard.

(V) ADMINISTRATIVE SAFEGUARDS

As it is clear from the previous discussion that different safeguards have been incorporated in the Constitution of India to uplift the down trodden condition of Scheduled Castes and Scheduled Tribes; so that their social, economic, political and educational condition could be strengthened and ameliorated. Our Constitution-framers were aware of the fact that only it will not be sufficient to enumerate the safeguards in Constitution but it must also be seen that whether these safeguards are being implemented properly. So the Constitution of India has some provisions relating to administration, monitoring and control of various activities towards securing Social justice and rightful share for the most under privileged and marginalised section to the society. The provisions are as under:

- **(A) Article 244** : Administration of Scheduled Areas and Tribal Areas.
- **(B) Article 339** : Control of the Union over the administration of Scheduled Areas and the welfare of Scheduled Tribes.
- **(C) Article 338** : National Commission for Scheduled Castes.
- **(D) Article 338A** : National Commission for Scheduled Tribes

(A) Article 244 : Administration of Scheduled Areas and Tribal Areas

(1) The provisions of the fifth Schedule shall apply to the administration and control of the Scheduled Areas and Scheduled Tribes in any State other than the State of Assam, Meghalaya, Tripura and Mizoram.

The fifth Schedule of the Constitution is related to the provisions concerning the administration and control of Scheduled Areas and Scheduled Tribes. The Part A Para 3 of the fifth Schedule provides that the Governor of each State having Scheduled Areas therein shall annually or whenever so required by the President make a report to the President regarding the administration of the Scheduled Areas in that State and the executive power of the Union shall extend to the giving of directions to the State as to the administration of the said areas.

The fifth Schedule, Part B, Para 4 provides for the setting up of Tribes Advisory Councils in certain States. It states that:

(1) There shall be a Tribes advisory council established in each State having Scheduled Areas therein and if the President so directs, also in any State having Scheduled Tribes but not Scheduled Areas therein, a Tribe Advisory Council consisting of not more than twenty members of whom, as nearly as may be, three-fourths shall be the representatives of the Scheduled Tribes in the Legislative Assembly of the State.
Provided that if the number of representatives of the Scheduled Tribes in the Legislative Assembly of the State in less than the number of seats in the Tribes Advisory Council to be filled by such representatives, the remaining seats shall be filled by other members of those tribes.

(2) It shall be the duty of the Tribes Advisory Council to advise on such matters pertaining to the welfare and advancement to the Scheduled Tribes in the State as may be referred to them by the Governor.

(3) The Governor may make rules prescribing or regulating as the case may be.
   (a) The number of members of the Council, the mode of their appointment and the appointment of the Chairman of the council and of the officers and servents thereof;
   (b) The conduct of its meetings and its procedure in general; and
   (c) all other incidental matters.

The introduction of the Tribes Advisory Council forms a notable feature of the special provisions made for the welfare of Scheduled Tribes in the Constitution. The representatives of Scheduled Tribes are made to study the welfare schemes for their advancement, and make suggestions to the Government as regards to their working. The Advisory Council go a long way in the formulation of welfare schemes, in accordance with the needs of the tribal population of the area concerned. Another novel feature of these councils is the inclusion of non-tribal members in the councils which makes them broad-based.

There are eight States having Tribes Advisory Councils, viz. Andhra Pradesh, Bihar, Gujarat, Himachal Pradesh, Madhya Pradesh, Maharaşhtra, Orissa and Rajasthan. In addition to these eight States Tamilnadu and West Bengal which do not have any Scheduled Areas, also have statutory Tribes Advisory Councils. Part B, Para 5 of the fifth Schedule deals with the powers of the Governor over the Scheduled areas. It states:

(1) Notwithstanding anything in this Constitution, the Governor may by public notification, direct that any particular Act of Parliament or of the Legislature of the State shall not apply to a Scheduled Area or any part thereof in the State or shall apply to a Scheduled Area or any part thereof in the State subject to such exceptions and modifications as he may specify in the notification and any direction given under this sub-paragraph may be given so as to have retrospective effect.

(2) The Governor may make regulations for the peace and good Government of any area in a State which is for the time being a Scheduled Area. In particular and without prejudice to the generality of the foregoing power, such regulations may:
    (a) Prohibit or restrict the transfer of land by or among members of the Scheduled Tribes in such area;
    (b) regulate the allotment of land to members of the Scheduled Tribes in such area; and
    (c) regulate the carrying on of business as money-lender by persons who lend money to members of the Scheduled Tribes in such area.

(3) In making any such regulation as is referred to in the sub-paragraph (2) of this paragraph, the Governor may repeal or amend any Act of Parliament or of the

Legislature of the State or any existing law which is for the time being applicable to the area in question.

(4) All regulations made under this paragraph shall be submitted forthwith to the President and, until assented to by him, shall have no effect.

(5) No regulation shall be made under this paragraph unless the Governor making the regulation has in the case where there is a Tribes Advisory Council for the State, consulted such council.

Part C of the fifth Schedule deals with Scheduled Areas it states:

(1) In this Constitution the expression "Scheduled Areas" means such areas as the President may by order declare to be Scheduled Areas,

(2) The President may at any time by order

(a) directs that the whole or any specified part of a Scheduled Area shall cease to be a Scheduled Area or a part of such an area,

(aa) increase the area of any Scheduled Area in a State after consultation with the Governor of that State,

(b) alter but only by way of rectification of boundaries, any Scheduled Area,

(c) on any alteration of the boundaries of a State or on the admission into the Union or the establishment of a new State, declare any territory not previously included in any State to be, or to form part of, a Scheduled Area, and

(d) rescind, in relation to any State or States, any order or orders made under this paragraph and in consultation with the Governor of the State concerned, make fresh orders redefining the areas which are to be Scheduled areas and any such order may contain such incidental and consequential provisions as appear to the President to be necessary and proper, but save as aforesaid, the order made under sub-paragraph

(i) of this paragraph shall not be varied by any subsequent order.

Part D of the fifth Schedule provides that Parliament may from time to time by law amend by way of addition, variation or repeal any of the provisions of this schedule and when the schedule is so amended, any reference to this Schedule in this Constitution shall be construed as a reference to such schedule as so amended.

According to the provision of Article 244(1), it is clear that the fifth Schedule does not apply to Assam, Meghalaya, Tripura and Mizoram. The provisions relating to these four States are there in Article 244(2).

Article 244(2) provides that:

> "The provision of the sixth schedule shall apply to the administration of the Tribal Areas in the State of Assam, Meghalaya, Tripura and Mizoram".[161]

The sixth Schedule contains provisions relating to the administration of the Tribal Areas in the States of Assam (North Cachar Hills District and Karbi Anglong District), Meghalaya, Tripura (Autonomous Hill District) and Mizoram.

There are autonomous district councils and autonomous regional councils in these areas which have a long tradition of self-management system.

These autonomous councils not only administer the various departments and developmental programmes but also have the power to make laws on a variety of subjects, e.g. land, forest, cultivation, village or town, police, public health and sanitation inheritance of property, marriage and divorce and social customs.

(B) Article 339 : Control of the Union over the Administration of Scheduled Areas and the Welfare of Scheduled Tribes

Now the problem is, what should be the criteria for

161. Substituted by the Constitution (Fourty-nineth Amendment) Act, 1984 and later by the State of Mizoram Act, 1986.

classifying Scheduled Areas. Article 339 provides for the appointment of a commission to study the problems of Scheduled Tribes and Scheduled Areas. To study the problems of Scheduled Tribes, Scheduled Areas and Scheduled Tribes Commission can be appointed by the President in pursuance of Article 339.

Article 339 states that:

(1) The President may at any time and shall, at the expiration of ten years from the commencement of this Constitution by order appoint a commission to report on the administration of the Scheduled Areas and the welfare of Scheduled Tribes in the States.
The order may define the composition, power and procedure of the commission and may contain such incidental or ancillary provisions as the President may consider necessary or desirable.

(2) The executive power of the Union shall extend to the giving of directions to a State as to the drawing up and execution of schemes specified in the direction to be essential for the welfare of Scheduled Tribes in the State.

(C) Article 338 : National Commission for Scheduled Castes

The framers of the Constitution felt the need for providing safeguards to Scheduled Castes and Scheduled Tribes; so they made special provisions to promote social, educational, economic and service interests of these two weakest of the weak section of the society (i.e. Scheduled Castes and Scheduled Tribes) and issued guidelines for implementation of these safeguards. In order to ensure that the provisions and guidelines were effectively implemented the Constitution of India establishes National Commission for Scheduled Castes under Article 338. The responsibility of commission is to oversee, monitor and investigate various activities towards securing justice and rightful share for the most underprivileged and marginalised section of the society, Fifty-nine years working of the Constitutional safeguards has shown that though the Scheduled Castes have benefited to some extent in terms of socio-economic development and reservation in services, yet there are many areas such as literacy, education , legal aid, land reforms, check on atrocities and general integration of Scheduled Castes in the mainstream of the society, where much more need to be done. The commission as a watchdog body is expected to direct and monitor the functioning of various organs of the State in order to protect and promote the interests of the Scheduled Castes.

Primarily, in order to ensure that the provisions and guidelines were effectively implemented the Constitution appointed a special officer under Article 338(1). He was responsible to investigate all matters relating to the safeguards provided to Scheduled Castes and Scheduled Tribes and to report to the President of India about the working of such safeguards. On 18 Nov., 1950, the office of the special officer was designated as Commissioner for Scheduled Castes and the Scheduled Tribes. He was assisted by ten Assistant Regional Commissioners, each incharge of a region. The Commissioners used to submit to the President every year a report which was laid before each House of the Parliament.

Article 338, however was amended in 1990 through the Constitution (Sixty-fifth Amendment) Act, to provide for a National Commission for Scheduled Castes and the Scheduled Tribes.

Amended Article 338 further amended by the Constitution (Eighty-nineth Amendment) Act, 2003, by this Amendment the words 'and Scheduled Tribes" omitted from Article 338. The Amended Article 338 runs as follows:

(1) There shall be a commission for the Scheduled Castes to be known as the National Commission for Scheduled Castes.

(2) Subject to the provisions of any law made in this behalf by Parliament, the commission shall consist of a Chairperson, Vice-Chairperson and three other members and the conditions of service and tenure of office of the Chairperson, Vice-Chairperson and other Members so appointed shall be such as the President may by rule determine.

(3) The Chairperson, Vice-Chairperson and other

Members of the commission shall be appointed by the President by warrant under his hand and seal.

(4) The Commission shall have the power to regulate its own procedure.

(5) It shall be the duty of the commission:

(a) to investigate and monitor all matters relating to the safeguards provided for the Scheduled Castes under this Constitution or under any other law for the time being in force or under any order of the Government and to evaluate the working of such safeguards;

(b) to inquire into specific complaints with respect to the deprivation of rights and safeguards of the Scheduled Castes;

(c) to participate and advise on the planning process of socio-economic development of the Scheduled Castes and to evaluate the progress of their development under the Union and any State;

(d) to present to the President, annually and at such other times as the commission may deem fit, reports upon the working of those safeguards;

(e) to make in such reports recommendations as to the measures that should be taken by the Union or any State for the effective implementation of those safeguards and other measures for the protection, welfare and socio-economic development of the Scheduled Castes; and

(f) to discharge such other functions in relation to the protection, welfare and development and advancement of the Scheduled Castes as the President may, subject to the provisions of any law made by Parliament by the rule specify.

(6) The President shall cause all such reports to be laid before each House of Parliament along with a memorandum explaining the action taken or proposed to be taken on the recommendations relating to the Union and the reasons for the non-acceptance; if any, of any of such recommendations.

(7) Where any such report, or any part thereof, relates to any matter with which any State Government is

concerned, a copy of such report shall be forwarded to the Governor of the State who shall cause it to be laid before the Legislature of the State along with a memorandum explaining the action taken or proposed to be taken on the recommendations relating to the State and the reasons for the non-acceptance, if any, of any of such recommendations.

(8) The commission shall, while investigating any matter referred to in sub-clause (a) or inquiring into any complaint referred to in sub-clause (b) of clause (5), have all the powers of a civil court trying a suit and in particular in respect of the following matters, namely:

(a) summoning and enforcing the attendance of any person from any part of India and examining him on oath;

(b) requiring the discovery and production of any document;

(c) receiving evidence on affidavits;

(d) requisitioning any public record or copy thereof from any court or office;

(e) issuing commissions for the examination of witnesses and documents; and

(f) any other matter which the President may by rule, determine;

(9) The Union and every State Government shall consult the commission on all major policy matters affecting Scheduled Castes.

(10) In this Article, references to the Scheduled Castes shall be construed as including references to such other backward classes as the President may, on receipt of the report of a Commission appointed under clause (1) of Article 340 by order specify and also to the Anglo-Indian community.

According to Article 338, the Commission shall consist of a Chairperson, a Vice-Chairperson and three other members. Previously there were five members in the commission, but by the (Eighty-nineth Amendment) Act, 2003 the number has been reduced to three. They shall be appointed by the President of

India. The first Commission was constituted on 12 March, 1992 with Ram Dhan as Chairman and the present Commission is constituted with Sri Suraj Bhan as a Chairperson but due to his death the position is presently vacant and Fakir Bhai Vaghela as a Vice-Chairman and Shri P.C. Verma, Smt. S. Lambutre and Shri Devender V. as a member of Commission. Every member of the Commission holds the office for a term of three years.

(D) Article 338(A): National Commission for Scheduled Tribes

Geographically and culturally, the Scheduled Tribes are different from the Scheduled Castes and their problems are also different from Scheduled Castes. Keeping this point of view, in Oct. 1999, a new Ministry of Tribal Affairs was created to provide a sharp focus to the welfare and development of Scheduled Tribes. It was felt necessary that the ministry of Tribal affairs should co-ordinate all activities relating to the Scheduled Tribes. In order to safeguard the interests of Scheduled Tribes more effectively, it was proposed to also set-up a separate National Commission for Scheduled Tribes. A new Article 338A is inserted in the Constitution by (Eighty-nineth Amendment) Act, 2003 and the commission for Scheduled Tribes has been establishd by the Article 338A.

Article 338A runs as follows:

(1) There shall be a commission for the Scheduled Tribes to be known as the National Commission for Scheduled Tribes.

(2) Subject to the provisions of any law made in this behalf by Parliament, the commission shall consist of a Chairperson, Vice-Chairperson and three other members and the conditions of service and tenure of office of the Chairperson, Vice-Chairperson and other Members so appointed shall be such as the President may by rule determine.

(3) The Chairperson, Vice-Chairperson and other Members of the commission shall be appointed by the President by warrant under his hand and seal.

(4) The Commission shall have the power to regulate its own procedure.

(5) It shall be the duty of the commission:

(a) to investigate and monitor all matters relating to the safeguards provided for the Scheduled Tribes under this Constitution or under any other law for the time being in force or under any order of the Government and to evaluate the working of such safeguards;

(b) to inquire into specific complaints with respect to the deprivation of rights and safeguards of the Scheduled Tribes;

(c) to participate and advise on the planning process of socio-economic development of the Scheduled Tribes and to evaluate the progress of their development under the Union and any State;

(d) to present to the President, annually and at such other times as the Commission may deem fit, reports upon the working of those safeguards;

(e) to make in such reports recommendations as to the measures that should be taken by the Union or any State for the effective implementation of those safeguards and other measures for the protection, welfare and socio-economic development of the Scheduled Tribes; and

(f) to discharge such other functions in relation to the protection, welfare and development and advancement of the Scheduled Tribes as the President may, subject to the provisions of any law made by Parliament by the rule specify.

(6) The President shall cause all such reports to be laid before each House of Parliament along with a memorandum explaining the action taken or proposed to be taken on the recommendations relating to the Union and the reasons for the non-acceptance, if any, of any of such recommendations.

(7) Where any such report, or any part thereof, relates to any matter with which any State Government is concerned, a copy of such report shall be forwarded to the Governor of the State who shall cause it to be laid before the Legislature of the State along with a memorandum explaining the action taken or

proposed to be taken on the recommendations relating to the State and the reasons for the non-acceptance if any, of any of such recommendations.

(8) The commission shall, while investigating any matter referred to in sub-clause (a) or inquiring into any complaint referred to in sub-clause (b) of clause (5), have all the powers of a civil court trying a suit and in particular in respect of the following matters, namely :

(a) summoning and enforcing the attendance of any person from any part of India and examining him on oath;

(b) requiring the discovery and production of any document;

(c) receiving evidence on affidavits;

(d) requisitioning any public record or copy thereof from any court or office;

(e) issuing commissions for the examination of witnesses and documents; and

(f) any other matter which the President may by rule, determine.

(9) The Union and every State Government shall consult the commission on all major policy matters affecting Scheduled Tribes.

The new Commission for Scheduled Tribes shall consist of a Chairperson, Vice-Chairperson and three other members. The Present Commission comprises Shri Kunwar Singh as a Chairperson, Shri Lama Lobzang, Smt. Prem Bhai Mandvi and Shri Buduren Srivaslu as a member. The post of Vice-Chairman fell vacant on 31.03.2004 when Shri Tapir Gao (who joined as Vice-Chairman on 2.3.2004), Shri Gajendra Singh Rajkheri has assumed office on 29.5.2006 as Vice-Chairman of the Commission.

Both Commission has framed its own rule of procedure which is known as Rule of procedure of the National Commission for Scheduled Castes and Rule of procedure of National Commission of Scheduled Tribes.

The Commission sends its annual report to the President of India. The report must be on the working of the safeguards and the recommendations regarding the measures that should be taken by the Union or any State Governments for the effective implementation of those safeguards *vis-a-vis* other measures for the protection, welfare and socio-economic development for the Scheduled Castes and the Scheduled Tribes.

The President should cause all such reports to be laid before each House of Parliament along with a memorandum explaining the action taken or proposed to be taken on the recommendations relating to the State and the reasons for non acceptance, if any, of such recommendations. Where any such report or any part thereof relates to any matter with which any State Government is concerned, a copy of such report shall be forwarded to the Governer of the State who shall cause it to be laid before the legislature of the State along with memorandum explaining the action taken or proposed to be taken on the recommendations relating to the State and the reasons for non-acceptance, if any, of any of such recommendations.

Some observations and recommendations by Scheduled Castes and the Scheduled Tribes Commission are as follows. All the observations and recommendations are of before the (Eighty-nineth Amendment) Act, 2003:

(1) About 200 million people in this country are classified as Scheduled Castes and the Scheduled Tribes.
(2) Even today, of the 39% who are below poverty line, 90% are Scheduled Castes and the Scheduled Tribes.
(3) Of the total dalit main workforce in the primary sector 64.54% are landless agricultural labourers. It is this section of dalit mass which is the prime victim of caste riots.
(4) In the Union Government services the proportion of Scheduled Castes in class I, II, III and IV (excluding sweepers) posts is presently 10, 13, 16 and 21 percent for the Scheduled Tribes, it is 3, 3, 6, and 7, percent respectively.
(5) Though the Constitution has provided 22% of reservations for Scheduled Castes and Scheduled Tribes, less than 2% out of the 67,500 reserved teaching posts has been filled in 239 Universities and 7000 Colleges country-wide.

(6) The Scheduled Castes and the Scheduled Tribes are under represented in the middle and higher echelons of the judiciary.

(7) The general perception is that the benefits of protective discrimination are always concerned by the creamy layer.

(8) The Scheduled Castes and the Scheduled Tribes have the lowest level of literacy. They are least represented in the higher level of bureaucracy and administration. Most of them work as scavengers, sweepers and casual labourers. Inspite of 50 years of independence, the situation of Scheduled Castes and the Scheduled Tribes has not shown any improvement and they continue to be victims of oppression.

(9) In the Constitution Scheduled Castes and the Scheduled Tribes have been accorded special treatment. The preferential treatment on the part of the State is meant to bring about social transformation. However, with the high level of caste bias and prejudices of the upper castes, the provision in the Constitution are hardly materialised. The bias and prejudices in the system, have taken away from Scheduled Castes and the Scheduled Tribes whatever was theirs. At the level of promises, everything is given to Scheduled Castes and the Scheduled Tribes and the other marginalized. In practice however there are large gaps.

(10) Exploiting the Scheduled Castes and the Scheduled Tribes vote bank has been a wining formula for politicians ever since independence. However, the tall promises remain mere rhetorics.

(11) A change in attitude is needed. It is not because more time is required but because efforts are made half-heartedly. Atrocities continue to occur. Political will is lacking to improve the condition of Scheduled Castes and the Scheduled Tribes.

(12) Since the main reason for dispute is found to be regarding the right over land; amendments to the relevant land laws are immediately required to protect the interest of cultivators and agricultural labourers.

(13) Since development in tribal areas is based on rich natural resources, Government should ensure that the original inhabitants of the areas are not merely labourers but equal partners in the development process with rights to lead a life of respect and dignity.

(14) The Government in consultation with the State Government and State Scheduled Castes and the Scheduled Tribes commission should come out with an appropriate national level policy.

(15) The Government must set-up a Scheduled Castes and the Scheduled Tribes development authority on the line of Planning Commission with Prime Minister as Chairman and a non-official as Vice-Chairman. Similar arrangements must be made in the States.

(16) The Government must provide reservation to the Scheduled Castes and the Scheduled Tribes in the Defence Forces, Scientific establishment and Judiciary.

(17) There should be a provision for providing of reservation in the private sector because the private sector enjoyed Government partronage in terms of concessional land, financing, excise and sales tax relief.

(18) Community certificates should be issued by following a foolproof procedure. Reservations should be legalised while 33% quota should be reserved for Scheduled Castes and the Scheduled Tribes women. Land reforms should be expend and the minimum wages formula should be introduced. Opportunities for higher education and specialisation should also be afforded to the Scheduled Castes and the Scheduled Tribes.

(19) Cases of atrocities committed on Scheduled Castes and the Scheduled Tribes should be tried in a Special Court and steps should be taken to provide them with adequate relief and rehabilitation mandatorily.

(20) Urgent steps must be taken by the Government to improve the condition of the Scheduled Castes and the Scheduled Tribes. The steps include, adequate

allocation of Funds, increasing vigilance on crimes against these sections, speeding up land reforms and a separate agency on the model of the CAT to deal with Scheduled Castes and the Scheduled Tribes service matters.

(21) In the past there was lot of delay in preparing the Action Taken Report (ATR). The recommendations of the commission should be placed in Parliament first and only then the ATR should be prepared.

(22) The Commission must examine why recommendations of the previous Commissions have not been implemented.

(23) The National Commission for Scheduled Castes and the Scheduled Tribes be vested with more powers, at par with the Election Commission of India, enabling it to pass strictures against the erring officials or State. Implementation of its orders should be made mandatory.

Different provisions of our Constitution make it clear that our Constitution-makers were not only willing to make safeguards in favour of Scheduled Castes and the Scheduled Tribes but also wanted that these safeguards must be effectively implemented; so they incorporated some provisions which could work as watchdog over the implementation of the above discussed safeguards. There are certain areas which are notified Scheduled Areas. For the better administration of these areas, Constitution-makers provided for Articles 244(1), 339. and 338. These Articles provide for some type of Administrative safeguards regarding Scheduled Castes and the Scheduled Tribes. A commission has been constituted to see that how the condition of the Scheduled Castes and the Scheduled Tribes could be uplifted and strengthened. The provisions of constitution regarding commission has been dealt at length in above discussion. The need of the hour is to implement the recommendations and suggestions of the commission in right spirit so that the down-trodden conditions could be ameliorated.

Conclusion and Suggestions

The Constitution of India is basically a compact socio-political document whose foundation can be traced in the freedom struggle of our country. With the dawn of Independence a new chapter commenced in the socio-political history of India.

The framers of the Constitution have not only devised a suitable constitutional framework for the country but also conceived the remedies for social problems. The incorporation of provisions relating to the cause of doing justice to Scheduled Castes and Scheduled Tribes constitute a glorious chapter in the Indian Constitution.

The imbalance in the society caused by the caste system is sought to be corrected by doing justice to backward class of citizens on the social, economic and political plane. This objective of the Constitution finds expression mainly in the Preamble, Fundamental Rights and Directive Principles of State Policy.

The Preamble to the Constitution accords primacy to Justice, social, economic, and political, in the making of state policy and in state action. Accordingly, an impressive array of legislative enactments and executive orders have provided a firm legal framework for government action to abolish the most outrageous aspects of the caste system, viz., untouchability; to anchor in law the scheme of reservations for the Scheduled Castes and Scheduled Tribes in political institutions of governance and to provide for reservation in government services and educational institutions; to reform land relations in order to enable the weaker sections, predominantly belonging to the Scheduled Castes and Scheduled Tribes, to access productive assets so that they may work with freedom and dignity; to protect the incomes of landless labour and marginal land holders through minimum wage legislation; to provide financial and organizational resources for the Scheduled Castes children to receive elementary, secondary and higher education; to prevent and penalise atrocities; to allocate plan resources under specially designed schemes for economic, educational and social development of the Scheduled Castes and Scheduled Tribes and to provide the plan mechanism of Special Component Plan for Scheduled Castes and Tribal Sub-plan to channelise more developmental resources to them and to integrate the Scheduled Castes and Scheduled Tribes with the mainstream of social and economic life in the country. There is a misconception that the problems of Scheduled Castes and Scheduled Tribes are sectional and marginal. In reality these are part of the central and core problems of the country. These categories of people constitute about a good population of the country and almost the entire physical labour force of the country is drawn from them. It is the failure to tackle their problems so as to remove their disabilities and secure their full potential for national development that lies at the root of the many weaknesses faced by post-Independence India to this day. Therefore, these issues and the remedial measures should be approached as central and core concerns of India.[1]

It is true there is some progress in breaking the mould of social inequality and caste oppression and in the economic and educational spheres but there is a long way to go before social equality, educational equality, freedom from caste oppression, freedom from economic dependence are achieved. The traditional sanction for inequality has been decisively

1. Subash Kashyap, Constitution-making since 1950, pp. 445-48.

questioned and to some extent undermined. What is most important is the cultural and intellectual upsurge in the dalit communities across the country evidenced in their literary and intellectual productions. This is a development which fills us with hope for the future.

Yet, one still waits for a cultural revolution that would uproot inherited attitudes, values, institutions, practices, and postures, replacing them with values and attitudes relevant to a modern, egalitarian society. Education has still to perform the role of dissolving the encrusted debris of birth sanctioned superiority and birth-based discrimination, deprivation and exploitation. Vast numbers of landless and marginal farmers still hope for a change in institutional arrangements that would end their abject dependency on the existing power structures in the rural areas.

However, even when faced with the reality of the gap between aspiration and achievement, we cannot but pay our humble tribute to the foresight and wisdom of the Constitution-makers in frontally tackling an issue of immense significance to nation-building. It remains for us to carry forward the task of bringing about social, economic and educational equality fortified by the mandates of our Constitution. Reservation, no doubt, helped the deprived sections to secure a share, though not to an adequate extent, in governance. Reservation was intended to be part of a comprehensive package of an entire gamut of economic, educational and social measures. This comprehensive package has not been provided in its fullness. Consequently, reservation alone by itself has not been able to bring about the total social transformation envisaged in the Constitution.

The outcome of the failure to provide the comprehensive package envisaged by the Constitution gives material for a sobering thought. More than half century after the Constitution, the bulk of the Scheduled Castes families remain agricultural wage labourers as in the past many centuries. The bulk of Scheduled Tribes continue to remain in remote areas and are being progressively deprived of their lands converting many of them into agricultural labourers. All the categories continue to be the victims, in varying forms and degrees, of all-round deprivations, discriminations and disabilities, in all spheres—

economic, educational, social—in the case of Scheduled Castes extending to the extreme of untouchability and in the case of Scheduled Tribes to the extreme of isolation.

This book is based on those provisions of Constitution which provides for different safeguards in favour of Scheduled Castes and Scheduled Tribes. In earlier chapters different provisions under relevant heads have been dealt within depth. In this chapter it has been attempted to conclude those chapters.

Chapter First introduces the subject. The very first Quotation in Chapter I quoted by Supreme Court from *William Black's* 'Auguries of innocence' in N.M. Thomas case[2] itself explains the down-trodden conditions of Scheduled Castes and Scheduled Tribes. Initially our society is a casteless society. But later on it had been divided into various castes based on their work. Work-based division of class has been converted into birth-based caste. The origin of social stratification has lost its antiquity.

The framers of the Constitution were great social engineers and the Constitution of India is an excellent piece of social engineering. The Constitution aims at peaceful social change by balancing the conflicting interests in the Indian Society.

Chapter I envisages the condition of depressed classes and also various steps taken for their enhancement through social engineering which have helped a lot in their upliftment.

The Second Chapter deals with various dimensions of social justice. Our society is a complex society divided in various castes. There are too much disparities between the same castes settled in different parts of country. But overall their conditions are very poor and miserable. For the sake of civilzed society as well as for the development of our country, it is very much necessary to take proper measure for their enhancement. Without the development of all the sections of society, we can't think about the development of our country. Various jurists and social workers such as Kelson, Plato, Aristotle, Herbert Spencer, Ulpian, etc. has propounded and developed their theory in this connection.

2. State of Kerala *v.* N.M. Thomas, AIR 1976 S.C., p. 490.

Chapter II also deals with the concept of Social justice from ancient times to modern era. Various jurists such as Holmes, Friedman, Roscoe Pound, Rawls, etc. have done a lot of work. Our Constitution also incorporates their views while framing the Constitution specially relating to the provisions concerned with Scheduled Castes and Scheduled Tribes.

This chapter deals with the various articles relating to social justice which have been incorporated in the Constitution of India to further Social Justice which is one of the main object of our Constitution-makers such as Preamble, Fundamental Rights and Directive Principles of State Policy of Indian Constitution. Articles 330, 332, 334, 338, 338A also deals with the safeguards for Scheduled Castes and Scheduled Tribes. The views of Jurists, Constitutional provisions and judgements of Courts have helped a lot in enhancing the conditions of depressed sections. The aim and object dealt in this chapter have helped a lot for the upliftment of depressed classes.

In the Chapter Three Historical Perspective and Origin of Scheduled Castes and Scheduled Tribes have been elaborately discussed. In tracing the origin of caste, people are greatly influenced by the facts recorded about this institution in the ancient sacred works such as Vedas, Upanishad, Puranas and Dharmshastras. The commonly known theory of caste is *Chaturvarna*. This idea of *Chaturvarna* is mentioned in *Purrushshuta* hymn in *Rigveda*.[3] This four-fold division of society was referred to in the Bhagvat Gita as : The four orders of society (viz. the Brahmin, the Kshatriya, the Vaishya and Shudra) were created by me classifying them according to their netal qualities and apportioning corresponding duties to them; though the author of this creation, know me, the immortal lord to be a non-doer.[4]

Coming to the critical theories of caste, *Nesfield* was of the firm conviction that function and function only, was the foundation upon which the whole caste system of India was built up. An intensive study of the social institution of caste points to the direction that a number of factors have contributed

3. Brahmanoasya mukhamaseda bahu rajanhya kritah uru tadasya yadyssyoh padmyam sudro ajayatah. Rigveda X 90.12.
4. The Bhagvat Gita, Chapter 4-12.

to the genesis, and growth of this institution at different intervals. 'Guna' or character was emphasised in the Varna theory of caste which is incidentally the oldest and the widely accepted theory. But with the lapse of time we find references being made to the factor of "Birth" as the sole determinant of caste.[5]

About the meaning of Scheduled Castes it can be said that in earlier times the words, Untouchables, Sudras, Depressed classes, Exterior Castes, Excluded Castes were used for Scheduled Castes. The term Scheduled Castes was first used in Government of India Act, 1935 and it is there in our present Constitution also with some addition. Articles 341 and 366(24) relate to the definition and meaning of Scheduled Castes.

Tribes are those nomadic and aboriginal groups who have their own distinct culture. They are socially separated and geographically isolated. The term Scheduled Tribes is of recent origin and came in vogue with the advent of the Constitution. Prior to that Scheduled Tribes were variously termed as Aboriginal, Adivasis, Forest Tribes, Hill Tribes, Primitive Tribes, Bangaras and Waderers. Articles 342 and 366(25) are related to the meaning of Scheduled Tribes.

From the chapter of Historical perspective and origin of Scheduled Castes and Scheduled Tribes it can be concluded that origin of Scheduled Castes and Scheduled Tribes can be chiefly attributed to different Dharmshastras and birth theory. For the purpose of clarity of the meaning of Scheduled Castes and Scheduled Tribes is included in our Constitution.

The chapter next to Historical Perspective and Origin of Scheduled Castes and Scheduled Tribes has dealt with those causes which were responsible for the degradation of Scheduled Castes and Scheduled Tribes. The idea of 'Karma' and 'Rebirth', the idea of pollution, the belief in the lower origin of Sudras, low economic and social position of Sudras and some psychological factors can be attributed to the degradation of Scheduled Castes and Scheduled Tribes.

It is fact that society is not a static phenomenon and the then society was also changing. The miserable condition of the Scheduled Castes and Scheduled Tribes have given rise to the

5. For a detailed historical background of the Social structure in India, See Churye, Caste and Classes in India, 1953.

movement for their upliftment. Though the movement was not forceful enough to eradicate caste and untouchability and establish a casteless and equal society but still it had some significance in the history of providing safegurards in favour of Scheduled Castes and Scheduled Tribes.

It was felt at that time it was the urgent demand of the situation to redress the grievances of the Scheduled Castes and Scheduled Tribes. Many social reformers came forward with different ideology. So that there could not be a major crack and conversion from Hindu society. The social reformers worked in various parts of the country and toiled a lot to unify the Hindu society. Had their efforts been collective, they would had been able to uplift the condition of Scheduled Castes and Scheduled Tribes.

The depressed community, itself endeavoured to improve its condition. This class have tried to raise their social standard by sanskritizing their eating habits, their occupations and their names whereas they tried to raise their ritual status by emulating the religious practices of higher castes and also by changing their marriage practices.

Though the Britishers were not interested in the upliftment of socio-political status of Scheduled Castes and Scheduled Tribes and many a times the English Courts had given the judgments in favour of higher castes. But there are the instances where we can have some trace of legislation in favour of Scheduled Castes and Scheduled Tribes. The most unfortunate stigma attached to Scheduled Castes were their being pollutant and untouchable. They were denied temple entry. Initially the Brithish Government resisted those domestic enactment which conferred upon the right of temple entry to Scheduled Castes. (as in the case of Travancore, Madras, Bombay and Delhi Legislation)

A major breakthrough was the 1936 proclamation of Maharaja of Travancore followed by the Legislation of province of Madras.

The Bombay Legislative Council passed a resolution in 1923 that untouchables (the Scheduled Castes) be allowed to use all public watering places, wells, schools, dispensaries, etc. In the year 1925 similar type of bill was introduced in Madras legislative council also.

There were certain provisions of Government of India Act, 1935 also which rule out inequality. These were sections 275 and 298. The corresponding Article to section 275 of Government of India Act, 1935 is Article 16.

The Constituent Assembly debated elaborately about providing different safeguards to Scheduled Castes and Scheduled Tribes. The minority sub-committee advised certain Fundamental Rights for Scheduled Castes and Scheduled Tribes which were included in the Constitution of India that came into effect on 26th of January 1950.

Chapter Six is the core of the book. Infact, it is the chapter which deals with the topic directly. This chapter is the articulation of our Constitution-makers and it elaborately deals with different provisions which have been provided to Scheduled Castes and Scheduled Tribes by our Constitution. The survey of these Constitutional provisions for Scheduled Castes and Scheduled Tribes show that two opposing trends are put into operation. These opposite trends are the concept of equality and special preference. Discrimination of grounds of caste, creed and sex, etc. is ruled out on the one hand while on the other hand, special provisions have been made for Scheduled Castes and Scheduled Tribes. Special treatment of Scheduled Castes and Scheduled Tribes is accorded in the triple field, Education, Government services and Political representation. The tangle of equality and special treatment has been pictured by *Pt. Jawahar Lal Nehru:*

> "We arrive at a peculiar tangle, namely, that we cannot have equality because in trying to attain equality we came up against certain principles of equality laid down in the Constitution. That is a very peculiar position we can not have equality because we cannot have non-discrimination. For it you are thinking of raising those who are down, you are some how affecting the *status quo,* undoubtedly. You are, thus, said to be discriminating because you are affecting the *status quo*."[6]

It could be said in favour of constitutional provisions for

6. Jawahar Lal Nehru Speeches, 1949-53, p. 518.

Scheduled Castes and Scheduled Tribes that they are both justifiable and inevitable. The social condition in India are such that they necessitate the incorporation of special treatment for Scheduled Castes and Scheduled Tribes.

A wide range of safeguards are there in Parts III[7] and IV[8] of our Constitution, but there are certain special provisions in Part XVI[9] of the Constitution of India. The intention to provide safeguards is to uplift the Scheduled Castes and Scheduled Tribes and to integrate them with the mainstream of national life.

Under the sub-head of social safeguards Articles 14, 15, 17, 23, 24 and 25(2)(b) have been dealt. These Articles are concluded as under.

Article 14 includes within itself equality before law and equal protection of law. The scope of Article 14 is that those who are in equal situation would be treated equal. Because of the fact that there exists some dissimilarity in society, Article 14 itself permits some sort of discrimination. The import of Article 14 is not restricted to the concept of formal or legal equality. It is comprehensive enough to include the concept of substantive equality also.

Article 15(1) must be construed as that no legislation could be passed by the State which further degrade the condition of Scheduled Castes and Scheduled Tribes. Article 15(2) forcefully recognises the rights of Scheduled Castes and Scheduled Tribes to have access to shops, public restaurant, hotels and place of public entertainment and to use the wells, tanks, bathing ghats, roads and places of public resorts maintained wholly or partly out of State fund or dedicated to the use of general public.

Article 17 gets a special distinction in the Constitution for materializing *Gandhiji's* dream of doing away with untouchability because the complete abolition of Untouchability was one of the visions of *Mahatma Gandhi* in his "Ramrajya'.[10] This Article adopts the Gandhian ideal without any qualification. Article 17 is unique in the sense that it has given

7. Articles 12 to 35 especially 14, 15, 16, 17, 23, 24 and 25.
8. Articles 36 to 51 especially 38, 39(A), and 46.
9. Articles 330 to 342.
10. Basu, Durga Das, Commentary on the Constitution of India.

a death blow to the country old practice of untouchability. It reflects the spirit of the Constitution, the determination to restore the dignity of the individual and assure fraternity. Untouchability is not only prohibited but it is punishable under law. The Parliament has assumed the power to legislate on this matter uniformly in all the States.

Though, Articles 23 and 24 are construed for the upliftment of Scheduled Castes and Scheduled Tribes but the language is used under these Articles in a wider sense. The people of Scheduled Castes and Scheduled Tribes community were more subjected to Trafficking, Begar and Forced labour. Similarly, the lower socio-economic condition of the Scheduled Castes and Scheduled Tribes forced them to send their children to work in hazardous factories also. The inclusion of these two Articles in the chapter of Fundamental Rights have greately supported the cause for the upliftment of Scheduled Castes and Scheduled Tribes. Our Hon'ble Supreme Court has also interpreted these Articles in favour of Scheduled Castes and Scheduled Tribes through different Public Interest Litigations.

Due to the practice of Untouchability and the low social status of Scheduled Castes and Scheduled Tribes the entry in temple has been denied to them for centuries. Article 25(2)(b) of the Constitution of India authorises the State to throw open such institutions to all classes and sections of Hindus. This right to temple entry has assured the Scheduled Castes and Scheduled Tribes that they have the right to live with dignity and they are not out-caste before God.

Article 15(4), Article 46 and Article 275(1) have dealt with under the sub-head of educational and economic safeguards. Inportance of education is well known. Eradication of illiteracy by teaching the Scheduled Castes and Scheduled Tribes constitute the keynote of the problem of educational advancement. Education is not mere literacy. Article 15(4) aims at the development of Individual personality of Scheduled Castes and Scheduled Tribes. It is quite appropriate that the Scheduled Castes and Scheduled Tribes should look the Constitution for special favour to redress the wrongs done in the past by creating social disability. This Article requires for an affirmative action by the State to make the Scheduled Castes and Scheduled Tribes stand on their own feet. Article 15(4) is not the exclusive repository of the notion of compensatory discrimination. It is an exception of Article 15(1) and 15(2) and explanation of Article 14. By virtue of Article 15(4) the State can make specific provisions favouring Scheduled Castes and Scheduled Tribes.

Protection of the interest of Scheduled Castes and Scheduled Tribes are first charge on the State. It is the underlying principle of Article 46. This is a comprehensive Article comprising both the developmental and regulatory aspects. This Article finds place in the chapter of Directive Principles of State Policy which is though not enforceable by court of law,[11] but it imposes a duty on the State that it would take into consideration the interest of Scheduled Castes and Scheduled Tribes while framing any educational and economic policies.

Under Article 275(1) there is provision for grants from the Union to certain States for the implementation of welfare schemes to better the conditions of Scheduled Tribes, so that they can be ameliorated to the level of others.

Under the sub-heading of service safeguards, Article 16(4), 16(4A), 16(4B) and Article 335 are discussed. Article 16(4) favours the policy of making reservation for certain sections of society who are supposed to be backward class of citizens. Our Supreme Court has tried to define the Expression 'Backward classes of citizens' and held that Scheduled Castes and Scheduled Tribes are also included under the ambit of this expression. Article 16(4) is an exception of Article 16(2) and explanation to Article 16(1). The objective of Article 16(4) is to provide reservation in public employment to backward class of citizens so that their condition could be uplifted. In the *Mandal Commission case*[12] our Hon'ble Supreme Court has interpreted the expression beneficially in favour of Scheduled Castes and Scheduled Tribes that it has a broader connotation than the expression of Article 15(4). Article 16(4) tries to achieve the core

---

11. Article 37. Application of the Principles contained in this part. The provisions contained in this part shall not be enforceable by any court, by the principles therein laid down are nevertheless fundamental in the governance of the country and it shall be the duty of the State apply these principles in making laws.
12. Indra Sawhney *v.* Union of India, AIR 1993 SC, p. 477.

commitment of equal opportunity and social justice as envisaged in our Constitution. By providing protective discrimination it has been endavoured to equate the Scheduled Castes and Scheduled Tribes with rest of the society. Further by the Seventy-seventh, Eighty-first, and Eighty-fifth Amendments of the Constitution these backward class of citizens have more protected and these amendments provide them a better opportunity to achieve something extra-ordinary. In addition to this, a more specific provision is made in Article 335 for making appointments to various services from the members of Scheduled Castes and Scheduled Tribes. Article 335 imposes a Constitutional duty to take into consideration the claims of the members of Scheduled Castes and Scheduled Tribes, consistent with the maintenance of efficiency of administration.

Our Constitution-makers have tried to give proper representation to Scheduled Castes and Scheduled Tribes. They incorporated Article 330, Article 332 and Article 334 and Article 164(1) in the Constitution initially (which came into effect on 26th of January (1950) later by incorporating Seventy-third and Seventy-fourth Constitutional Amendment Act, inserted Article 243(D) and Article 243(T). By providing political representation of Scheduled Castes and Scheduled Tribes through reservation it has been attempted that they could participate in Government so that they can forcefully put forward their grievances at any appropriate forum and get them solved with their own participation. The Amendments made later are of great significance because the very elementary level the opportunity of political participation is provided to Scheduled Castes and Scheduled Tribes. It is pertinent to note that initially the reservation in legislature was for the period of ten years but at present the limit is extended to sixty years. By the Constitution Seventy-ninth Amendment Act, 1999, it is in the conformity with the norms of International Human Rights Law which authorises such measures to protect the interest of the vulnerable section of society.

It is evident that different Constitutional provisions provide for the safeguard of Scheduled Castes and Scheduled Tribes. The safeguards would become only decorative if the Administration and monitoring of these safeguards not be done. For the purpose of administration and monitoring Article 244,

Article 338, Article 338A and Article 339 have been specifically incorporated. Article 244 is for the Administration and control of Scheduled Area and Scheduled Tribes. Because of the fact that these area are highly oppressed, so a separate provision for the administration of these areas is incorporated. To ensure that the provisions and guidelines were effectively implemented the Constitution of India establishes National Commissions for Scheduled Castes and Scheduled Tribes under the Article 338. This commission is entrusted with the responsibility to oversee, monitor and investigate various activities towards securing justice and rightful share for the most underprivileged and marginalised section of society. The commission make recommendations and suggestions from time to time for the betterment of Scheduled Castes and Scheduled Tribes. Article 339 authorises the Union to control the administration of Scheduled Areas and the welfare Scheduled Tribes. Under the Article a commission is appointed to study the problems of Scheduled Tribes and Scheduled Areas. The commission is appointed by the President. The Executive of the commission can direct the State Government for the welfare of Scheduled Tribes in the State.

SUGGESTIONS

The Constitution of India was shaped by the guiding hand and genius of Dr. Ambedkar with the goodwill of Pt. Nehru, Sardar Patel and Dr. Rajendra Prasad and other stalwarts of the Constituent Assembly under the inspiration of Mahatma Gandhi and contains distinct provisions for the protection and promotion of the interests of Scheduled Castes, Scheduled Tribes and other weaker sections so that an egalitarian society could be built up. If these provisions had been implemented in the right spirit, the problems bedevilling the masses of the people and country as a whole should have disappeared by now. Taking the realities of the recent decades and the failure to implement these constitutional provisions, it is necessary to strengthen these provisions by amendments, transfer of certain articles to Part III Fundamental Rights, and certain other similar steps should be taken. So certain suggestions can be put forward for effective upliftment of Scheduled Castes and Scheduled

Tribes so that the objective of our Constitution could be affirmatively achieved.

The Hindu social system has accorded lower place to Scheduled Castes and Scheduled Tribes classifying them as polluters, Sudras, Untouchables and Adivasis; thus, lower position in society has made their life miserable. To correct this historic wrong Article 17 of Constitution abolishes the Untouchability and the practice of Untouchability is forbidden. To give effect to this Article Parliament made an enactment viz. Untouchability (Offence) Act, 1955. To make the provision of this Act more stringent, the Act was amended in 1976 and was also renamed as a Protection of Civil Rights Act, 1955. To prevent the atrocities against Scheduled Castes and Scheduled Tribes Parliament passed another important Act in 1989. This Act is known as Scheduled Castes and Scheduled Tribes (Prevention of Atrocities) Act, 1989. For carring out the provisions of this Act the Government of India have notified the Scheduled Castes and Scheduled Tribes (Prevention of Atrocites) Rules, 1995.

Despite all these measures which have been taken by the legislature there is a little respite to Scheduled Castes and Scheduled Tribes. Infact, these legislative measures have not been able to give substantive relief to Scheduled Castes and Scheduled Tribes Community. It is suggested that some sort of reformative measures must be adopted which could spread awareness in the society about the problem of Untouchability. Some affirmative action must be taken to strengthen the brotherhoodness between the lower and higher castes. Besides this, with regard to legal structure, the Scheduled Castes and Scheduled Tribes (Prevention of Atrocities) Act, 1989 needs to be strengthened and its effective enforcement ensured. This include the establishment of special courts exclusively to try offences under this Act, inclusion of certain crimes in the list of atrocities, certain penal provisions where they do not exist, appropriate plugging of certain loopholes and comprehensive rehabilitation of victims and so on.

Regarding untouchability which continues to be widely prevalent in old classic forms as well as in new forms in line with modern developments, multipronged measures covering human rights education, moral education, building up of a strong democratic movement against untouchability and effective punitive action under the Protection of Civil Rights Act, 1955 are required.

Apart from the social basis of untouchability there is an economic basis also. It is well known fact that the vast majority of the Scheduled Castes population remain landless agricultural labourers and marginal peasants and the Scheduled Tribes have been steadily losing their land and adding to the landless agricultural labour force. Without access to productive assets and firm legal protection for their title, ownership, possession and peaceful enjoyment, it is difficult to see how there can be a real and significant change in the position of the Scheduled Castes and Scheduled Tribes in the village society. In addition, we need to inject new vitality in the operation of minimum wage legislations to benefit agricultural labour. It is suggested that land reforms involving distribution and allotment of lands from different sources (i.e. Government lands not required for genuine public use, bhoodan lands, ceiling surplus lands, etc.) to the Scheduled Castes and Scheduled Tribes along with supportive mechanism in the shape of supply of subsidized capital and credit and extension be made, and development of these lands through irrigation and other means be undertaken. And strong legal action is needed to prevent alienation of lands belonging to the tribal communites and effective prior rehabilitation of tribals before displacement due to the developmental projects.

To further the objective enshrined in Article 23 and Article 24 Parliament has passed Bonded Labour System (Abolition) Act, 1976 and The Child Labour (Prohibition and Regulation) Act, 1986 respectively. For effective implementation of these Acts schemes for identification, liberation and rehabilitation must be put in order. So that the oppressed class could get benefited from these enactments. It is suggested that the Government should implement its socio-economic programmes in toto and appropriate rehabilitation plans must be effectively implemented. The proper rehabilitation of Bonded labour and Child labourers would substantially help in raising their socio-economic standards.

The Government must introduce a scheme of special preferential policy in providing education to the students of

Scheduled Castes and Scheduled Tribes. There is a great need for imparting vocational guidance to these students and to inform them of all the available employment opportunity. Education, being a vital aspect of all development schemes for the advancement of Scheduled Castes and Scheduled Tribes, the Government must put it at top priority.

The term backwardness is relative and it could be attributed to a number of factors which are interrelated. Chain action and reaction of social, educational, economic, environmental and habitual factors have contributed to backwardness. It should be noted that number of untouchables who are actually in higher civil services such as classes I and II is not by any means large. It appears that most of them do come from educated and well-off sections of Scheduled Castes community. This raises the question as to what extent the policy of protective discrimination has really benefitted the bulk of Scheduled Castes and Scheduled Tribes. From the available evidence it appears that only a small section of Scheduled Castes and Scheduled Tribes have been benefitted from the policy that too especially elite, while the large majority among them have remained where they were before independence. The Government should endeavour to investigate the problem with objective test and scientific measures must be adopted so that it could be find out that whether the marginalised section is actually getting the benefit or not.

Reservation in legislature has been provided to Scheduled Castes and Scheduled Tribes. No doubt this legislative reservation has given substantial social and political leverage to the community of Scheduled Castes and Scheduled Tribes to enhance their socio-economic status. In practice, their effect is insignificant. Most of the members of Parliament belong to the national political parties and once elected, represent their parties rather than representing exclusively their community. It is suggested that there must be some sort of forum for these reserved category members where they can freely discuss the problem of their own community and search for the solutions.

Many developmental schemes have been designed to uplift the Scheduled Castes and Scheduled Tribes to a better status. These includes, among others, provision of free house sites, subsidies for the construction of houses, allotment of lands, health measures such as provisions of wells, mobile, dispensaries maternity facilities, encouragement of cottage industries, etc. Administering these schemes has never been successful. Lack of planning and imaginative leadership, delay in release of grants from the Union, lack of coordination and co-operation between various government departments are the reasons behind the slow progress in regards the upliftment of Scheduled Castes and Scheduled Tribes. It is suggested that there must be better co-operation and understanding between the Government Departments so that the Constitutional objective to uplift the Scheduled Castes and Scheduled Tribes could be achieved.

A separate ministry of social justice is created at the Union level. The minister-in-charge of this ministry is usually the weakest in cabinet and if he is a bit serious in his job other ministers do not cooperate with this ministry and do not comply with the directions and promises of this department. It is suggested that the minister must be given more authority so that he could get his schemes implemented fully.

The most complex problem regarding tribals is their integration with the rest of society. As Nehrujee remarked, "What we ought to do is to develop sense of oneness, with these people a sense of unity and understanding. That involves a psychological approach."[13] This integration could be achieved through voluntary agencies, tribal council and cultural research institutes. It is suggested that tribal council must try to win the faith of different tribal groups and to solve their problems at local level. Opening of educational institutes and publication of literature on tribal would help to ameliorate their condition.

The tribals differ so widely in their social and economic environment, culture, language and customs. The social fabric of tribals calls for a cautions scrutiny and scientific investigation in the process of their transformation. Any scheme of ameliorative measures should cater first and foremost, to the preservation of tribal culture. As the Scheduled Areas and Scheduled Tribes Commission pointed out, "The problem of problems is not to disturb the harmony of tribal life and

13. Jawahar Lal Nehru Speeches, 1949-53, p. 518.

simultaneously work for its advance; not to impose anything upon the tribals and simultaneously work for their integration as member and part of Indian family."[14]

The following suggestions can be put forward for this:

- The Government must try to encourage in every way their own traditional art and culture.
- Tribal rights in land and forests must be respected.
- The Government should avoid introducing too many outsiders into the tribal territory.
- The Government should try to train and buildup a team of their own people to do the work of administration and development.
- The Government should not over administer these areas of overwhelm them with a multiplicity of schemes.

The integration of Scheduled Castes and Scheduled Tribes with the mainstream of national life is first and foremost priority. To achieve this objective social reform programmes at different levels must be implemented with the help of Governmental and Non-Governmental Organisations.

The Scheduled Castes and Scheduled Tribes community has been given different legal rights and different schemes are being run for them. The need is to make them aware so that they can know about their legal rights and the scheme for their benefit.

To get their legal rights enforced some simple machinery should be evolved by the Governments, so that their grievances may be redressed easily and they may feel more secure.

No help is better than self-help. The Scheduled Castes and Scheduled Tribes community must come forward for their own help. They must assert for their rights in a Gandhian way (i.e. through non-violence)

The Constitution has provided for different safeguards and protective measures in favour of Scheduled Castes and Scheduled Tribes. In furtherance of these provisions different

14. Report of the Scheduled Castes and Scheduled Tribes Commission, 1961-62, para, 1.27, p. 6.

enactments, schemes and commission have been made. Ultimately, it can be said that a lot more has to be done to realised the objective and dream of our Constitution-makers. Even after more than six decades of the commencement of the Constitution, the position of Scheduled Castes and Scheduled Tribes has not been substantially improved. The need of the hour is to make sincere attempt for the upliftment of Scheduled Castes and Scheduled Tribes community because they are not downtrodden but our brothers. We must honestly endeavour to integrate them with the mainstream of national life, so our nation could march to a new height with our brothers of Scheduled Castes and Scheduled Tribes community.

List of Cases

Bibliography

Constituent Assembly Debates, Volume III, VII.

Acts

Bonded Labour System (Abolition) Act, 1976.
Protection of Civil Right Act, 1955.
Scheduled Castes and Scheduled Tribes (Prevention of Atrocities) Act, 1989.
The Child Labour (Prohibition and Regulation) Act, 1989.
Untouchability Offence Act, 1955.

Books

Ambedkar, B.R., The Untouchables, who were they? And why they became Untouchables?
Austin, Granville, The Indian Constitution: Cornerstone of a Nation.
Basu, Durga Das, Commentary on the Constitution of India.
Bakshi, P.M., The Constitution of India.
Balsara, S.D., Social Legislation in India.
Chaturvedi, R.G., Natural and Social Justice.
Gajendragadkar, P.B., Law, Liberty and Social Justice.
Gandhi, M.K., Removal of Untouchability.
Ghurye, G.S., Caste and Race in India.
Grangrade, K.D., Social Legislation in India.
Hutton, J.H., Caste in India: Its Nature, Function and Origin.

Jain, M.P., Indian Constitutional Law.
Jaswal, P.S., Directive Principles: Jurisprudence and Socio-economic Justice in India.
J. Krishna lyer, Social Justice : Sunset or Dawn.
J. Wed, S.B., Caste and the Law in India.
Kagzi, M.C.J., Segregation and Untouchability Abolition.
Kashyap, Subash, Constitution making since 1950 (An overview).
Krishna Murthy, Impact of Social Legislation on Criminal Law in India.
Kshirasagar, R.K., Untouchability in India. (Implementation of the Law and Abolition)
Pandey, J.N., Constitutional Law of India.
Prem Prakash, Political Gains of Scheduled Castes and Scheduled Tribes.
Pylee, M.V., India's Constitution.
Rawls, John, A Theory of Justice.
Revankar, Ratna G., The Indian Constitution: A Case Study of Backward Classes.
Seervai, H.M., Constitutional Law of India : A Critical Commentary.
Sharma, B.R., Socio-economic Justice under Indian Constitution.
Sharma, Kusum, Ambedkar and Indian Constitution.
Shukla, V.N., Constitution of India.
Singh, Bakshish, The Supreme Court as an Instument of Social Justice.
Sivaramaya, B., Inequalities and the Law.

Articles

Balsara, S.D., Legal Aspect of Untouchability.
Bhargava, B.S. and Samal, Avinash, Protective Discrimination and Development of Scheduled Castes: An Alternative Model for Good Governance.
Borale, P.T., Problem of Untouchability and Former Untouchables.
Dr. Anirudh Prasad, Social Engineering and Problem of Widening the Scope of Protective Discrimination
Errabi, B., Protective Discrimination : Constitutional Prescription and Judicial Perception.

Jariwala, C.M., Reservation in Admission to Higher Education : Development and Directions.

Nandu Ram, Law and the Atrocities on Weaker Sections.

Rai, R.P., Child labour—A Myth or Reality—In the Sphere of Human Rights.

Rajeev, D., Basis of Protective Discrimination : A Jurisprudential Enquiry.

Samuel, C.J., Right against Exploitation.

Singh, Parmanand, (a) Social Justice for Harijans: Some Socio-legal Problems of Identification, Conversion and Judicial Review. (b) Equal Opportunity and Compensatory Discrimination : Constitutional Policy and Judicial Control. (c) Some Reflections on Indian Experience with Policy of Reservations.

Singh, M.P., Jurisprudential Foundation of Affirmative Action : Some Aspects of Equality and Social Justice.

Srivastava, S.C., Constitutional Protection to Weaker and Disadvantaged Section of Labour.

Reports

National Crime Records Bureau, Ministry of Home Affairs, 2006.

5th Report of National Commission for Scheduled Castes and Scheduled Tribes.

Central Bureau of Investigation Report of Atrocities, 2006.

Websites

http://ncsc.nic.in/
http://socialjustice.nic.in/
http://ncrb.nic.in
www.ilidelhi.org
http://indiacode.nic.in/

Index